LET THEM EAT CAKE!

Amusing Slices from History

by

Geoffrey Regan

With 20 cartoons by
Will Morrison

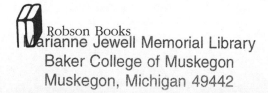

Robson Books

First published in Great Britain in 1994 under the title *Histrionics*.
This edition first published in 2001 by Robson Books,
10 Blenheim Court, Brewery Road, London N7 9NY

A member of the Chrysalis Group plc

British Library Cataloguing in Publication Data
A catalogue record for this title is available from the British Library.

ISBN 1 86105 457 2

Typeset by FiSH Books, London WC1
Printed by Creative Print & Design (Wales), Ebbw Vale

❦ CONTENTS

For Neil and Lucia

INTRODUCTION

The ancestry of the anecdote is long and distinguished. Many scholars have written extensively on its origin and development as a literary form, tracing it originally from the Greeks for whom the anecdote meant something secret or unpublished. However, it was not really until the eighteenth century that great wits like Samuel Johnson, Horace Walpole and others turned their attention to defining something that was essentially in need of no definition. Johnson called the anecdote a 'biographical incident; a minute passage of private life', and, thanks to his friend James Boswell, his own life has come down to us littered with such 'incidents', which have truly illuminated passages of the private Johnson. It is this private man that the reader wants to see in any biography, not merely the public man as he wished us to see him. Anecdotes give us glimpses of a 'secret history' and readers love secrets, for the secrets of great men and women are more interesting and entertaining if they prove that kings, queens and presidents are as prone to follies and foibles as lesser folk. And so anecdotes work in a cathartic manner, reassuring their readers or hearers that the great are really not so great after all.

My intention in assembling this collection of anecdotes, or episodes, or moments in history – call them what you will – has been to entertain rather than to instruct. During the eighteenth and nineteenth centuries there were many collections of such stories, most of which were selected by the editor with the intention of illustrating laudable qualities such as loyalty, duty, perseverance in the face of adversity and so forth. But each age needs to collect its own anecdotes. The humour of Prince Albert, for example, like much of the music of that favourite Victorian composer Felix Mendelssohn, can seem very pale to us today. When Winston Churchill called anecdotes the 'gleaming toys of history' he was very close to achieving a definition for 'all seasons'. Yet even the toys of yesteryear must gleam and glisten for each generation of readers. Worthy Victorian anecdotes may have served their purpose but they were too functional. They did not allow the imagination to leap, they tied it securely to the ground. But the anecdotes of Samuel Johnson, Sydney Smith and Oscar Wilde can still amuse us today, hundreds of years after they first saw the light of day.

My book, then, is no history of the anecdote, nor even a collection aimed at being representative of the vast range available. I have been deliberately selective, aiming to stimulate and entertain. The result, I hope, is more a potpourri than an anthology, a jumble of good things, an assortment of episodes, curiosities, memoirs and snippets, funny stories and terrible, even fearful ones. I have held out my hands to catch the thistledown of history and hopefully have produced something for everyone. Some of the stories deal with oddities in the byways of the past. In the past as today normality requires a sauce of abnormality if it is not to seem unendurably dull. The popular press wants to know the details of what makes people different and prints it for our entertainment every day. Yet it has not been my intention to sensationalize the past. The anecdote has always been a more subtle form than that. It serves as a basis for conversation, for after-dinner entertainment, for relaxed contemplation. The subtleties of some of the stories defy immediate understanding and yield their secrets grudgingly.

In order to give some structure to what otherwise might appear a kind of literary jumble, I have imposed thirteen divisions on the material which may help the reader to find his way about the maze. However, the divisions were made after rather than before the stories were assembled and there are many that could with equal ease appear elsewhere. As my field of operation was no less than the whole of human history I found it necessary to impose some limits of my own. My preference for the wits of the eighteenth century may see them possibly over-represented and yet I think they are worth it. Few anecdotes are included merely because they are worthy of inclusion, as might have been said at one time of King Canute and the waves, Robert the Bruce and the Spider, and King Richard and Sultan Saladin. All of these I regard as apocryphal anyway, and so dated in their message that they are out of step with our time. So, the choice has been mine throughout, and I take no responsibility for what has been omitted, save to say that I hope you find the result as entertaining to read as I found it to assemble. The vast majority of the anecdotes have been rewritten for this book, though some do appear in their original form, particularly those by such masters as Samuel Pepys, John Evelyn, Fanny Burney, Horace Walpole and so on. If I have a personal favourite out of so many, it is the Pythonesque encounter between the Federal Agent Izzy Einstein and the Bartender, during the period of Prohibition in the United States. It should have been filmed, and played by Laurel and Hardy.

1. LET THEM EAT CAKE!

❦ The gentle sex (1)

During the sixteenth century, Caterina Sforza was known throughout Italy as the Virago. She was noted not just for her beauty but for her courage and her ruthlessness.

During a siege of the Castle de St Angelo she strode around the battlements wearing armour over her satin dress. When the besiegers threatened to murder her children, she lifted up her skirt and bluntly replied, 'Look, I have the mould to make more.'

❦ The bulb's gone

In Holland during the seventeenth century, tulip bulbs became so valuable that fortunes were spent in buying them.

In one extraordinary incident a rich merchant – and notable collector of tulips – received news from a sailor that his cargo of Levantine goods had arrived at the docks. The merchant welcomed the sailor into his counting-house, where there were piles of goods of all kinds, and rewarded him for his good news with a large red herring for his breakfast. The sailor thanked the merchant and, seeing what he assumed to be a discarded onion lying on the counter, took it and set off to eat his breakfast in the fresh air. Unfortunately, of course, the onion was not an onion at all but a fantastically valuable Semper Augustus tulip bulb worth 3,000 florins. The merchant at once noticed that his prize was missing and instigated a frantic search, but to no avail. Then he remembered the sailor and assumed that he must have stolen the bulb. The merchant set up a hue and cry but it was all too late. By the time they found the sailor, seated on a pile of ropes down by the quayside, he had eaten the herring and the 'onion'. In spite of his protestations of innocence the sailor was charged with stealing the tulip and was thrown into gaol.

❦ And all because the lady loves ... sheep's dung

When English privateers first seized the rich cargoes of Spanish ships travelling home from the Caribbean or South America, the English sailors tipped the chocolate beans overboard, thinking them no better than 'sheep's dung'. This blunder prevented chocolate reaching the English market for many years.

In an attempt to wean his fellow Englishmen away from their irrational contempt for chocolate, the seventeenth-century English sailor Thomas Gage, who had been a prisoner of the Spaniards for a number of years, instructed them to serve the chocolate with a variety of flavourings including sugar, cinnamon, rose water and even pepper. Gage himself had a portable chocolate-making kit, and became the forerunner of a whole industry of British chocolate makers. Gage's other recommendation to his English readers did not catch on so well – hedgehog and iguana savouries.

❦ Mache Potetesse

The French were resistant to the potato. The frequent dearths of wheat during the eighteenth century resulted in hundreds of thousands of deaths from starvation. In spite of this, the majority of Frenchmen could not be convinced that the potato was not poisonous.

It was not until, in 1814, Antoine Beauvilliers published a cookbook extolling the virtues of such English dishes as Woiches Rabettes, Plomb Poutingue and Mache Potetesse that the French came to understand the English predilection for potatoes. But a century or more of neglecting the vegetable had cost France the lives of many thousands of peasants who succumbed to starvation rather than risk the poisonous or leprous 'spud'.

❦ A clerical error

At public executions in the eighteenth century the mobs that gathered to watch, and sometimes even the hangman himself, were thoroughly drunk.

In 1738, at one execution the hangman, already intoxicated, was convinced that he was supposed to be hanging three men instead of the two who were presented to him. As a result he tried to put the rope around the neck of the parson who was attending the two condemned criminals and was only with difficulty prevented from hanging him as well.

❦ Heads in the clouds

By 1798, pre-eminence in air warfare rested with the French, who by then had two 'balloon companies' attached to the Republican Army. But one man put an end to military ballooning and that was Napoleon Bonaparte himself. The problem was that the gallant French aeronauts were regarded as the 'glamour boys' of the French army and the French hot air balloons were used less and less for military purposes and more for amorous ones.

When not on duty the 'daring young men in their floating machines' took their girlfriends to heaven and back. Bottles of champagne and hampers of food were often taken aboard before each flight. When one French aeronaut, Lieutenant Beauchamp, was hauled down to the ground with his female companion, he could only stammer out an apology to his commander and express a willingness to marry the young lady. In 1799, Napoleon suppressed his aerial corps on the grounds that it was unnecessary and immoral.

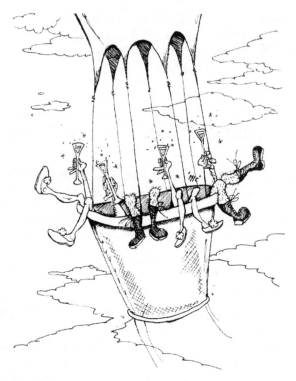

❦ The demon drink

*Prohibition in the United States encouraged many people to take
up drinking alcohol who had never bothered before. It challenged
the ingenuity of the ordinary American who resented the heavy-
handed legislation. However, some of the homemade products
were quite alarming.*

As a result of distilling alcohol from paint and anti-freeze, thirty-
four people died in New York during a four-day period in 1928.
Unscrupulous distillers used alcohol from hair tonic, cosmetics
and even, in one case, 'Parisienne solution for perspiring feet, 90
per cent alcohol'. The distilled liquor circulated under the names
of 'Kentucky Tavern', 'Pebble Ford', 'Coffin Varnish' or 'Rot Gut'.

Rich and poor alike fell victim to vile concoctions of corn mash or potato whisky. When one cautious drinker had his bootlegged liquor tested by a chemist he received the alarming and baffling answer, 'Dear sir, your horse has diabetes.'

❦ Screwing up

The laying of the first transatlantic cable encountered unexpected hitches.

The plan had been for the British ship *Agamemnon* and the American ship *Niagara* to set off from their respective coasts carrying with them half of the entire cable. They would rendezvous in mid-Atlantic and there join the two ends of the cable. Unfortunately, the two cables had been manufactured by separate contractors and certain details of construction had not been agreed in advance. As a result, the direction of the 'lay' of the wire armouring was different on the two cable ends, one being 'right-handed' and the other 'left-handed'. Thus to tighten one end by turning in one direction was to loosen the other. Faced with catastrophe the cable-layers botched together a link that enabled a few faint messages to reach Newfoundland from Ireland. But it was never going to last and within weeks the entire cable fell silent.

❦ The follies

William Beckford, builder of Fonthill Abbey, Britain's great 'folly', was a true eccentric.

Beckford surrounded Fonthill Abbey with a wall seven miles long and twelve feet high, topped with sharp spikes, and its grounds were patrolled by armed men with ferocious dogs. Beckford preferred not to mix with the common people, who irritated him by asking for charity. His usual response was to turn on any beggars and give them a thorough horse-whipping. For exercise, Beckford used to ride madly around his estate in the middle of the night before throwing himself fully clothed into a green pond. Those who witnessed these weird nocturnal ceremonies were convinced that the rider was no living man and his horse nothing less than a demon steed.

❦ Vice versa

The British embassy in Paris is one of Britain's oldest and most prestigious. Sometimes the ambassadors were oddballs or worse.

When Lord Bertie of Thame was British ambassador in Paris he kept pornographic prints on the wall of his study on the back of pictures of less provocative subjects. When expecting visitors it was the task of his young secretary to turn the pictures round before the guests entered the inner sanctum.

❦ A spirited response

After a dinner at 10 Downing Street in the 1950s, Prime Minister Winston Churchill spoke to the Prime Minister of Pakistan.

'Will you have a whisky and soda, Mr Prime Minister?' asked Winston.
  'No thank you,' was the reply.
  'What's that?'
  'No, thank you.'
  'Why?'
  'I am a teetotaller.'
  'A teetotaller? Christ! I mean, God! I mean, Allah!' gasped Churchill.

❦ Mao goes up the wall

During the Cultural Revolution worship of Chairman Mao in China almost became a state religion.

In one newspaper story a peasant was praised for sticking thirty-two portraits of Mao on his bedroom walls so that he could see

Chairman Mao's face as soon as he opened his eyes. The peasant was later beaten up when the truth got out that he had only used the portraits because he could not afford any other wallpaper and the pictures were being given away free.

❦ Matching the greatest

President Amin, brutal dictator of Uganda, tried to bully the leaders of surrounding states.

Eventually, Amin pushed the Tanzanian leader, Julius Nyerere, too far. He offered to marry him, saying that he loved Julius in spite of his grey hair and wanted to have his children. Nobody, however, was laughing when, in October 1978, Amin invaded Tanzania with 3,000 troops, who raped and massacred as they advanced. The better-trained Tanzanian troops drove Amin's men back, only for the Ugandan president to offer to settle the war with a boxing match between himself and the diminutive Tanzanian leader, with Muhammed Ali as referee.

❦ What's in a name?

In 1943, the famous British pianist, Solomon, was touring Algeria with ENSA. He often found the pianos he was asked to play poor to say the least.

On one occasion, in Algiers, Solomon found the piano absolutely decrepit with broken pedals and sticking notes. He was in despair. Groups of Allied soldiers were using the concert hall as a canteen and one of them noticed that Solomon was looking dismally at his piano.

'Would you like me to put the piano straight for you?' asked one American GI.

'I am afraid it is hopeless,' replied Solomon, much amused.

'Give me a coupla hours,' said the GI, 'and I'll fix it.'

Solomon returned later and found the GI replacing the lid. He played a few notes and found to his astonishment that it was much improved.

'You seem to know a lot about pianos,' said Solomon. 'What's your name?'

'Steinway.'

❦ A plaintiff note

At a certain social event the British actor Samuel Foote was irritated by the sound of a man nearby singing.

'Why are you singing that one tune all the time?' Foote asked.

'Because it haunts me,' the man replied.

'I am not surprised,' retorted Foote, 'since you are for ever murdering it.'

❦ Spelling rules

When the Earl of Denbigh asked the famous novelist, Henry Fielding, a relation of his, why his family spelt their name 'ie' whilst the earl's family spelt theirs 'ei', he was told, 'I cannot be certain, my lord, except that perhaps my branch of the family was the first that knew how to spell.'

❦ A change of address

The German writer Lessing could be very forgetful.

Once he returned home after dark without his key. He knocked on the front door and a servant peered out of an upstairs window, not recognizing him in the dark.

'Professor Lessing is not at home,' called out the servant.

'Very well,' said Lessing, turning away. 'Tell him I will call another time.'

❦ Man the lifeboats!

British author Somerset Maugham always travelled in French ships. When asked why he replied, 'Because there's none of that nonsense about women and children first.'

❦ Ethical trade

The actress Mae West was seen wearing the most extravagant pearls. One of her female companions exclaimed, 'Goodness, Mae, where did you get those beautiful pearls?'

'You can take it from me, sister,' replied Mae, 'that goodness had nothing to do with it.'

❦ Mummy's boy

The American painter James Whistler was cornered at a party by a very snobbish Bostonian lady who asked him where he had been born. Whistler told her that he came from Lowell, Massachusetts.

The lady winced. 'Whatever possessed you to be born in a place like that?' she asked haughtily.

'I wished to be near my mother,' replied Whistler.

❦ The cost of living

Irving Cobb was one of the most famous American newspaper reporters. In 1914 his reports from the battlefronts in France and Belgium alerted the world to German atrocities.

During the First World War Irving Cobb was in Belgium covering the German invasion with several of his press colleagues. On one occasion he was travelling by taxi to the Belgian Army headquarters when he was captured by the Germans and questioned. The interrogation went on for hours, during which Cobb became increasingly anxious. Finally he called out to the German officer interrogating him, 'Whether or not you intend to shoot us, for God's sake tell the taxi driver to turn off his meter.'

❦ Faulty execution

Nurse Edith Cavell was shot by the Germans in 1915 for helping Allied prisoners escape and subsequently became a national heroine.

When the war ended a statue of Nurse Cavell was erected outside the National Portrait Gallery in London. At the unveiling of the statue the artist James Pryde, unconvinced by the sculptor's work, was heard to remark as the curtains were pulled back, 'My God, they've shot the wrong person.'

❧ My dad's a picture

Some children were so young when their fathers went to war in 1939 that they only remembered them from the framed photographs their mothers kept.

One little girl was just four when her father came back from the war. Her mother had taken her to Cambridge railway station to meet him and kept reminding her that he would have legs – a friend of hers who had not seen photos of her father until he had arrived home had said, on first seeing him, 'He's not my father. He's got legs.'

❧ Nude bathing

During the interwar years public attitudes towards nudity on American beaches reached a severity never known before or since.

In one such case at Atlantic City a woman was arrested and sentenced to a month in jail for removing her stockings and sunbathing barefoot.

❧ Property is theft

At the opening of the Second World War the evacuation of women and children from the big cities into the countryside was not always a happy experience.

A householder who lived alone in Datchet found that the authorities billeted a woman and her eight children from London in his house. Quite unable to cope with the change in his life, he left his house and went to live with his mother, leaving the Londoners in possession of his property. The woman contacted her husband, who had remained behind in London, and he sold their house and moved to Datchet to be with his wife. The new occupants refused to pay any rent to the owner as they were 'evacuees' and the authorities stopped paying him any allowances for the Londoners as he was no longer in the house himself. Living with his mother actually cost the owner rent which he had to pay to another landlord.

❦ Where there's muck there's money

In 1939 during the evacuation of children from the big cities one country woman tried to persuade her evacuee child to wash himself. As she said, 'If you will wash your hands I will give you a penny, and if you wash your face as well I will give you tuppence.'

The boy replied, 'Cor blimey! I might as well have a whole bath and make me fortune.'

❦ Hardboiled

The evacuation programme revealed that many women from poorer urban areas had few domestic skills.

One young housewife from the East End dropped an egg into a pot of boiling water and stirred it round for a long while. Eventually, in exasperation, she said to the country woman with whom she was staying, 'This is hopeless. I've been cooking this bloody egg for half an hour now and it ain't got soft yet.'

❦ Free speech? Five shillings

In 1939 and 1940 defeatism was very much in the air in Britain and the government acted to stamp it out. This resulted in some absurd incidents.

One evening in a London public house a woman overheard what she believed were pro-German opinions expressed by a group of men. She reported the incident to a policeman and a man was arrested. What had apparently happened was this:

Three men were drinking together and a French soldier lifted his glass and said, '*Vive La France*,' while another soldier added, '*Vive L'Angleterre*.' An Englishman nearby joined in with, 'To hell with Hitler.'

The woman whistle-blower had told the policeman, 'That's him. I heard him say, "Heil Hitler!"'

When confronted with the evidence, the Englishman, somewhat the worse for drink, denied the accusation, abused the woman and became so angry that he was eventually arrested and charged with insulting words and behaviour. He was fined five shillings by the magistrate.

❦ Tripping the light fantastic

The blackout during the war was applied as rigorously in the countryside as in the towns. This resulted in the need to improvise by many farmworkers.

One magical example was the West Country landgirl, bereft of batteries for her torch, who found her way home by the glimmer given off by a handful of glow-worms.

❦ A touching moment

A train was travelling through the countryside during the blackout in 1940. A young lady's voice was heard to announce in the pitch darkness: 'Here, take your hand off my knee! No, not you, *you!*'

❦ Meeting targets

One farmer in the West Country, for example, had been prosecuted for showing a light in the middle of one of his fields. He complained that he could not identify the cows for milking but eventually resorted to painting large white numbers on each cow. To preserve the New Forest ponies from rampant motorists, the authorities first tried painting them to increase visibility but later found that their foals would not go near them in such camouflage and the idea was dropped.

❦ Making an asp of himself

In 1939 it was feared that thousands of German bombers would destroy London in a matter of days.

In order to comfort the legions of dead and dying who would succumb to the German bombers, Canon Barry of Westminster undertook a first-aid course. He was surprised to find that his first lecture was on the treatment of snake-bite.

❦ A happier land

When war became imminent advertisements began to appear in newspapers offering salvation for those who could afford it.

For Londoners wishing to avoid the inconveniences of war the city of Bath offered itself as an ideal alternative, as it claimed to be 'immune from all air-raid dangers'. Aldwick Bay, on the south coast near Bognor Regis, ambitiously claimed that it was 'immune from the international situation'. Readers of the *Tatler* were pleased to learn that – to ensure that the British way of life suffered no serious disruption – a hotel at St Leonard's-on-Sea assured its guests that 'the ballroom and adjacent toilets have been made gas- and splinter-proof'. Other advertisements promised, 'A garden of sunshine absolutely free of war's activities' and 'Live safely and comfortably during the war period in one of the many delightful out-of-the-way beauty spots of North Wales.'

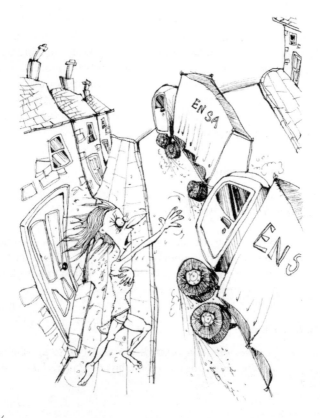

❦ Barely in time

During the early days after the Normandy invasion in 1944 ENSA sometimes found it difficult to ship its concert parties to France.

One group was trapped in a long traffic jam of military vehicles outside Southampton. The officer in charge let the artistes wander off, telling them they would be warned when to come back by the traffic hooters. When the signal was given all the artistes returned except for one pretty chorus girl who had managed to persuade a householder to let her take a bath. At the sound of the hooting she came running out of a house with just a towel wrapped round her, shouting, 'Hi, wait for me.'

❦ Rest cure

Many of the Allied troops fighting in Iraq and Iran complained that ENSA was ignoring them because of the unfriendly weather conditions. To rectify this, Joyce Grenfell agreed to fly out to Baghdad to entertain the troops. When she arrived at one hospital filled with men suffering from heat exhaustion she was introduced by the medical officer with the words, 'And now this wonderful lady has come all the way to Baghdad just to entertain you men in bed.'

2. ODDS AND ENDS

❦ It runs in the family

Lord Frederick North was one of the worst prime ministers in British history. His ridiculous policies between 1770 and 1782 led to the loss of Britain's American colonies.

One night at the opera, between acts, the man sitting next to Lord North asked him, 'Who is that plain-looking lady in the box opposite?'

'That is my wife,' said Lord North.

'Oh I don't mean her,' stuttered the embarrassed man, 'I mean the lady next to her.'

'That, sir, is my daughter: we are considered to be three of the ugliest people in London.'

❦ North awakes

Lord North was often accused of being asleep on the Treasury bench.

On one occasion, an opponent, enraged at the sight of the slumbering North, exclaimed, 'Even now, when voices of warning and protestations are raised against him, the noble Lord is asleep.' To which North, without opening his eyes, retorted, 'I wish to God I was.'

❦ A cool customer

William Pitt the Younger was one of Britain's greatest prime ministers and Revolutionary France's most formidable opponent.

In 1786 Pitt found that he was suffering from a tumour in the mouth. It was removed by surgeon John Hunter of Downing Street. Pitt would not let the surgeon tie him down during the operation and asked how long it would last. Hunter replied that it would take just six minutes. Pitt remained motionless during the operation even though he must have been in great pain. When the ordeal was over his only comment was, 'You have exceeded your time by half a minute.'

❦ The proudest moment

Arthur Wellesley, 1st Duke of Wellington, was both general and statesman and was widely known as the 'Iron Duke' or 'Old Nosey'.

In spite of his military prowess, Wellington was not a good shot. In 1819, Wellington managed to pepper a dog and a keeper's legs before going on to shoot a cottager in the arms as she was hanging out her washing. When the poor woman complained she was told, 'My good woman, this ought to be the proudest moment of your life. You have the distinction of being shot by the great Duke of Wellington.'

❦ A damned fool

The Duke of Wellington had a sharp wit and did not suffer fools gladly.

A man once helped Wellington across the crowded Hyde Park Corner, taking the opportunity to state, 'My lord, I have passed a long, and not uneventful life, but never did I hope to reach the day when I might be of assistance to the greatest man that ever lived.'

'Don't be a damned fool,' said Wellington.

❦ The wisdom of a little lady

Known as the 'lady with the lamp' and famous for her reforming

work in the medical services during the Crimean War, Florence Nightingale lived to the age of ninety, spending much of her later life as a self-proclaimed invalid.

Florence Nightingale kept a miniature owl as a pet and took it everywhere with her in a pocket.

❦ The wife who laboured

Lord Lytton's marriage had not been happy but he was loved by his children who often tried to find ways to please him.

On one occasion Lord Lytton's children presented a costume drama in which a knight was shown returning from the Crusades. The knight first told his tales of danger and adventure, whereupon his 'wife' produced a string of 'babies' and told him, 'I too, my lord, have not been idle.'

❦ Consorting with foreigners

One of Horace Walpole's descendants was a noted xenophobe. On the death of Prince Albert, he dressed in his brightest outfit and went about rejoicing that 'there was now one foreigner less in the world'.

❦ Rage over a lost penny

On one occasion Meyer de Rothschild, the famous banker, dropped a penny outside his bank in Piccadilly and spent so long searching for it that when he straightened up it was only to discover that someone had picked his pocket and made off with his gold watch.

❦ Beefsteak grilled by police

The Beefsteak Club was once raided by the police on the grounds that its exterior was so decrepit that it was thought to house a criminal gang. When the members were interrogated, the first who was asked his name replied, 'The Lord Chancellor'. The second claimed to be the Governor of the Bank of England and the third the Archbishop of Canterbury. The policeman, by now convinced he was dealing with a den of rogues, added sarcastically to the fourth, 'And I suppose you are the Prime Minister.'

'As a matter of fact I am,' replied Arthur Balfour with a smile.

❦ How inconvenient

Frederick Edwin Smith, 1st Earl of Birkenhead, was a barrister and a Conservative politician. He was renowned for being witty but was described by Margot Asquith as 'Very clever, but his brains go to his head'.

F E Smith was in the habit of dropping into the Athenaeum Club to use the toilet there, although he was not a member. One day he was taken aside by a porter who informed him that the Athenaeum was a private club and that he was, in fact, trespassing. Undeterred, Smith replied, 'I see. It's a club as well, is it?'

❦ Barometer under pressure

One rainy morning Sir William Eden came downstairs and tapped his barometer as usual. It was indicating sunshine. When it refused to change its mind, Sir William pulled it off the wall, walked to the front door and flung the barometer onto the front garden. 'Go and see for yourself, you damned fool,' he muttered.

❦ A diet of blood and iron

Prince Otto von Bismarck was a notably difficult patient and constantly squabbled with his doctors.

When Bismarck was diagnosed as having cancer, a young Berlin specialist, Ernst Schweninger, was brought in to give a second opinion. Schweninger was not overawed by his patient and tackled the great man head on, asking him about his habits and his previous medical history. 'I don't like questions,' Bismarck snapped. 'Then get a veterinarian,' replied Schweninger. 'He doesn't question his patients.'

❦ Afraid of the dark

The British physician William Harvey was most famous for discovering the circulation of the blood.

Dr Harvey was ever afraid of becoming blind: early one morning, for he always rose early, his housekeeper coming into his chamber to call him, opened the window shutters, told him the hour, and asked him if he would not rise. Upon which he asked if she had opened the shutters; she replied yes – then shut them again – she did so – then opened them again. But still the effect was the same to him, for he had awakened stone blind. Upon which he told her to fetch him a bottle (which she herself had observed to stand on a shelf in his chamber for a long time) out of which he drank a large draught, and it being a strong poison, which it is supposed he had long before prepared and set there for this purpose, he expired within three hours after.

❦ Value Added Tax

The great English scientist and mathematician Isaac Newton was not very worldly wise. His love of telescopes and optical devices blinded him to the value the world set upon his instruments.

One of Sir Isaac Newton's philosophical friends abroad had sent him a curious prism, which was taken to the Custom House, and was at that time a scarce commodity in this kingdom. Sir Isaac, laying claim to it, was asked by the officers what the value of the glass was, that they might accordingly regulate the duty. The great Newton, whose business was more with the universe than with duties and drawbacks, and who rated the prism according to his own idea of its use and excellence, answered 'that the value was so great that he could not ascertain it'. Being again pressed to set some fixed estimate upon it, he persisted in his reply, 'that he could not say what it was worth, for that the value was inestimable'. The honest Custom House officers accordingly took him at his word, and made him pay a most exorbitant duty for the prism, which he might have taken away upon only paying a rate according to the weight of the glass!

❦ A dinner to remember

Sir Isaac Newton was remarkably absent-minded.

On one occasion Newton invited a friend to dinner and forgot that he had done so. The friend arrived only to find Newton in a fit of abstraction and when just one dinner was brought up he decided to eat it while the philosopher continued to be absorbed with his thoughts. Suddenly Newton became aware of his friend's presence and seeing the empty dishes, said, 'Well, really, if it wasn't for the proof before my eyes, I could have sworn that I had not yet dined.'

❦ A mad monarch

In 1832, Lord Macaulay related to his sisters a conversation he had had with Lord Holland, who had been very entertaining. Holland had told the story of his visit to the court of Denmark and of his meeting with King Christian, known as the 'Madman', who was at last deprived of all real share in the government on account of his infirmity.

'Such a Tom of Bedlam I never saw,' said Lord Holland. 'One day the Neapolitan ambassador came to the levee and made a profound bow to His Majesty. His Majesty bowed still lower. The Neapolitan bowed down his head almost to the ground; when, behold! The King clapped his hands on his Excellency's shoulders and jumped over him like a boy playing leapfrog.'

❧ The naked truth

Lord Lytton was both a novelist and a politician. Famous for his historical novels, Lytton was also noted for his oddities.

Not long after their marriage Mr and Mrs Lytton Bulwer, as they then were, were travelling along the Riviera between Genoa and Spezzia; Mr Lytton Bulwer was dressed in a somewhat fantastic costume which at that period he affected. The vetturino drove. Mrs Bulwer's maid was sitting beside him: the happy couple were in an open carriage. Passing through one of the many villages close to the sea, they observed a singularly handsome girl standing at a cottage door. Mr Bulwer, with somewhat ill-advised complacency, turning to his wife, said, 'Did you notice how that girl looked at me?' The lady, with an acidity which developed itself later in life, replied, 'The girl was not looking at you in admiration: if you wear that ridiculous dress no wonder people stare at you.' The bridegroom thereupon with an admirable sense of logic said: 'You think that people stare at my dress; and not at me: I will give you the most absolute and convincing proof that your theory has no foundation.' He then proceeded to divest himself of every particle of clothing except his hat and boots: and taking the place of the lady's maid drove for ten miles in this normal condition.

❧ A want of latitude

Sir John Leslie was professor of mathematics at Edinburgh University.

Leslie once wrote an article on the North Pole which appeared in the *Edinburgh Review* and was attacked by a hostile reviewer named Lord Jeffrey. Incensed, Leslie called on Jeffrey just as he was getting on horseback, and in a great hurry. Leslie began with a grave complaint on the subject which Jeffrey interrupted with, 'O damn the North Pole.' Leslie went off in high dudgeon and soon after met Sydney Smith who, seeing him disturbed, asked what was the matter. He told him what he had been to Jeffrey about and that he had in a very unpleasant way said, 'Damn the North Pole.' 'It was very bad,' said Sydney; 'but do you know, I am not surprised at it, for I have heard him speak very disrespectfully of the Equator.'

❦ Off his head

The English poet Algernon Charles Swinburne was a renowned eccentric, whose heavy drinking and unconventional sexuality made him appear a scandalous figure in Victorian England.

Algernon Swinburne was leaving his club one day and looked around for his hat in the hall. He only found four tall top hats belonging to other members of the club. He tried on the hats one after another, and as they did not fit his large head, threw them in turn on the floor. When the hall porter, hearing a noise, appeared, he found Swinburne executing a war dance on the hats. The infuriated poet went for the hall porter, demanding, with that sanguinary power of invective which was his peculiar gift, where his hat was. The man replied that he believed Mr Swinburne had no hat when he entered the club that evening.

❦ Befogged

The Duke of Devonshire was one of the most important Liberal politicians at the end of the nineteenth century.

The Duke of Devonshire was awoken one morning from a heavy sleep by his valet. Gazing out of his window, he was aware of an impenetrable grey pall outside his window and replied to the

23

servant, 'I'm not getting up in this damn fog.' He therefore went back to sleep giving instructions to be woken two hours later. Exactly on time the valet wakened his lordship but the fog was still apparent outside. A further two hours passed and the valet wakened his lordship for luncheon. 'It's still foggy outside,' said the duke. 'I beg your pardon, Your Grace,' said the man, 'but that is not fog that you see outside your window. That is the tent that Her Grace has had erected in the garden for her party this afternoon.'

❦ The Double Duchess

Lottie von Alten – known to everyone in Victorian England as the 'Double Duchess', being at various stages both the Duchess of Manchester and the Duchess of Devonshire – was one of the beauties of her time. She was also a notorious 'social-climber' and at the coronation of Edward VII in 1902 her 'climbing' was her undoing.

As King Edward and Queen Alexandra left Westminster Abbey after the ceremony and descended the steps, Lottie – eager to assert her seniority as the wife of the Duke of Devonshire – scuttled after them, barging and pushing her way to the front. As she caught up with the royal couple her way was barred by the officer in charge of the Grenadier Guards. Undeterred, Lottie shrieked at the soldier and abused him loudly, trying to push past him and succeeding only in falling headlong down the steps of the Abbey. Lottie – by this time in her mid-sixties – was somewhat shaken but picked herself up, dusted herself off and, with the help of Mrs Asquith, the wife of the chancellor of the exchequer, tidied her hair and replaced her coronet. She then took up the chase once again and pursued the king and queen to their coach.

❦ With friends like that...

Lord Berners – George Tyrwhitt-Wilson – was an eccentric British artist and composer.

One of Lord Berners's acquaintances was in the habit of telling him how much he had been sticking up for him. He repeated this once too often and Lord Berners replied, 'Yes, but I have been sticking up for you. Someone said you weren't fit to live with pigs, and I said you were.'

❦ A return ticket

William Arden, 2nd Baron Alvanley, was a friend of Beau Brummell and the Prince Regent, and one of the leaders of fashionable society during the Regency period.

After emerging unscathed from a duel fought in a discreet corner of London, Lord Alvanley handed the cab driver a guinea. The coachman was surprised at the size of the fee and protested, 'But, my lord, I only took you a mile.' Alvanley laughed. 'The guinea is not for taking me, my man, it is for bringing me back.'

❦ Ze librettist

Italian appreciation of William Shakespeare's plays has not always been as sophisticated as in some other countries.

Whilst staying in Birmingham, the Italian conductor and composer Luigi Arditi was advised by a friend to spend a day at Stratford-upon-Avon. 'It would be a pity to leave the area without visiting the birthplace of Shakespeare,' said a friend. 'Who is this Shakespeare?' asked Arditi. His friend looked at him in amazement. 'Haven't you heard of the man who wrote *Othello*, *Romeo and Juliet*, and *The Merry Wives of Windsor*?' 'Ah,' replied Arditi, after a moment's thought, 'You mean ze librettist.'

❦ The last laugh

The French novelist Honoré de Balzac was frequently in debt.

One night a thief broke into Balzac's single-room apartment, while the novelist was asleep in bed. The thief tried to pick the lock on Balzac's desk and the sound awoke the sleeper. The thief was startled by a laugh from the bed, where Balzac was now watching him with an amused expression on his face. 'Why are you laughing?' asked the thief. 'I am laughing to think of the risks you have taken to break in here by night and try to find money in my desk when I can never find any there by day.'

❦ Spartan tartan

Cameron of Lochiel was a stickler for the old virtues of endurance and resolution.

Sir Ewan was out camping in the Highlands with his grandson, Donald Cameron. It had been snowing heavily and as darkness fell they looked for somewhere to sleep in the open. The Cameron of Lochiel noticed that the boy had rolled a large snowball to make a pillow for his head. Sir Ewan kicked the snowball away. 'I'll have no effeminacy here, boy.'

❦ A man of good proportions

Doctor Samuel Johnson, as well as being a great lexicographer, was also a chauvinist when it came to discussing other nations or peoples.

While he was compiling his great dictionary Johnson was asked by his former tutor at Oxford how long the task would take him. He replied that his dictionary would take three years, whereupon his tutor pointed out, 'But the French academy, which consists of forty members, took forty years to compile their dictionary.'

Unabashed, Johnson replied, 'Sir, thus it is. This is the proportion. Let me see; forty times forty is sixteen hundred. As is three to sixteen hundred, so is the proportion of an Englishman to a Frenchman.'

❦ Keeping his word

Dr Samuel Johnson was a man of his word – unfortunately so, as this example shows.

Johnson was travelling in a coach when he passed by a poor woman carrying her baby in the rain. He ordered his coach to stop and offered the woman a lift on condition that she used no baby talk to the child. At first the woman sat quietly in the corner while the baby slept. But soon the jerking of the carriage woke the baby and it began to cry. The woman leaned over the baby and said, 'The little dearie, is he going to open his eyesie-pysies then.'

'Stop the coach,' cried Johnson, and he promptly turned the woman and her baby back out into the rain.

🏵 Much ado about nothing

When Doctor Johnson was preparing a new edition of Shakespeare he took subscriptions to offset the cost.

A bookseller's apprentice delivered the money from a new subscriber to Dr Samuel Johnson and was amazed when the great man put the money in his pocket and took no note of the subscriber's name. When he asked Johnson how he would remember the name so that it could be printed on the list of subscribers that would appear at the front of the book, Johnson replied, 'I shall print no list of subscribers.' When the apprentice looked perplexed, Johnson added, 'Sir, I have two very cogent reasons for not printing any list of subscribers – one, that I have lost all the names, the other, that I have spent all the money.'

🏵 The noblest prospect

Doctor Johnson had no great love for Scotland or the Scots.

While on his tour of Scotland with James Boswell, Dr Samuel Johnson replied to one of the natives who had boasted to him about Scotland's many noble, wild prospects, 'I believe, sir, you have a great many. Norway, too, has noble wild prospects; and Lapland is remarkable for prodigious noble wild prospects. But, sir, let me tell you, the noblest prospect which a Scotchman ever sees, is the high-road that leads him to England.'

❦ The unfair sex

Samuel Johnson was a male chauvinist when it came to the question of considering the abilities of the female sex.

After listening to a woman preach at a Quaker meeting one Sunday, Boswell hastened to tell Samuel Johnson about what he had heard. Johnson was not impressed. As he said, 'Sir, a woman preaching is like a dog's walking on his hind legs. It is not done well, but you are surprised to find it done at all.'

❦ Bell, book and candles

Robert Stephen Hawker was an idiosyncratic poet and antiquary who lived in Cornwall during the nineteenth century.

When attending church, Hawker was usually accompanied by nine or ten cats, which entered the chancel with him and played around during the service. Whilst saying prayers, Hawker would pat and stroke his cats and scratch them under their chins. Generally there were ten cats who attended his church but one was discovered to have killed a mouse on a Sunday and was excommunicated and banned from going to church with him.

❦ The misplaced garter

Viscount Castlereagh represented Britain at the Congress of Vienna in 1814–15. However, his wife who travelled with him was not well received by the Viennese.

Lady Emily Castlereagh was not regarded by the Viennese as one of the beauties of the Congress. The Austrian Count Nostitz described her as 'colossal, ungainly, her manner uncivilized and unconcerned'. She committed one appalling *faux pas* by attending a ball given by Princess Metternich with her husband's Order of the Garter wrapped around her head. The Austrians were shocked because, only the day before, Emperor Francis I had been installed as a member of the Order of the Garter by

Garter King-of-Arms Sir Isaac Heard, who had travelled all the way from England for that purpose.

❦ Mrs Baird's resolution

Mrs Baird of Newbyth, the mother of General Sir David Baird, had always been spoken of as a grand specimen of a resolute Scottish lady.

When the news arrived from India of the gallant but unfortunate action of 1784 against Hyder Ali, in which Mrs Baird's son, then Captain Baird, was engaged, it was stated that he and other officers had been taken prisoners and chained together, two and two. The friends were careful in breaking such sad intelligence to the mother, who was, however, too Spartan in her nature to require such considerate treatment. When she was made fully to understand the position of her son and his gallant companions, disdaining all weak and useless expressions of her own grief, and knowing well the restless and athletic habits of her boy, all she said was, 'Lord pity the chiel that's chained to our Davey.'

❦ Divine understanding

Dean Ramsay relates that during the long French war two old ladies in Stranraer were going to the kirk, when one said to the other, 'Was it no' a wonderful thing that the Breetish were aye victorious over the French in battle?'

'Not a bit,' said the other old lady. 'Dinna ye ken the Breetish aye say their prayers before gaen into battle?'

The other replied, 'But canna the French say thir prayers as weel?'

The reply was most characteristic: 'Hoot! Jabbering bodies, who could understan *them*?'

❦ The bogeyman

At the time of the renewal of war, after the peace of Amiens, a gentleman, who was fishing in a sequestered spot not far from

London, was accosted by an old woman of the neighbourhood, who entered into conversation with him on various matters. After a while he asked her if she were not alarmed about Bonaparte's landing on the island.

'Oh dear, no!' she answered. 'I am up to all that. He was expected here when I was a young woman, and he nearly came. At that time they called him the Pretender, and now they call him Bonaparte.'

❦ A lady of breeding

Prince Charles Maurice de Talleyrand-Périgord once wrote in his Memoirs *an anecdote about his wife.*

On one occasion Princess Talleyrand had nearly set the whole province in uproar by an unseasonable display of what the Prince was wont to call her *impertinence régente*. A large party had been invited to dinner at the château, a party in honour of the arrival of some high and illustrious visitor at Valençay. I think there were even scions of Royalty among the guests. In short, it was one of the gaudy days of the castle, when the flaming yellow liveries, and the antique silver and the Royal gifts were all displayed. Of course, the Prefect of the department, the Mayor of Valençay, the Curé and, in short, all the authorities of the place, had been invited, and with true provincial punctuality had arrived at the exact hour named in the invitation, which, as usual in modern times, was long before the princely host expected to receive his guests, and, when they were ushered into the drawing room, they found that none of the family had as yet appeared, and that they would be consequently compelled to amuse themselves as they best could until the ringing of the bell, which would gather together the stray members of the household. In a short time, however, the great doors of the drawing room were thrown back with a loud fracas and in sailed, in all the majesty of stiffened silks and fluttering plumes, her Highness the Princess T. The troubled provincials immediately with one accord turned from the chimney, where they had been talking in mysterious murmurs concerning the mighty individuals whom they were to meet at dinner, and moved in a body, with sundry low bows and a great display of gymnastic prostrations, towards the fair Princess. The latter stood for a moment, and gazed as they advanced, then turning suddenly round to the grinning domestic, who had remained standing at the door, 'Fool!' exclaimed she indignantly. 'Did I not bid you ascertain if anybody had arrived, before I troubled myself to come down to the salon?'

'Yes, Princess, and I came myself to see,' answered the servant, looking rather puzzled and embarrassed, first at his mistress and then at the guests, who stood wondering where the questioning would lead to, 'and when I found these gentlemen here – '

'Idiot!' interrupted the Princess, 'not to know your business better; remember that such as these are not *anybody* but *nobody*.'

With these words she tossed out of the room, pointing with her fan over her shoulder at the poor stupefied provincials, whose rage and mortification defy description.

❦ A very remarkable man

By definition saints have to be different from ordinary mortals, but perhaps St Beuno took matters too far.

During the renovation of the chapel reputed to hold the bones of St Beuno, it was found necessary to open the tomb of the saint. Archaeologists took the opportunity to examine the bones and found to their surprise that the pelvis contained the bones of a foetus. But the church authorities were not surprised: 'Saint Beuno,' they said, 'was a very remarkable man.'

❦ A connoisseur of unhappy endings

George Selwyn had an obsession with death and never missed a chance to see a corpse, appearing at the site of accidents or natural disasters or, preferably, attending executions.

Of executions, Selwyn was reputed a connoisseur and so great was his reputation that when he went to Paris to see Damiens broken on the wheel, the executioner held up the proceedings until Selwyn had arrived. He even asked the crowds to part to allow the Englishman through to the front, saying, 'Make way for the gentleman; he is an Englishman and an enthusiast.'

❦ The voice of reason

William Cecil, later Lord Burghley and Queen Elizabeth I's great minister, attended the Inns of Court in London. He was certainly no eccentric but once he was forced to employ rather devious methods against one of his fellow students.

In his youth he was something of a gambler and on one occasion he lost a lot of money to a fellow student. Learning that his adversary slept in an adjacent room, with his head against the partition where Cecil himself slept, William devised a speaking tube which passed through the wall and under the other student's pillow. During the night Cecil began calling to him in the name of the Almighty to forsake gambling for ever or face everlasting Damnation. It worked. The next morning the shaken student came to Cecil's door and returned the money he had won.

❦ The flagship taken for a ride

The Royal Navy – the Senior Service – usually considers itself up to most things, even if it involves laughing at itself.

In February 1909, the British Home Fleet was lying at anchor off Weymouth when they received the signal that the Emperor of Abyssinia with a small party was coming to pay a visit to the *Dreadnought*. The emperor's party duly arrived, consisting of four Abyssinians, a Foreign Office official and a translator. They were taken aboard the battleship, which was dressed in flags with its band playing, and were given the full red carpet treatment by the admiral and his senior officers, resplendent in their dress uniforms. The Abyssinian party was shown round the entire ship, even entering one of the gun turrets and having the gun barrels elevated and lowered. All the time the translator communicated the admiral's words to the emperor. When explaining the different uniforms of the marines, the translator told the emperor, 'Entaqui, mahai, kustufani,' and the emperor nodded, replying, 'Tahli bussor ahbat tahl aesque miss.' The naval officers were splendid hosts, demonstrating to the Abyssinians the wonders of modern science, like the electric light. Declining the prepared lunch on religious grounds, the emperor and his party were taken ashore and returned to London. It had all been a great success.

However, a few weeks later the *Daily Mirror* broke the news that it had all been a hoax. The 'emperor' had been a young man named Anthony Buxton, wearing greasepaint and a turban. The language he had spoken to the translator was a mixture of Swahili and a mispronunciation of part of the fourth book of the *Aeneid*. One of the Abyssinians had even been a woman, suitably disguised, none other than the future Virginia Woolf.

The Navy felt humiliated, questions were asked in Parliament about security, and when the admiral came home on leave children followed him in the street chanting, 'Bunga, Bunga.' Although the hoaxers tried to apologize to the First Lord of the Admiralty, a red-faced Reginald McKenna was in no mood to listen.

❦ A box of tricks

The French actress Sarah Bernhardt was one of the most interesting characters of the period 1870–1910, and numbered the Prince of Wales among her numerous lovers. As a result of an accident, she lost a leg in her later years and wore a false one.

In her declining years Sarah Bernhardt painted her face chalk white and made herself a coffin of rosewood, with silver handles. She frequently used this to entertain guests, employing it as a table for drinks. Sometimes she slept in the coffin and had herself photographed in it, with her eyes closed and her hands crossed on her chest.

❦ On the hoof

The British explorer James Bruce travelled extensively in Ethiopia and discovered the source of the Blue Nile. However, he was widely suspected of exaggeration in many of his stories.

After his travels in Abyssinia Mr Bruce says he met a party of Abyssinian soldiers who drove a cow before them, and in his presence cut several slices of flesh from her, after which they covered the wound with skin and proceeding made the miserable animal accompany them to serve for their future repasts.

❦ A birch tree

Dr Birch was very fond of angling, and devoted much time to that amusement.

In order to deceive the fish Birch had a dress constructed which, when he put it on, made him appear like an old tree. His arms he conceived would appear like branches, and the line like a long spray. In this sylvan attire he used to take root by the side of a favourite stream, and imagined that his motions might seem to the fish to be the effect of the wind. He pursued this amusement for some years in the same habit, till he was ridiculed out of it by his friends.

❦ Johnson going downhill

Dr Samuel Johnson was sometimes as energetic as he was unusual in his activities.

After breakfast we walked to the top of a very steep hill behind the house. When we arrived at the summit, Mr Langton said, 'Poor dear Dr Johnson, when he came to this spot, turned back to look down the hill and said he was determined "to take a roll down". When we understood what he meant to do, we endeavoured to dissuade him; but he was resolute, saying, "I have not had a roll for a long time"; and taking out of his lesser pockets whatever might be in them – keys, pencil, purse or penknife – and laying himself parallel with the edge of the hill, he actually descended turning himself over and over, till he came to the bottom.'

❦ The turkey trot

The English lords of the eighteenth century were as eccentric as they were extravagant.

According to Horace Walpole, in 1756 Lords Rockingham and Orford made an extraordinary wager on a race from Norwich to London between five turkeys and five geese. The finishing point of the race was to be at Mile End turnpike.

❦ Love at first sight

Giuseppe Garibaldi, the Italian revolutionary fighter, may well be the only man to have chosen a wife by telescope.

Garibaldi was once standing on the deck of a ship off the coast of Brazil at Laguna, when he decided to find himself a wife, to dispel his melancholy. He thereupon picked up a telescope and scanned the shoreline until he saw some houses and a young woman standing by them. He decided that this was the woman for him and had himself rowed ashore. At first he found it difficult to find the right house and so he took coffee in one house while he prepared to continue his search. But fate was on his side for inside the house he found the girl of his dreams, whose name was Anita. Garibaldi remembered the first glimpse of Anita, adding that the two gazed at each other in silence. It was love at first sight.

❦ Two men in a boat

Theodore Hook – 1788–1841 – the British journalist and wit, was renowned for his practical jokes.

Hook was rowing up the Thames on one occasion with his friend Charles Mathews, the comic actor. Their attention was drawn to a sign at the bottom of one of the gardens they passed saying that unauthorized landings were forbidden. This annoyed the two men who decided to take up the challenge. They moored their boat and disembarked. They then used their fishing lines as surveyor's tapes and paced up and down as if they were taking measurements. It was not long before the owner came out, a civic dignitary from the City of London, who wanted to know what the deuce they were doing there. Hook said that he was an official from a canal company which was planning to cut a new canal which would pass through the alderman's garden, right under the windows of his house. At this news the alderman's face dropped and he invited his impromptu guests into his house where they were served excellent food and wine, trying to dissuade them from ruining his property. Only after they had drunk the last bottle of his wine did Hook and Mathews admit to their hoax.

❦ A splenetic fury

The nineteenth-century Austrian anatomist Joseph Hyrtl was professor of medicine at Vienna.

Hyrtl was once examining a particularly nervous candidate for his medical degree. He asked the young man, 'What can you tell me about the function of the spleen?' The candidate winced and then tried to bluff his way through. 'I did know exactly what it was,' he stammered, 'I knew it just a minute ago. But now I've forgotten.'

'Miserable creature,' shouted Hyrtl in mock horror. 'You are the only man in the whole world who knows anything about the function of the spleen – and now you have forgotten it!'

❦ Ducks and birds and geese better scurry

Sir Edward Coke, owner of Holkham Hall, was a quirky character.

Hearing that nobody but royalty was allowed to drive six horses in the London streets, Sir Edward Coke harnessed a coach to five horses, plus a donkey as the leader, and drove up and down in front of Buckingham Palace. Coke, in fact, had refused a peerage for more than thirty years, saying, 'I would rather remain first of the ducks than be the last of the geese.'

❦ You can look but you better not touch

Henry Cyril Paget, 5th Marquis of Anglesey, was one of the wealthiest and weirdest men in Victorian England.

Henry married his cousin Lilian Florence Maud Chetwyn, daughter of Lady Florence Paget. Lilian was a beautiful young woman and Henry liked to use her almost as a mannequin on which to display the wonders of his jewellery collection. On their honeymoon in Paris, Lilian was gazing in awe at the window display of Van Cleef and Arpels. Noticing this, Henry purchased the whole display for his new wife. Then, ignoring her tearful request not to be turned into such a spectacle, he made her wear the whole display to the races. Their marital relations were difficult from the start. Henry liked to waken his wife in the night and order her to strip naked, whereupon he covered her body in jewels. Having done so, he made her return to bed and sleep wearing the jewellery. After a short while Lilian sued for divorce which she was granted on the grounds of non-consummation.

❦ Resurrection squared

The nineteenth-century mathematician Charles Babbage designed a machine that was the forerunner of the computer. Unfortunately he also devoted his considerable talents to more eccentric academic pursuits.

Babbage once tried to investigate statistically the credibility of the biblical miracles. In the course of his analysis he made the assumption that the chance of a man rising from the dead was 1 in 10^{12}.

❦ Seeing triple

The eighteenth-century Greek scholar Richard Porson was as famous for his drinking bouts as he was for his scholarship. Presumably there were times when his eyesight might have supported all kinds of miraculous things.

Porson was walking with a Trinitarian friend; they had been speaking of the Trinity. A buggy came by with three men in it: 'There,' said his friend, 'is an illustration of the Trinity.' 'No,' said Porson, 'you must show me one man in three buggies if you can.'

❦ An unkind cut

Francis Bacon, 1st Baron Verulam and Viscount St Albans, was the most brilliant man of the late Elizabethan and Jacobean world. Both a lawyer and a philosopher, Bacon rose to be Lord Chancellor under King James I.

While Lord Chancellor of England, Bacon presided over a criminal appeal in which the plaintiff was a man called Hogg. Hogg facetiously pleaded that he should be let off on the grounds of his kinship with the judge. 'For,' he claimed, 'Hogg must be kin to bacon.' 'Not until it has been hung,' replied the chancellor grimly.

❦ A critic

The British chemist Sir Humphry Davy was one of the greatest scientists of the nineteenth century.

On his return from a visit to Paris, Davy was asked what he thought of the art galleries he had seen there. 'The finest collection of frames I ever saw,' he replied.

❦ A grammarian's funeral

Thomas de Mahay, Marquis de Favras, was a French aristocrat who tried to help Louis XVI escape from France in 1790. He was arrested and executed for high treason by the revolutionaries. His reputation as a literary critic was high.

Favras's trial lasted nearly two months; the evidence against him was inconclusive and the witnesses disagreed, but in the end he was found guilty. Before being led to the scaffold he was handed his death sentence, written down by the clerk of the court. He read it through, then said, 'I see, monsieur, that you have made three spelling mistakes.'

❦ Old habits die hard

The French philosopher, Bernard de Fontenelle, had been a great lover of women in his youth.

In his great old age (he lived to be 100) Fontenelle feebly but gallantly tried to pick up a fan a young lady had dropped. As she moved to help him, he exclaimed, 'Ah, if I were only eighty again.'

❦ Strange meeting

The French soldier, Marshal MacMahon, crushed the Paris Communards in 1871 and was President of France from 1873 to 1879.

Visiting a field hospital one day, the marshal addressed a few words to a soldier who lay ill with a tropical fever. 'Yes, that's a nasty disease you've got there. You either die of it or go crazy. I've been through it myself.'

❦ Spoiled for choice

The British prime minister Lord Palmerston had no time for foreigners.

A certain Frenchman, eager to flatter the patriotic Lord Palmerston, once remarked, 'If I were not a Frenchman I should wish to be an Englishman.' Palmerston was unimpressed. 'If I were not an Englishman,' he replied, 'I should wish to be an Englishman.'

❦ A good judge

The Scottish explorer Mungo Park travelled extensively in West Africa.

While exploring a particularly wild and uncultivated region of West Africa, Park unexpectedly came across a gibbet. 'The sight of it,' he later remarked, 'gave me infinite pleasure, as it proved that I was in a civilized society.'

❦ A painful scene

Thomas Pelham Holles, 1st Duke of Newcastle, was not one of Britain's better prime ministers.

In 1754 the Duke of Newcastle grieved on hearing of the death of his brother. 'Either grief for his brother's death, or joy for it had intoxicated him. He flung himself at the king's feet, sobbing and crying "God Bless your Majesty" and lay there howling and embracing the King's knees, with one foot so extended that Lord C—, who was luckily in waiting, begged the standers by to retire, with "For God's sake, gentlemen, don't look at a great man in distress", endeavoured to shut the door, caught his grace's foot, and made him roar out with pain.'

❦ At your convenience

In social matters, as in the affairs of state, the Duke of Newcastle could be relied upon to do the wrong thing.

'The Coronation is over: 'tis a more gorgeous sight than I imagined. Of all the incidents of the day, the most diverting was what happened to the Queen. She had a retiring chamber, with *all* conveniences behind the altar. She went thither – in the *most convenient* what found she but – the Duke of Newcastle.'

❦ Pillow fight

William Pitt the Elder, 1st Earl of Chatham, was a great English orator and statesman, who led the country successfully through the Seven Years' War.

During one of Pitt's illnesses Newcastle visited him in bed to discuss vital matters concerned with the Seven Years' War. There was no fire in the room so Newcastle, to keep warm, eventually leapt fully dressed into another bed. When the under secretary came in he was astonished to find his two ministers both sitting up in bed shouting at each other.

🐝 3. POTPOURRI

🐝 Name dropping

The Volstead Act of 1919 ushered in the period of Prohibition in the United States. As a result the 1920s was the time when crime rates in most American cities reached record levels. It was the period of Al Capone and the Chicago gangs, and the federal authorities found it almost impossible to contain the outburst of criminality. The problem was that the main effort was being made to combat drink-related offences and in this work nobody was more successful than two Federal Agents known as Izzy Einstein and Moe Smith. Izzy and Moe often used unconventional methods.

Izzy Einstein once entered a speakeasy – an illegal bar – and asked the bartender for a drink.

But the bartender refused to serve him, saying, 'I don't know you.'

'Why,' said Izzy, laughing, 'I'm Izzy Epstein, the famous prohibition detective.'

'Get the name right, bud,' said the bartender. 'The bum's name is Einstein.'

'Epstein,' said Izzy, 'don't I know my own name?'

'Maybe you do, but the low-life you are trying to act like is named Einstein. E-i-n-s-t-e-i-n.'

'Brother,' said Izzy, 'I ain't never wrong about a name. It's Epstein.'

'Einstein!' roared the bartender.

'Epstein!' shouted Izzy.

'You're nuts!' yelled the bartender. 'I'll bet you anything you like that it's Einstein.'

'OK,' said Izzy, 'I'll bet you the drinks.'

The bartender called for quiet in the bar and asked his customers who was right. Was it Epstein or Einstein? Eventually, after some discussion, it was unanimously agreed that the bartender was right. The correct name was Einstein. So Izzy lost and had to buy nine drinks – at the government's expense. Once the bartender had served out the drinks, Izzy promptly arrested him for serving illegal liquor.

❦ Am I too late?

Sir Walter Scott relates a story from the time of the 1745 Jacobite Rebellion.

As the Highlanders occupied Carlisle, one old lady was particularly apprehensive about the danger of violence to her person. She shut herself away in a closet, in order that she might escape ravishment. But no one came to disturb her solitude, and she began to be aware that poor Donald was looking out for victuals or seeking for some small plunder, without bestowing a thought on the fair sex; by and by she popped her head out of her place of refuge and enquired, 'Good folks, can you tell me when the ravishing is going to begin?'

❦ The Paris waterworks

The indignation felt by all Italians over the denial of their rights to the Adriatic coast at the Peace of Paris in 1919 caused the temporary return of Italy's delegate to the Paris conference to Rome for new instructions. His departure was the occasion for a considerable display of the Latin temperament.

On the day Orlando was leaving, one of Britain's delegates in Paris – Lord Balfour – told his friends at dinner, 'I must go and put on my wading boots.' His friends were nonplussed until Balfour told them, 'To say goodbye to Orlando. He was in tears when I left him and I have no reason to suppose that he has stopped crying since.'

❦ Warts and all

While Lord Protector of the Realm, Oliver Cromwell had his portrait painted by Peter Lely.

Lely had a reputation for improving the appearance of noblemen and their wives in his portraits and Cromwell, ever the Puritan, had no time for such vain activities. He sternly told Lely, 'Mr Lely, I desire you would use all your skill to paint my picture truly like me and not flatter me at all; but remark all these roughnesses, pimples, warts, and everything as you see me, otherwise I will never pay a farthing for it.'

❦ Setting up shelfs

After the restoration of the monarchy in 1660, King Charles II brought to justice the men who had authorized the execution of his father. These men were known as the Regicides and on 13 October 1660, Samuel Pepys recorded the execution of one of their number.

To my Lord's in the morning, where I met with Capt Cuttance. But my Lord not being up, I went out to Charing Cross to see Maj-Gen. Harrison hanged, drawn and quartered – which was done there. He looking as cheerfully as any man could do in that condition. He was presently cut down and his head and his heart shown to the people, at which there was great shouts of joy. It is said that he said that he was sure to come shortly at the right hand of Christ to judge them that now have judged him. And that his wife doth expect his coming again. Thus it was my chance to see the King beheaded at Whitehall and to see the first blood shed in revenge for the blood of the King at Charing Cross. From thence to my Lord's and took Capt Cuttance and Mr Sheply to the Sun taverne and did give them oysters. After that I went by water home, where I was angry with my wife for her things lying about and in my passion kicked the little fine Baskett which I bought her in Holland and broke it, which troubled me after I had done it. Within all the afternoon, setting up shelfs in my study.

❦ A sharp customer

Sir Walter Ralegh was one of the greatest of all Elizabethans and it was perhaps his misfortune that he survived into a meaner age. Ralegh had always made enemies and during the reign of King James I these men were able to engineer first his imprisonment and then his execution. Even facing execution, Ralegh showed his qualities as a wit.

Putting off his doublet and gowne he desired the headsman to shew him the Axe, which not being suddenly granted unto him, he said, I prithee let me see it, dost thou thinke I am afraid of it, so it being given unto him, he felt along the edge of it, and smiling spake unto Mister Sheriffe saying, this is a sharpe medicine, but it is a physician that will cure all diseases.

❦ Taking the initiative

During the famous siege of Sidney Street in the East End of London, two anarchists held the police and troops at bay for several hours.

The Home Secretary, Mr Winston Churchill, and his advisers who were with him at the end of the street began to feel hungry. A man suddenly appeared wearing an apron and carrying a tray of sandwiches, which he sold to Churchill and his fellows at high prices and which they greedily consumed. Nobody had bothered to enquire as to the identity of the sandwich man. It later turned out that he was the local cat's meat seller.

❦ An act of presumption

Henry Morton Stanley's meeting with Dr Livingstone at Ujiji in 1871 was one of the most famous incidents in the history of exploration. Livingstone, who had been presumed lost, had become a legend in his own lifetime and the Welsh-American Stanley was determined to make a reputation for himself by finding him. In this extract Stanley describes the moment of meeting:

As I advanced slowly towards him I noticed he was pale, looked wearied, had a grey beard, wore a bluish cap with a faded gold band round it, had on a red-sleeved waistcoat and a pair of grey tweed trousers. I would have run to him, only I was a coward in the presence of the mob – would have embraced him only, he being an Englishman, I did not know how he would receive me. So I did what cowardice and false pride suggested was the best thing – walked deliberately up to him, took off my hat and said, 'Doctor Livingstone I presume?' 'Yes,' said he with a kind smile, lifting his cap slightly. I replaced my hat on my head, and he puts on his cap, and we both grasp hands, and I then say aloud – 'I thank God, Doctor, I have been permitted to see you.' He answered, 'I feel thankful that I am here to welcome you.'

❦ An unwelcome guest

During the suppression of the Hungarian rising of 1849 the Austrian general Haynau – nicknamed the Hyena – earned himself a grim reputation for brutality, notably through shooting officers, abusing women and for his psychopathic lust for blood.

In 1851 General Haynau visited England and inspected a brewery there, but the draymen, apprised of his coming, attacked him and threw him in the dirt shouting, 'Down with the Austrian butcher.' Lord Palmerston, the British Foreign Secretary, was not sorry for what happened and made no official apology.

❦ A painless experience

The first public operation using a general anaesthetic was conducted by the great Scottish surgeon Robert Liston.

Chloroform was used to anaesthetize the patient, Frederick

Churchill, and the leg was painlessly removed. Unfortunately, so swift was Liston in cutting off the leg and so thorough was his follow-through that he also succeeded in amputating the patient's left testicle and two of his assistant's fingers.

❦ The Great Fire of London

An example of one of history's poorest predictions.

In spite of the enormous damage caused by the Great Fire of London – 13,000 houses were destroyed and an area of 436 acres laid waste – the authorities did not take it very seriously at first. When the Lord Mayor, Sir Thomas Bludworth, came to inspect the scene on the first day, he uttered the words 'Pshaw! A woman might piss it out.'

❦ An eminence grise

When war broke out between France and Germany in 1914, and German troops invaded Belgium, Britain presented Germany with an ultimatum. The outbreak of a great European war, the first for a century, was a shattering blow to all the diplomats who had struggled so hard to avoid it.

As the British ultimatum to Germany expired on 4 August 1914 the British Foreign Secretary, Sir Edward Grey, standing at the window of his office overlooking St James's Park, said to a friend, 'The lamps are going out all over Europe; we shall not see them lit again in our lifetime.'

❦ Auto-da-fé

Thomas Cranmer, Archbishop of Canterbury under King Henry VIII and King Edward VI, was sentenced to be burned at the stake for heresy by Queen Mary. At first Cranmer abjured his religion to save his life but later he changed his mind and willingly died for his faith. He decided that the right hand that had signed his recantation should burn first.

47

And when the wood was kindled, and the fire began to burn near him, stretching out his arm, he put his right hand into the flame, which he held so steadfast and unmovable (save that once with the same hand he wiped his face) that all men might see his hand burn before his body was touched.

❦ Singeing the king of Spain's beard

When the English learned that the Spanish king, Philip II, was preparing an Armada against England, steps were taken to delay its sailing. Sir Francis Bacon described the raid on Cadiz carried out by Sir Francis Drake.

As for the expedition of Sir Francis Drake in the year 1587, for the destroying of the Spanish shipping and provision upon their own coast, as I cannot say that there intervened in that enterprise any sharp fight or encounter, so nevertheless it did straightly discover, either that Spain is very weak at home, or very slow to move, when they suffered a small fleet of English to make an hostile invasion or incursion upon their havens and roads from Cadiz to Cape Sacre, and thence to Cascous and to fire, sink and carry away at the least ten thousand ton of their greater shipping, besides fifty or sixty of their smaller vessels, and that in the sight and under the favour of their forts and almost under the eye of their great Admiral, the best commander of Spain by sea, the Marquis de Santa Cruce, without ever being disputed with in any fight of importance: I remember Drake, in the vaunting stile of a soldier, would call the enterprise the Singeing of the King of Spain's beard.

❦ As easy as cracking eggs

The Genoese navigator Christopher Columbus made the first modern voyage across the Atlantic in 1492 on behalf of the Spanish rulers, Ferdinand and Isabella.

A shallow courtier present, impatient of the honours paid to Columbus, and meanly jealous of him as a foreigner, abruptly asked him whether he thought that in case he had not discovered the Indies, there were not other men who would have been capable of the enterprise. To this Columbus made no immediate answer, but, taking an egg, invited the company to make it stand on one end. Everyone attempted it, but in vain; whereupon he struck it upon the table so as to break the end, and left it standing upon the broken part; illustrating in this simple manner that when he had once shown the way to the New World, nothing was easier than to follow it.

❦ All for one and one for all

American statesman, writer and scientist Benjamin Franklin was one of the fathers of the American nation and one of the five men who signed the Declaration of Independence.

During the drafting of the Declaration of Independence in 1776 there were numerous disputes between the men from the various states. John Hancock said to his fellows, 'We must be unanimous – we must all hang together.' 'We must indeed all hang together,' said Franklin, 'or most assuredly we shall all hang separately.'

❦ Away with such baubles

In 1653, the Lord Protector Oliver Cromwell decided to dismiss the Long Parliament, which had been sitting for more than twelve years, during which time the country had been riven by civil war.

With the backing of the army Cromwell was prepared to use force to dissolve Parliament and entered the Commons with a band of musketeers. The Speaker was arrested and the MPs dispersed by soldiers. In front of the Speaker's chair lay the mace – the emblem of Parliament's authority – and one of the soldiers called out, 'What shall we do with the mace?' 'Away with such baubles,' cried Cromwell.

❦ Putting on a brave face

Georges Jacques Danton played a leading part in the overthrow of King Louis XVI. However, in 1793, his moderate policies were rejected by the Committee of Public Safety led by Citizen Robespierre and Danton was denounced and guillotined.

At the height of the Terror, Danton was put on trial, charged with betraying the French people. He treated the charges with contempt and though condemned to death told his executioners, 'Show my head to the people. It's worth it.'

❦ Ralegh put out

Sir Walter Ralegh was renowned for bringing tobacco back to England from the New World and for popularizing smoking. The novelty caused much comment and some confusion.

Sir Walter Ralegh was once enjoying a pipe of tobacco when one of his servants, seeing his master enveloped in smoke and apparently on fire, quickly emptied a bowl of water over his head.

❦ Set meals

The Paris mob, instrumental as it was in bringing about frequent political change in France throughout the centuries, was very aware of mealtimes. An eyewitness to the French Revolution, Helen Williams, wrote:

Here I will make one remark. During the frequent insurrections which took place in Paris in the course of the Revolution, it has been observed that the people always dispersed at mealtimes. The same characteristic was observed in the previous century by Cardinal de Retz who, on receiving the order to disperse the crowd on the first day of the Fronde rebellion, replied: 'That will not give me much trouble. It will soon be supper time.'

❦ For those in peril on the sea

Sir Humphrey Gilbert, half-brother to Sir Walter Ralegh, established a settlement in Newfoundland. In Richard Hakluyt's Principal Navigations, *the death of Sir Humphrey Gilbert is recorded by Edward Hayes, who was sailing in the* Golden Hind, *and saw Gilbert's ship sink.*

Monday, the ninth of September, in the afternoon, the frigate was near cast away, oppressed by waves, yet at that time recovered; and giving forth signs of joy, the General, sitting abaft with a book in his hand, cried unto us in the *Hind*, so oft as we did approach within hearing: 'We are as near to heaven by sea as by land!'; reiterating the same speech, well beseeming a soldier, resolute in Jesus Christ, as I can testify he was.

❦ Prussian blues

The Prussian delegation at the Congress of Vienna in 1814 was made up, primarily, of military men. Their training as soldiers made them horrified at the evidence of extravagance in the Austrian capital.

At the grand balls that accompanied the Congress of Vienna, the ladies wore such a glittering array of jewels that one of the Prussian representatives remarked, 'Good God, you could run three campaigns on this.'

❦ He died laughing

The death of the Huguenot, the Comte de La Rochefoucauld, in 1571, was a tragi-comedy. He even called on his killers not to tickle him.

During the Massacre of St Bartholomew's Day the Comte de La Rochefoucauld was asleep in bed when the murderers came to his room. He had only recently returned from a party and when he was awoken by the noise of intruders he found his bed surrounded by men in masks. He burst out laughing, thinking it was his friends playing a prank on him, and was still laughing as the soldiers hacked him to death.

✋ Your time is up

King Louis Philippe of France – known as the 'Citizen King' – had come to the throne after the deposition of Charles X in 1830. But by 1848 his liberal policies had been rejected and he was overthrown by left-wing elements, pressing for more social reform. The king found refuge in England.

King Louis Philippe was taking luncheon with some of his family, when the Duc de Montpensier burst into the room shouting that the army had thrown in its lot with the Reds.

'You must abdicate immediately,' Montpensier told him.

The old man turned up the table cloth and began to write his abdication proclamation on it while Montpensier kept banging on the table saying, 'Hurry, Sire.'

The king finished the proclamation, pulled the table cloth off the table and handed it to his son, who was standing nearby. 'Even to abdicate takes a little time,' he added sadly.

✋ The man without qualities

Prince Felix Schwarzenburg symbolized Habsburg rule in their empire: ingratitude and brutality, both conducted with an air of superficial gentility.

After the collapse of the Hungarian Revolt in 1850, as a result of considerable Russian help, the Austrian politician Prince Felix Schwarzenberg, when asked if he felt a sense of great obligation to Tsar Nicholas I for his help, replied, 'Austria will astonish the world by the magnitude of her ingratitude.' When he was later asked if, in response to appeals for clemency from throughout the civilized world, he would be lenient to the Hungarian rebels, he replied, 'Yes, yes – a very good idea. But first we will have a little hanging.'

❦ Climbing the family tree

Alexander Dumas the elder, author of The Count of Monte Cristo *and* The Three Musketeers, *was notoriously short-tempered. He was once questioned on his ancestry by a very insistent newspaper reporter.*

'Is it true that you are a quadroon?' asked the reporter. Dumas replied that he was.

'So your father was a mulatto?'

'Yes,' said Dumas.

'And your grandfather was a negro?'

'Yes,' said Dumas, growing impatient.

The reporter persisted.

'And your great-grandfather?'

'A baboon, sir,' roared Dumas. 'A baboon. Which means that my family begins where yours ends.'

❦ A play on words

American writer Mark Twain enjoyed teasing his companions.

On one occasion after attending a church service given by the self-important Dr Doane, later Bishop of Albany, Twain congratulated him on an enjoyable sermon. 'I welcomed it as an old friend,' he went on. 'I have a book at home containing every word of it.' Doane bristled. 'I am sure you have not, sir,' he replied huffily. 'Indeed, I have,' Twain persisted. 'Every word of it.' 'Well I would like to have a look at it then,' said Doane. 'Could you send it to me?' The following day Twain sent him a dictionary.

❦ Not feeling himself

British theologian Richard Chenevix Trench suffered a fall, fracturing both his knees. He never fully recovered and lived in fear of paralysis.

Once at a dinner, a lady seated next to Trench noticed that he seemed agitated and was muttering, 'It has come at last. I can't feel a thing. I am paralysed.' The lady asked Trench what was wrong and he replied, 'I have been pinching my leg for the last five minutes and I can't feel a thing.' The lady went red and said, 'It is all right your grace. It is my leg you've been pinching.'

❦ A mathematical error

When not writing delightful children's books, Lewis Carroll (Charles Dodgson) was in fact a mathematician.

Queen Victoria was delighted by Lewis Carroll's *Alice in Wonderland* and wrote to the author telling him that she would willingly receive any other works by him. A little later, however, she was disconcerted to receive Dodgson's *Syllabus of Plane Algebraical Geometry.*

❦ The brass butterfly

After the death of Oscar Wilde, a committee headed by Robert Ross commissioned the sculptor Epstein to make a memorial for the great writer's tomb in Paris. Epstein took up the challenge and designed a superb sculpture of Wilde as the Sphinx. Unfortunately, the nude figure was too specific for the sensitivities of the Paris Police and when it was unveiled in the cemetery Père Lachaise, it was immediately covered by an official with a tarpaulin, in spite of the sculptor's objections that he had not even completed it yet. Not to be deterred, every afternoon Epstein with a group of supporters visited the cemetery, removed the tarpaulin and continued working on the memorial. As soon as the police were informed they replaced the tarpaulin and so the day's work came to an end. This continued for some time until the police lost patience and arrested Epstein and his friends.

Meanwhile, Robert Ross was disturbed to hear about the antics performed daily around the memorial he had commissioned. He approached Epstein and asked if the offending article could be covered in some way, but the sculptor refused. Ross, frustrated that his memorial to Wilde was now totally hidden by the police tarpaulin, came up with a compromise. A bronze plaque, in the shape of a butterfly, would be positioned strategically so as to remove any possible threat to public decency. The police were satisfied, Epstein infuriated. Ross next approached the poet Aleister Crowley and asked if he would officially unveil the memorial. Crowley agreed, 'in the interests of art'.

The unveiling passed off without a hitch and there the matter might have ended except that, a few weeks later, a man in full evening dress turned up at the Café Royale in Piccadilly with a long cord around his neck. On the end of the cord was the bronze butterfly plaque removed by the poet Crowley, for it was he, 'in the interests of art'. As he told guests at the restaurant, the tombstone of Wilde was now exactly as Epstein had conceived it.

❦ Rewriting history

When the French painter Alphonse Legros adopted British citizenship he was asked by one of his French colleagues what he hoped to gain by this defection.

'To begin with,' Legros replied, 'I win the battle of Waterloo.'

❦ Smooth talker

The American dramatist Marc Connelly was almost totally bald. One day a drinking companion playfully ran his hand over Connelly's bare head, remarking, 'That feels just like my wife's behind.'

Connelly stroked his head thoughtfully. 'So it does,' he replied.

❦ The missing note

During a performance of Beethoven's *Leonora III Overture*, the offstage trumpet call twice failed to be played. The conductor, Leopold Stokowski, was enraged. As soon as the overture was finished he left the rostrum and went to search for the missing trumpeter. He found him in the wings wrestling with the janitor, who was saying, 'You can't blow that damned thing here. I tell you there's a concert going on.'

❦ Stamping his authority

The great actor and impresario, Sir Herbert Beerbohm Tree, was noted for his offbeat character.

Once when visiting a post office to buy a stamp the assistant showed him a whole sheet of them. Tree scrutinized the sheet for a moment and then pointed to one right in the middle. 'I'll have that one, please.'

❦ For tomorrow you diet

The German composer Brahms liked good cooking but it did not always agree with him.

Once when suffering indigestion, Brahms consulted his doctor, who recommended a strict diet. Brahms complained, 'But this evening I am dining with Strauss and we shall have chicken paprika.' 'Out of the question,' said the doctor. 'Well then,' said Brahms, 'please consider that I did not come to consult you until tomorrow.'

❦ Guests who?

In 1940 Lord Berners once sent a spoof invitation to one of his friends, a well-known 'social climber'. It was in the form of a brief note saying, 'I wonder if by any chance you are free to dine tomorrow night? It is only a tiny party for Winston and GBS. I think it important that they should get together at this moment. There will be nobody else except for Toscanini and myself.' He then deliberately obscured the signature and the address for a reply, driving his victim mad with frustration.

❦ Physician heal thyself!

Grimaldi was the most famous clown of his time.

A doctor once received a visit from a very gloomy patient. 'You need amusement,' he advised. 'Go and hear the comedian Grimaldi. He will make you laugh and that will be better for you than any medicine.' The patient was not impressed: 'I am Grimaldi,' he replied.

❦ An early riser

Richard Harris Barham was a difficult student at Oxford and often failed to turn up for chapel in the morning.

His tutor demanded an explanation and Barham told him: 'The fact is, it is too late for me. I am a man of regular habits and I cannot sit up until seven o'clock in the morning. Unless I get to bed by four or five at the latest I am good for nothing next day.'

❦ Paper boy

The Italian poet D'Annunzio found inspiration for his poetry in many unusual ways, including writing with a quill pen on paper balanced on an upturned umbrella, and keeping stillborn babies pickled in bottles on shelves in his study. Furthermore, he loved to shock the Italian Establishment, which he regarded as harmful to the progress of his country.

On 9 August 1918, in the last months of the war, the skies of Vienna were filled with pieces of coloured paper – red, white and green – dropped by planes of the Italian Air Force. The squadron responsible was led by Gabriele D'Annunzio. It was a propaganda coup, the text of the pamphlets reading, 'Viennese, we could now be dropping bombs on you. Instead we drop a salute.'

❦ Choice material

Mr Wilby Lunn, one of ENSA's entertainers, took his Spotlight Concert Party to a camp in the West of England. On his arrival the Entertainments Officer came to ask him if there was anything in the programme to which exception might be taken as the C.O. and his daughter were going to attend. He was told that there was nothing. The officer returned, just fifteen minutes later, to tell Lunn that the C.O. was not coming after all, only his daughter, adding, 'So you can make it as dirty as you like.'

❦ It ain't 'arf 'ot, Mum

In ENSA one comedian was renowned for complaining about every assignment he was given. When he was told that his party was being sent to Khartoum, in the Sudan, he moaned, 'You cannot send me there. It is a hell of a place. They tell me that it is 120 degrees in the shade.'

'Don't worry about that, old boy,' he was told, 'there's no shade there at all.'

❦ A horse's tale

The cricketer Charles Burgess Fry was one of the twentieth century's 'Renaissance Men'. Besides being an exceptional scholar, cricketer, footballer and athlete – he held the world long jump record – he was also offered the vacant throne of Albania.

When Fry told a friend that, at the age of seventy, he was thinking of interesting himself in the Turf by setting up a racing stable, his friend replied, 'What as, Charles, a trainer, jockey or a horse?'

❦ Cat flap

When DDT was used to destroy mosquitoes in Sarawak it resulted in the death of the cat population who were poisoned by the chemical. As a result there was a plague of rats and the threat of bubonic plague. In order to solve the problem and restore balance to the ecosystem of Sarawak, the World Health Organization had to call on the RAF to drop cats by parachute on isolated villages in the interior. This remarkable first, known as 'Operation Cat-Drop', was less ridiculous than it seemed.

❦ Beating the bully at his own game

Dr Keate became headmaster of Eton in 1809 at a time when discipline was slack and he felt the need to raise standards by the most brutal regime in educational history. The flogging campaign of May to June 1810 has to have been the activity of a madman.

On one occasion, Keate decided to beat all one hundred members of the fifth form. He did the deed in public, with the culprits lined up witnessing justice in action and other members of the school watching the beating. The cruelty of the occasion, the blood so clearly being spilled and the cries and screams of the injured soon drove the watching boys into a kind of communal frenzy. They began shouting, jeering and stamping their feet. Next they began throwing eggs and tomatoes at the headmaster who ignored their missiles and continued thrashing like an automaton. As the situation grew more serious stones began striking Keate, who never for a moment lessened his stroke, and other masters were forced to patrol the crowd of schoolboys to suppress the violence with their own canes and birches. With each boy receiving six strokes delivered with his full strength Keate must have been an enormously strong man. The six hundred blows he administered so strained his ligaments that he was confined to bed for a week after this demonstration of discipline.

❦ Prodigies

In 1673 Mrs Basua Makin's school for girls was set up in Tottenham. It advertised that in its establishment eight-year-olds 'that can read well' were able to learn Latin, French, English Grammar, Greek, Hebrew, Italian and Spanish.

❦ The tables turned

When Winston Churchill was seven he was being taught by his governess, Miss Hutchinson. On one occasion the bell rang in the servants' quarters and a maid went up to the room where the lessons were taking place. The maid entered and enquired of the governess if she had rung. Instead, Winston replied, saying, 'I rang. Take away Miss Hutchinson, she is very cross with me. Please show her out.'

❦ Eager to please

The high reputation of British nannies was recognized worldwide. Both for reasons of snobbery and for their efficiency they were in demand in many countries. However, they rarely earned high military rank except in Russia.

In 1899 the Empress of Russia decided to employ a British nanny for the royal children. Nanny Eager was appointed and given virtually absolute power in the nursery. When the Romanov princesses grew old enough tutors were appointed to teach them, each tutor being given the military rank of a general. However, Nanny Eager outranked them all, being given the rank of field marshal.

❦ Child care

Before formal training for nannies was introduced many had no training at all and, as they were frequently very young and inexperienced, they discovered child care the hard way. One elderly nursemaid was once asked what she did if her child screamed incessantly from morning to night. The old woman replied, 'Oh, I dunno. I just sits and bears it.'

❦ Priorities

During a daylight air-raid in Plymouth in 1940, a two-year-old asked his nanny, 'What's that noise, Nanny?' Nanny replied, 'Bombs dear. Now, elbows off the table.'

❦ Painting the world red

Cecil Rhodes was popular with Queen Victoria as he added so much territory to the British Empire.

Meeting the great man at Windsor in December 1894, the Queen asked Rhodes, 'What have you been doing since I last saw you, Mr Rhodes?' Rhodes modestly replied, 'I have added two provinces to Your Majesty's dominions.' The Queen concluded, 'Ah, I wish some of my Ministers, who take away my provinces, would do as much.' In fact, Rhodes had won control of both Matabeleland and Mashonaland from their native rulers, and was administering the whole area as Rhodesia.

❦ The cycles of history

The Jameson Raid depended on the support of the Uitlanders in the Transvaal. Unfortunately, when Dr Jameson needed him the Uitlander leader was busy.

When Jameson kept his appointment to meet Frank Rhodes in Johannesburg to discuss the distribution of weapons he found a message from Rhodes, apologizing for breaking the appointment but explaining that he was busy teaching a lady to ride a bicycle.

❦ Wedding reception

The great Islamic leader Saladin was renowned for his courtesy. Once when besieging Kerak, the castle of Reginald of Chatillon, he interrupted a wedding celebration.

The mother of the bridegroom, Stephanie de Milly, personally prepared some dishes from the bridal feast, and sent them out to Saladin who received them in his tent. In return the great warrior enquired as to which of Kerak's towers was being used by the newly-weds, and promptly ordered his engineers to cease the bombardment in that area so that the honeymooners could get some peace.

☙ Sightseers

In England in 1678 fears of a French invasion were widespread.

A story came from Dorset, along with the sworn statements of men who had witnessed the episode, that a French army had landed on the Isle of Purbeck and had drawn up in line, with their officers at their head. The Earl of Danby, the lord lieutenant of Dorset, spurred his horse towards Hyde Park, sword in hand and shouting to everyone to take arms as the French were coming. But the observers of the French landing had been mistaken, or more likely drunk. The French line of battle turned out to be a hedge and the officers nothing more than some horses grazing in a meadow.

☙ Wee Pilliewinkie

By the 1620s witch-hunting was common in Calvinist Scotland and nearly three times as many witches were executed there as in the rest of Britain.

During one witchcraft trial in North Berwick, a woman named Gellie Duncan was put to the terrible torture of the pilliewinkies. It persuaded her to admit to joining some 200 witches and warlocks in naked frolics in a kirk on the edge of the city. There they were told by the devil to assassinate King James I who was, according to the evil spirit, 'the greatest enemy he ever had'. When the king heard this he was privately delighted. He ordered Gellie Duncan to attend him at court and play the same reel that she had played at the witches' frolics in the church.

☙ Medical profession

Quack doctors made a good living during the eighteenth century.

On one occasion, a meeting took place between a famous doctor and a famous quack, both men foremost in their respective professions. But the doctor, for all his qualifications and medical successes, was still far less wealthy than his streetwise opponent. The doctor asked the quack to explain why this was so. The quack replied by asking the doctor how many of the hundred people who had just passed by possessed common sense. The doctor answered that no more than one possessed real common sense. 'Well,' said the quack, 'that one comes to you for help and the other ninety-nine come to me.'

❦ Lucy in the sky

During the Middle Ages bread was sometimes contaminated by ergot.

At Modena in 1592, unscrupulous dealers added darnel to the flour to create 'dazed bread', which was known to have stupefying effects on its victims, in which they danced about like madmen, beat their heads against walls or even killed themselves in a frenzy. St Vitus's dance, which was common among medieval peasantry, almost certainly stemmed from the presence of ergot containing lysergic acid (LSD) in their bread.

4. A FANFARE OF STRUMPETS

❦ A revealing gesture

During the 1860s Edward, Prince of Wales, was the most eligible bachelor in Europe. He travelled widely but spent much time in Paris, where he found the life of the Second Empire much to his taste.

When the Prince of Wales was introduced by the Duc de Grammont-Caderousse to the courtesan Guila Braucci in his private dining room, Guila curtsied and then dropped her clothes to the floor, standing naked in front of the prince. When the duke reprimanded her for her forwardness, she replied, 'But you told me to be on my best behaviour with His Royal Highness and I showed him the best I have for free.'

❦ Lady and the tramp

Not all of the Prince of Wales's mistresses came out of the 'top drawer'. The cockney whore, Rosa Lewis, eventually opened the Cavendish Hotel on her earnings, but she never lost the common touch.

On one occasion Edward took a night-time ride in a Hackney coach with Rosa. They travelled around for some considerable time and Edward eventually gave the cabbie a shilling, not knowing what the proper fare should be for so long a drive.

'What's this bleeding bob for?' asked the cabbie, who had not recognized the Prince of Wales, and was furious at being short-changed.

'Your fare, my man,' said the prince.

'A bleeding bob for two hours' driving and ten miles?' yelled the cabbie.

At this moment Rosa leant forward and gave the man two sovereigns. This quietened him considerably.

'I knowed you was a lady as soon as I seen you,' said the driver to Rosa, 'but where did you pick 'im up?'

❦ The cook's special

Cora Pearl – an English girl born Emma Elizabeth Crouch in Plymouth – became the most famous courtesan of Paris during the Second Empire, numbering princes among her many lovers. She was fond of the elaborate practical joke.

Cora was staging a lavish dinner party at the exclusive Café Riche, in Paris, to which only the most eligible clients – princes, dukes and senators – had been invited. She then proposed a bet, that she would offer them a dish that evening that none of them could eat. Amidst laughter she took the bets and then excused herself

while the dish was prepared. Some time passed and an air of expectancy was relieved by a round of applause from the diners as the doors to the kitchen were opened and the chef appeared, to a flourish from a trumpeter, leading a column of waiters, two of whom were staggering under the weight of an enormous silver serving dish. Having placed the dish in the centre of the dining table, the chef took off the cover to reveal Cora, naked and curled up on a bed of flowers. Sprinkling Cora's belly with parsley, the chef bowed to the guests and returned to the kitchens. Cora leapt to her feet laughing and collected her winnings.

❦ Still at the top

The great French actress Sarah Bernhardt had in her prime been the target for many men of wealth and distinction.

In her later years Sarah Bernhardt lived on the top floor of a Paris apartment. An old admirer arrived at her door one day, out of breath after the long climb. When he had recovered he asked her, 'Madame, why do you live so high up?' 'My dear friend,' replied the actress, 'it is the only way I can still make the hearts of men beat faster.'

❦ Dishonourable intentions

The British scholar and explorer Sir Richard Burton was one of the most extraordinary men of his time, visiting Mecca disguised as an Arab and translating erotic Arab and Indian texts into English. He travelled widely in Africa in search of the source of the River Nile.

After his return from Sind, Burton encountered an attractive young lady in Boulogne who turned out to be Louisa, sister of his future wife, Isabel Arundell. Unfortunately, unsavoury rumours surrounded Burton's time in Sind, and Louisa's mother decided that she had better meet the famous explorer. So she summoned him to her presence because, she told him, she felt it was her duty to ask him what his intentions were towards her daughter. Burton, who was merely flirting with the young girl, replied to the mother,

'My intentions towards your daughter, Madame, are, alas, strictly dishonourable.'

❦ Abreast of the truth

Ninon de Lenclos was the most famous courtesan of the seventeenth century. Even in old age both men and women consulted her for advice on the art of love.

A lady once asked Ninon de Lenclos, 'How large should a woman's breast be to attract a lover?' Ninon replied, 'Large enough to fill the hand of an honest man.'

❦ False hopes

When the eccentric nineteenth-century English adventuress Jane Digby was in Greece she was robbed while engaged in painting a picture.

Jane Digby was standing on some steps by the town of Mount Lycabettus when she became aware that a well-dressed and handsome young Greek was standing near her. He edged towards her and finally snatched a golden chain from her neck and ran away. She told the story to some friends in Athens who asked her why she had let the man come so close to her without registering alarm. 'How could I guess,' said Jane candidly, 'that he was only interested in my chain?'

❦ Blanching

The French courtesan Blanche d'Antigny spent four years in St Petersburg, finally becoming the lover of the Russian chief of the secret police, Count Mezensteff.

Blanche committed a blunder when she decided to attend the gala performance at the opera in St Petersburg wearing a dress that would outshine everyone, including the royal family. She found at her couturier exactly the dress that she wanted.

Unfortunately it was one that the empress had ordered and intended to wear to the gala evening. Overriding every protest from the couturier, she bought the dress and the following evening wore it to the opera house and paraded it in full view of the royal box. The next morning Count Mezensteff received a message from the palace and Blanche d'Antigny was expelled from Russia.

❧ Twinkle toes

The stage debut of the courtesan Cora Pearl, at the Théâtre des Bouffes-Parisiens, as Cupid in Offenbach's comic opera Orphée aux Enfers, *was a significant one for students of jewellery and unusual footwear.*

One onlooker described Cora Pearl as looking like a jeweller's window while another wealthy patron offered fifty thousand francs for the boots she was wearing. An Englishman at the first performance remarked that 'the buttons on her boots were large diamonds of the first water...and in one last extravagant gesture she threw herself flat on her back and flung her legs up in the air to show the soles of her shoes that were one mass of diamonds.'

❧ A binding agreement

Cora Pearl once received a beautifully bound book from one of her admirers. When she opened it she found that every page was a thousand-franc note.

❧ La toilette des pieds

Princess Borghese – the beautiful sister of Napoleon Bonaparte – who had modelled for Canova's sculpture of Venus, was inordinately proud of her feet and liked to display them to her admirers.

Princess Borghese would issue regular invitations to attend *La toilette des pieds*. When the guests arrived in the morning they found the princess stretched out on a couch, with her feet on a velvet cushion. Then two or three maids would come in, wipe the feet with a sponge and dust them with special powder. It is said that the Duke of Hamilton, son-in-law of the famous English eccentric William Beckford, would sit close to the princess and place one of her feet inside his waistcoat 'like a little bird'.

❦ In bondage to La Païva

The courtesan, Thérèse Lachmann, known to the world as La Païva, lived in splendour at Pontchartrain. She employed one servant whose job was to open and shut the 150 windows, beginning his work at six in the morning and not finishing his daily task until late in the evening. La Païva was obsessive about the condition of her gardens and fined her gardeners fifty centimes for every leaf that she found on the grass.

❦ A private viewing

Richard Burton told the story of a group of Englishmen who visited a Muslim sheikh in the desert.

As they watched, the sheikh's wife fell off a camel, revealing her private parts. The Englishmen were thoroughly embarrassed and were amazed when the sheikh seemed entirely unconcerned. It was only later that they learned that the sheikh had in fact been delighted that his wife had managed to keep her face covered while she fell.

❦ The Harleian Miscellany

George Gordon, Lord Byron, was one of the most significant British Romantic poets. He was also a notorious rake.

Shortly after breaking off his affair with Lady Caroline Lamb, Lord Byron moved in with Jane Elizabeth Scott, the forty-year-old wife of Lord Edward Harley, Earl of Oxford. Lady Jane was as notorious in her way as Byron, having had so many lovers during her marriage that her brood of children were known as the Harleian Miscellany.

❦ At a loose end

Cesare Borgia was the son of Pope Alexander VI. His father originally intended him to enter the Church and he became a cardinal, but he later gave up the religious life to pursue a career of conquest.

On 12 May 1499, Cesare Borgia married Charlotte d'Albret, daughter of the Duc de Guyenne. Their marriage night proved to be an eventful one. Somebody played a practical joke on Cesare, substituting laxatives for the aphrodisiac pills that he had intended to take to improve his performance. The result was that Cesare spent as much time in the privy as he did with his bride.

❦ A womb with a view

In 1809 Napoleon married Princess Marie Louise of Austria, daughter of the emperor.

The Austrian princess had been brought up so strictly that she had not even been allowed to see male animals. But Napoleon was less concerned with her ignorance of sexual matters than with the question of whether she could provide him with a son and heir. He inspected her as if she was a brood mare, concluding that she had 'the kind of womb I want to marry'.

❦ A noble heart

The Countess de Castiglione was sent to France by the Piedmontese prime minister Cavour to become the Emperor Napoleon's lover and to influence his policy, notably towards helping Italy achieve freedom from Austrian domination. Naturally 'Nicchia' or 'La Castiglione' was much hated by the Empress Eugénie.

'Nicchia' once attended a grand ball given by the emperor and empress of France. She wore a most daring costume, consisting of a thin gauze dress, under which she was completely naked. Her nipples were covered with two small hearts, and her *mons veneris* was concealed by a larger heart shape. Otherwise, the costume was so transparent that everything was visible. She caused a sensation when she entered the room but the Empress Eugénie was not prepared to let the Italian steal the show in this way. She calmly walked up to La Castiglione and said, 'Countess, your heart seems to have slipped.' She asked her to leave the palace, which Nicchia tearfully did. But she was soon back wearing an equally amazing dress, cut up the sides from ankle to shoulder, revealing that she was still naked beneath.

❦ Cheap at twice the price

Kitty Fisher was one of the most renowned courtesans in eighteenth-century England and the prices she was able to charge were legendary. Curiously, Kitty died at an early age from the effects of her lead face paint.

On one occasion Kitty Fisher was engaged by Edward Augustus, Duke of York, a younger brother of King George III. Kitty felt that this was her greatest conquest but she was in for a disappointment. After spending the night with her the duke gave her just fifty pounds instead of her normal fee of one hundred guineas. Furious at his parsimony, she chased him out of the house and then had his fifty pounds baked in a pie, which she later ate for lunch. She never slept with a royal duke again without settling the price in advance.

❦ The Bride of Christ

Rodrigo Borgia, who later became Pope Alexander VI, had numerous mistresses even after his elevation to the papacy.

One of Rodrigo Borgia's mistresses, the sixteen-year-old Giulia Farnese, was already married when he became her lover. The Romans, more amused than censorious, called Giulia the 'Bride of Christ'.

❦ A union meeting

Royal mistresses needed staying power and many of them seemed to possess it in abundance.

Let Them Eat Cake!

At the coronation of King George I an unusual meeting took place.
Lady Dorchester, a former mistress of James II, espied the Duchess
of Portsmouth, one of Charles II's mistresses, and Lady Orkney,
who had fulfilled the same function for William III, walking into
the abbey. 'Good God!' she exclaimed. 'Who would have thought
that we three whores would have met together here.'

❦ Splitting hairs

*Noah Webster, the lexicographer and author of the famous
dictionary, was a man of great precision, notably when it came to
finding excuses for his infidelities.*

Going unexpectedly into the parlour of their house one day,
Mrs Webster discovered her husband embracing their maid.
'Noah, I am surprised!' she exclaimed. Webster released the
maid and re-assumed his professional dignity. 'No, my dear,' he
corrected his wife, 'it is I who am surprised; you are merely
astonished.'

❦ The chaperone

*Princess Marie Pauline Borghese, sister to Napoleon I, was one of
the most beautiful women of the First Empire. Of all Napoleon's
relations, Pauline was the only one to stand by him in exile after
his defeat at Waterloo.*

On one occasion a lady expressed herself surprised that Pauline
Bonaparte, the Princess Borghese, should have posed naked while
Antonio Canova modelled his famous statue of her as Venus Victrix.
'But,' said the princess demurely, 'there was a fire in the room.'

❦ Advice to fathers

*The great English diarist and naval administrator Samuel Pepys
was no stranger to sins of the flesh.*

My Lord (Sandwich)... telling me the story of how the Duke of

Yorke hath got My Lord Chancellor's daughter with child, and that she doth lay it to him, and that for certain he did promise her marriage and had signed it with his blood, but that he by stealth had got the paper out of her Cabinett. And that the King would have him marry her, but that he would not. So that the thing is very bad for the Duke and for them all. But my Lord doth make light of it, as a thing that he believes is not a new thing to the Duke to do abroad. Discoursing concerning what if the Duke should marry her, my Lord told me that among his father's many old sayings that he had writ in a book of his, this is one: that he that doth get a wench with child, and marries her afterwards, it is as if a man should shit in his hat and then clap it upon his head.

❦ Stars in her eyes

The eighteenth-century British soldier and diplomat, the Earl of Albemarle, was sent as plenipotentiary to Paris in 1748, at the end of the Seven Years' War.

On this occasion, Albemarle took with him his mistress, a young actress named Lolette Gaucher, who was described by her contemporaries as 'cunning and rapacious'. One evening, seeing her gazing up at the stars, the earl warned her, 'It's no good, my dear, I can't buy them for you.'

❦ Double-entendre

Sir Walter Ralegh was a dazzlingly attractive member of Elizabeth I's court and had his pick of the queen's ladies-in-waiting.

He loved a wench well; and one time getting up one of the Mayds of Honour up against a tree in a Wood ('twas his first Lady) who seemed at first boarding to be somewhat fearful of her Honour, and modest, she cryed, sweet Sir Walter, what doe you me ask? Will you undoe me? Nay, sweet Sir Walter! Sweet Sir Walter! Sir Walter! At last, as the danger and the pleasure at the same time grew higher, she cryed in the extasey, Swisser Swatter, Swisser Swatter. She proved with child . . .

❦ Dishes of the dey

The British politician Lord North was an unusually ugly man and was quite open about the way in which his looks offended the fair sex. On a diplomatic visit to North Africa he encountered Muslim sensibilities but in his case all rules were waived.

Once visiting the dey of Algiers, Lord North was invited to see the harem. When it was pointed out that visitors were normally only shown one girl at each visit, the dey replied, 'He is so ugly, let him see them all.'

❦ No refunds

The actress Dorothea Jordan was the mistress of the Duke of Clarence and produced ten children for him in ten years. When the duke tried to reduce her allowance she handed him a slip of paper, which in those days was always attached to playbills. It read, 'No money refunded after the rising of the curtain.'

❦ The love of skittles

During the 1860s, Lord Hartington, the Duke of Devonshire – known to his friends as 'Harty-Tarty' – was involved in affairs with two notable courtesans, the more famous of whom was known as 'Skittles'. Hartington bought Skittles a house and maintained her at the rate of £2000 a year. However, Skittles lost the battle for the duke's affections when her rival – Louisa von Alten – eventually married him in 1892.

In 1876 Lord Hartington was visiting Coventry. For a joke the Prince of Wales, the future Edward VII, instructed the Mayor of Coventry to ensure that Hartington was taken to see the bowling alley as he was very fond of that game. The mayor duly obliged and when they reached the bowling alley he was surprised when Hartington showed no interest at all. So he explained that the Prince of Wales himself had asked specially for his lordship to be brought to the alley in tribute to his 'love of skittles'.

❦ The price of experience

Henri, Duc d'Aumale was well known in Parisian society for his numerous love affairs. But as old age overtook him he reflected, 'As a young man I used to have four supple members and one stiff one. But now I have four stiff ones and one that is supple.'

❦ Conscience pricks

Samuel Pepys was notably unfaithful to his wife, the French lady Elizabeth de Saint-Michel, who must have been a most tolerant woman. Surprisingly, in spite of Pepys's constant philanderings he and his wife remained in love and on good terms.

Samuel Pepys once received a salutary warning about attempting to make love in a public place. He was in church when his wandering eye espied the pretty maid who was standing next to him in the pew. He tried in vain to take her by the hand but she edged away from him, then his wandering hands began exploring again. 'At last I could perceive her,' said Pepys, 'to take pins out of her pocket to prick me if I should touch her again, which seeing, I did forbear and was glad I did spy her design.'

❦ No smoke without fire

The Marquis of Granby was once smitten by a beautiful young married lady at a house party. She seemed to return his affections and so later that evening, believing her husband to be fully engaged elsewhere, the marquis stealthily visited her room. The lady was asleep in bed and just as the marquis was about to awaken her, the door to the room opened and in came the husband. Showing enormous presence of mind, the marquis held up a warning finger to the husband and whispered, 'Hush, don't disturb her, she is fast asleep. I was passing and I thought I smelled smoke but all's well.' The husband thanked him heartily and the two men parted as good friends.

❦ Bertie in the buff

In 1874, Edward, Prince of Wales, visited the castle of Mellon, owned by the Princess Jeanne de Sagan, with whom he had been conducting a relationship for some time, behind her husband's back.

One afternoon the princess's eldest son walked into his mother's boudoir and found a man's clothes draped across a sofa. Angrily he picked up the clothes, ran outside and threw them into a fountain. Hearing a noise, a naked Prince of Wales peeped out of the bedroom door and saw that he had nothing to wear. Worse still, the prince's stoutness meant that he could not borrow the clothes of another gentleman of the household. When he left the castle he was wearing borrowed trousers that were literally heaving at the seams.

❦ 5. THE ART OF THE POSSIBLE

❦ A precise answer

William Ewart Gladstone and Benjamin Disraeli, leaders of the Liberal and Conservative parties respectively, were formidable political opponents. Their debates dominated politics in the middle of the Victorian era.

Disraeli was once asked to define the difference between misfortune and calamity. He answered, 'If Mr Gladstone fell into the Thames, it would be a misfortune; but, if someone pulled him out, it would be a calamity.'

❦ Miss Wilberforce for ever

In the days of the open hustings and before secret ballots, bribing the voters was a feature of most British elections.

When Mr Wilberforce was a candidate for Hull, his sister, an amiable and witty young lady, offered the compliment of a new dress to each of the wives of those freemen who voted for her brother; on which she was saluted with the cry of, 'Miss Wilberforce for ever!' When she pleasantly observed, 'I thank you gentlemen, but I cannot agree with you; for really I do not wish to be Miss Wilberforce for ever.'

❦ The senior service

Lady Astor, canvassing for her first parliamentary seat in Plymouth, because of her status and because she was new to the town, was allotted a senior naval officer as a minder, and together they went round knocking on doors.

'Is your mother at home?' asked Lady Astor when one door was opened by a small girl. 'No,' replied the child, 'but she said if a lady comes with a sailor they're to use the upstairs room and leave ten bob.'

❦ A family likeness

In spite of his reputation as a dour and serious politician, Gladstone had a biting wit, sharpened by his numerous verbal duels with Disraeli.

Gladstone, visiting an antique dealer's shop, admired an early seventeenth-century oil painting depicting an aristocrat dressed in old Spanish costume, with a ruff, plumed hat and laced cuffs. He wanted it badly but thought the price too high.

Some time later, at the house of a rich London merchant, he came upon the portrait he had so admired. His host, noticing Gladstone's absorption, approached him. 'You like it? It's a portrait of one of my ancestors, a minister at the court of Queen Elizabeth.' Said Gladstone, 'Three pounds less and he would have been an ancestor of mine.'

❦ Heading in the wrong direction

In 1832, the Duke of Wellington, the leader of the Tory Party, was strongly opposed to the reform of the House of Commons by changes in the electoral system. As an arch-traditionalist he was critical of anything that suggested a more democratic approach to government.

Asked what he thought of the Reformed Parliament, when for the first time he surveyed the new Members of Parliament from the Peers' Gallery, the duke replied, 'I have never seen so many bad hats in my life.'

❦ A chastity belt

European diplomats, by the late nineteenth century, were members of an élite club which met on occasions of international crisis. Lord Salisbury, the Foreign Secretary in 1885, accompanied Lord Beaconsfield to the Congress of Berlin.

At the end of the Congress of Berlin in 1885, Lady Salisbury was presented by the Sultan of Turkey with the Order of Chastity, Third Class. When her husband, Lord Salisbury, queried this he was told that only the wives of crowned monarchs received the order first class. Other royal ladies received the order second class, while the wives of diplomats were awarded third class.

❦ A hell of a choice

The eighteenth-century politician John Wilkes was a lively campaigner. He needed to be, for the open hustings of the time was no place for faint hearts.

A voter once answered Wilkes's canvass with the words: 'I'd sooner vote for the devil than you.'

'And if your friend isn't standing?' enquired Wilkes.

❦ Free as the air

Dean Swift, author of Gulliver's Travels, *had a ready wit but a cold hostility towards English rule in Ireland.*

Lady Carteret, wife of the English viceroy in Ireland, was on friendly terms with Swift. One day when she happened to remark on how good the air was in Ireland, Swift fell on his knees and besought her, 'For God's sake, Madame, don't say that in England, for if you do, they will surely tax it.'

❦ Court jester

Disraeli and Gladstone continue their battle of wits.

Gladstone once challenged Disraeli on the topic of the latter's famous wit, claiming that Disraeli had the reputation of being able to make a joke on any subject. Disraeli replied that this was quite true. 'In that case I challenge you to make a joke about Queen Victoria,' said Gladstone.

'Sir,' replied Disraeli, 'Her Majesty is not a subject.'

❦ Too soon

It was claimed that Lord North could sleep through anything.

In 1769 North was being attacked by Lord Grenville, who was making a seemingly endless speech on the history of taxes and revenues. So North asked a neighbour to wake him up when Grenville reached modern times. After a while, his neighbour duly prodded him. North listened to Grenville again for a few moments and then protested, 'Zounds, you have waked me a hundred years too soon.'

❦ The three-card trick

The British politician, Sir Robert Peel, served his country in many capacities, including that of prime minister. He repealed the Corn Laws, introduced a postal service and a police force.

A few years before his death, Sir Robert, with one or two friends, happened to be going to the Alexandra Park to witness a balloon ascent, or something of that sort (as a matter of fact I believe it was a parachute descent by the well known Professor Baldwin), when, making his way to the grounds, he found himself in close proximity to a man who was doing the three-card trick. Drawing himself up, as he used to do, he said to his companions, 'I thought this old swindle was extinct; however (with a wink) as we have come across it, I shall expose the rascal.' He at once proceeded to push himself to the front of the little crowd which stood round the illicit operator, but as soon as he got there his expression softened, and relenting, he whispered, 'The poor man is a sad bungler, he cannot do the trick at all.' Soon, however, Sir Robert yielded to the blandishments of the sharper whilst his friends were present (and no money was on), proving completely successful in spotting the court card, which he did almost every time. The rest of the party, having applauded his skill, said they would walk slowly on to the Palace, which they did; but finding sometime later that no Sir Robert appeared, someone went back to look for him, and to his great astonishment, discovered the missing baronet still in close proximity to the card-sharper, but now in a furious rage, all his money being lost. 'I ought to convict you,' he was saying, 'I am a magistrate and you, sir, (this in his grandest manner, his hat fiercely cocked and one hand in a Napoleonic pose just inside his coat) – you, sir, are a rogue, a thief, and a vagabond.'

❦ The happiest days

The future prime minister, Lord Salisbury, had been very unhappy at Eton, where he was frequently bullied.

He had written to his parents, 'I am bullied from morning to night without ceasing... I am obliged to hide myself all evening in some corner to prevent being bullied... When I come into dinner they kick and shin me and I am obliged to go out of dinner without eating anything.' Even during his holidays the horrors of his school fellows never left him. And if he was in London he kept away from the main streets for fear of bumping into a fellow Etonian. It was not until he was fifteen that Salisbury was able to persuade his father to take him away from Eton. Yet even though he kept his own sons at home until they were twelve he still had them educated at Eton. He gave them these few words of comfort, 'If you should ever be in danger of a flogging take the train home immediately.' So bad were his memories of the place that when it was time for his two younger sons to go he couldn't take them himself and entrusted the task to his wife.

❦ Down stream

The Liberal prime minister, Lord Rosebery, was both a statesman and a leader of fashion.

When he was in his final illness he instructed one of his servants to purchase a gramophone and play the 'Eton Boating Song' to him in his last moments.

❦ Hearsay

Lord Rosebery once made a speech in which he flatteringly likened two leading members of the audience to seventeenth-century parliamentary heroes, calling them 'the village Hampden and the village Pym'. The latter, after bearing this for a while, stalked out furiously, because he thought he had been called the village pimp.

❦ The cabinet waits

From about 1914 the Liberal politician David Lloyd George spent as much time as possible at his house at Walton Heath. This sometimes caused problems, especially when he had to attend evening functions in London.

Late one night Lloyd George was being driven back from a City function where he had been required to wear his elaborate Privy Councillor's uniform, including knee breeches, long stockings and silver buckled pumps. Suddenly his car broke down in the middle of nowhere. The chauffeur got out to investigate, failing to notice that Lloyd George had also got out of the car to stretch his legs. All too soon, Lloyd George heard the car engine splutter into life before it disappeared down the country lane without him. It was some time before the chauffeur noticed that the back seat was empty. Appalled at what he had done, he sped back along the same road and finally saw in the headlights of the car the weary figure of his employer trudging down the middle of the road. The incident became one of Lloyd George's favourite stories. In its final version he used to add that he eventually came to the doors of a lunatic asylum and in desperation rang the bell: 'I'm the chancellor of the Exchequer,' he announced as the warden answered the door. 'Come in,' invited the warden calmly. 'The rest of the cabinet is expecting you.'

❦ A public man

Conservative leader Stanley Baldwin was a man who did not relish the publicity that went with high office. Sometimes, however, he was regarded almost as H G Wells's 'invisible man', as this story shows.

During a weekend at Cliveden in 1935, Baldwin admitted it was true that during his previous premiership he had been wearing his old school tie in a railway compartment and had been asked by a fellow traveller: 'Were you not at Harrow in my time? What have you been doing since?'

❦ A relic of Munich

The name of Neville Chamberlain, prime minister between 1937 and 1940, will for ever be synonymous with the national betrayal at Munich. It is said that Hitler chuckled after Chamberlain had left, 'I only signed the document because I thought the old fellow wanted my autograph.'

In 1938 Chamberlain returned from Munich as a hero, boasting of peace in our time. He was fêted throughout Europe for his diplomacy and received many gifts, including innumerable fishing rods and salmon flies, 4,000 tulips from Holland and cases of Alsatian wine. The strangest request was from a man in Greece who asked for a piece of Chamberlain's umbrella to make a relic in an icon.

❦ Joking aside

Winston Churchill, Britain's greatest war leader, was renowned for a sharp wit that stood him in good stead in times of trouble.

When Churchill had finished giving his 'We shall fight on the beaches' speech in June 1940, he put his hand over the micro-phone and added, 'We will hit 'em over the head with beer bottles, which is all we have to fight them with.'

❦ A tart response

During a by-election campaign in 1931, Stanley Baldwin – the Conservative leader – launched a fierce attack on the press, claiming that it 'enjoyed power without responsibility, the privilege of the harlot'. To this the Duke of Devonshire replied, 'That's done it. He's lost us the tarts' vote.'

❦ A name to conjure with

When the Conservative member Sir Alfred Bossom was first elected to Parliament, he was introduced to Sir Winston Churchill, who commented, 'Bossom? Bossom? What manner of name is that? It is neither one thing nor the other.'

❦ When help was needed

The eighteenth-century politician Charles James Fox was not only a man of affairs and a great orator, but a gambler and bon viveur.

On one occasion a friend found Fox slumped across a table at Brooks's Club, surrounded by seven empty bottles of port. He asked the politician if he had emptied them unassisted, to which Fox replied, 'No. I was assisted by a bottle of Madeira.'

❦ A bad man to cross

Lord Kitchener, whose life had been spent in the army, where seniority counted for everything, found the world of politics far too democratic for his taste. Nevertheless, he believed that fate had something special in store for anyone who opposed him.

Someone once asked Kitchener how he dealt with his enemies. Kitchener replied, 'Oh I have no difficulty. You see such awful things happen to them quite independently of me.' When asked what he meant he explained, 'Well, George Curzon lost his wife, Sir Edmund Ellis lost his and his son was eaten by a crocodile, and Sir Denzil Ibbetson died of cancer.'

❦ A bombast fellow

The British politician and statesman Lord Curzon was an aristo-cratic figure in a democratic age and he was frequently ridiculed for his incapacity to come to terms with ordinary people. It may well have cost him the leadership of the Conservative party when Stanley Baldwin was preferred to him after Andrew Bonar Law retired in 1923.

Lord Curzon's first experience of taking a London bus was quite eventful. As he explained, 'This omnibus business is not what it is reported to be. I hailed one at the bottom of Whitehall and told the man to take me to Carlton House Terrace. But the fellow flatly refused.'

❦ A different species

Lord Curzon's experience of the working class was very limited. On seeing soldiers, on leave, in a swimming pool, he remarked, 'Good Heavens, I never knew that the working classes had such white skins.'

❦ A period piece

On one occasion Curzon kept the entire cabinet waiting, without sending any message of explanation or apology. At long last an office messenger arrived, bearing an antique footstool covered in green baize on which Curzon, who suffered from phlebitis, was accustomed to rest his leg. Derby said, 'The Marquess himself has not yet arrived but we see premonitory symptoms.' And he rose and bowed deferentially to the footstool.

❦ Forward planning

Curzon was very dynastic and paid great attention to adorning the tomb of his first wife and preparing his own in Kedleston Church. Shortly after his death, his widow went down into the vault to look at his coffin. On a nearby ledge she noticed a postcard, bearing in his handwriting the words: 'Reserved for the second Lady Curzon'.

❦ A cadaverous look

Curzon had expected to succeed Bonar Law as leader of the Conservative Party. Instead Stanley Baldwin was selected, much to Curzon's chagrin. Baldwin remarked on meeting his rival, 'I met Curzon in Downing Street from whom I got the sort of greeting a corpse would give to an undertaker.'

❦ The light of freedom

The American politician and statesman Stephen A Douglas was Abraham Lincoln's chief political opponent in Illinois and campaigned against him for the presidency in 1860. Known as the 'Little Giant', Douglas split the Democrat Party on the slavery issue.

In 1854, Douglas's stand on the slavery issue made him intensely unpopular in the northern states of America. On one occasion he admitted, 'I could travel from Boston to Chicago by the light of my own effigies.'

❦ Making friends and influencing people

The Scottish philosopher David Hume wrote the Treatise of Human Nature, *one of the most important philosophical works of the eighteenth century.*

A few weeks before his death, when there were dining with him two or three of his intimate companions, one of them, Dr Smith, happened to complain of the world as spiteful and ill-natured. 'No, no,' said Mr Hume, 'here am I, who have written on all sorts of subjects calculated to excite hostility, moral, political and religious, and yet I have no enemies, except indeed, all the Whigs, all the Tories, and all the Christians.'

❦ The Gaelic twilight

The ebullient Welshman David Lloyd George found his political ally, the Conservative leader Andrew Bonar Law, an uncongenial travelling companion. Bonar Law, a dour Scot, had no time for the

Welshman's high jinks. In alliance the two led their country through the greatest war it had ever faced. In this story they are travelling together by car in southern France.

I told Bonar that...I had been to a Mozart concert and the music was wonderful. Bonar casually and languidly remarked, 'I don't care for music.' As we motored along, there was the Mediterranean blue sea on one side and the rolling snow-capped Alpes Maritimes on the other. This inspired me to exclaim: 'Look, Bonar, what a wonderful scene that is.' 'I don't care for scenery,' remarked Bonar. Presently we came to a bridge...I said to Bonar: 'Look, Bonar, aren't those handsome women?' 'I don't care for women,' remarked Bonar very drily. 'Then what the hell do you care for?' I asked. Then in his very soft voice and quieter still Bonar replied, 'I like bridge.'

❦ A lot of hot air

Winston Churchill was well known as a prankster but sometimes his jokes misfired.

On one occasion in 1926, at the Oxford Union, Churchill passed the rather rotund R B Haldane and tapped his 'tummy' appreciatively, saying, 'What are you going to call the baby?' Haldane replied, 'If it's a boy I will call it George, after the king. If it's a girl, Mary after the queen. But if, as I strongly suspect, it is only wind, I shall call it Winston.'

❦ A false conception

Joseph Addison was an indecisive speaker, an unfortunate defect for a politician in the eighteenth century – the great age of parliamentary oratory.

On one occasion Addison stood up to speak in the house and began, 'Mr Speaker, I conceive – I conceive, sir – sir, I conceive – ' At this point he was interrupted by one of the other members calling out, 'The Right Honourable Secretary of State has conceived thrice and brought forth nothing.'

❦ The glow-worm

Winston Churchill was rarely guilty of underestimating his own abilities. Violet Asquith recounts this story of a conversation she once had with him in 1906, when he was still a Liberal.

Churchill was unusually quiet, and seemed sunk in abstraction. Then, suddenly aware of her existence again, Churchill asked her how old she was. Violet replied that she was nineteen. 'I am thirty-two already,' Churchill replied. 'On reflection, younger than anyone else who counts, though. Curse ruthless time! Curse our mortality. How cruelly short is the allotted span for all we must cram into it. We are all worms. But I do believe that I am a glow-worm.'

❦ Life, liberty and extinction

Winston Churchill, who was half-American through his mother Jenny Jerome, was not blind to the failures of the 'Great Republic'.

At a wartime reception, Churchill was accosted by an overbearing American lady. 'What are you going to do about those wretched Indians?' she demanded. 'Madam,' replied Churchill, 'to which Indians do you refer? Do you mean the second greatest nation on earth, which under benign and munificent British rule has multiplied and prospered exceedingly? Or do you mean the unfortunate North American Indians, which under your present administration are almost extinct?'

❦ Nothing to hide

Winston Churchill established an excellent personal relationship with President Roosevelt, which was vital to Britain in the early years of the Second World War.

On an occasion when Churchill was visiting the White House, President Roosevelt wheeled himself along to the British leader's bedroom and opened the door unexpectedly. Churchill was standing in the middle of the room stark naked and unembarrassed. 'You see, Mr President, we British have nothing to hide.'

❦ Churchill's cross

Winston Churchill and Charles de Gaulle were never exactly friends. Each was too full of himself to leave space for the other and each was very much – at least in his own eyes – the embodiment of his nation.

Once, during the war, a dinner given by Churchill at Chequers was interrupted by a telephone call from de Gaulle, who said he wanted to speak to the prime minister. In the middle of his dinner, Churchill refused to take the call, but de Gaulle was insistent and the British leader's butler scurried back with the Frenchman's demand to be heard. Churchill eventually gave way, apologized to his guests, and left the table to take the call. He returned ten minutes later, red in the face and trembling with anger. 'Bloody de Gaulle!' he said to his guests. 'He had the impertinence to tell me that the French regard him as the reincarnation of Joan of Arc...I found it necessary to remind him that we had to burn the first one.'

❦ The great compromiser

American statesman Henry Clay of Kentucky played a vital part in solving two crises over slavery in 1820 and in 1850, earning himself a reputation as a compromiser. Although he never became president, his influence on American history in the first half of the nineteenth century was incalculable.

American politicians John Randolph and Henry Clay were rivals and on one occasion the two men found they could not avoid walking towards each other on the same footpath. One of them would have to give way. 'I never give way to scoundrels,' said Randolph, standing his ground. 'I *always* do,' said Clay, stepping off the pavement to let Randolph pass.

❦ The price tag

The French politician Georges Clemenceau was nicknamed 'The Tiger'. During the First World War it was his tigerish qualities that helped France to survive.

Clemenceau once awarded the Legion of Honour to a businessman whose only claim to fame was that he contributed large sums to the President's political fund. As he pinned the decoration on the man's chest, Clemenceau whispered to him, 'Sir, you wanted the Legion of Honour. Here it is. Now all you have to do is deserve it.'

❦ An American Moses

President Woodrow Wilson seemed idealistic and sanctimonious to a seasoned political schemer and fighter like Georges Clemenceau.

As the First World War drew to a close in 1918, American president Woodrow Wilson issued his famous 'Fourteen Points', which were to act as a basis for the peace settlement. Clemenceau, unimpressed by the self-righteous American, remarked, 'Fourteen Points? Even God Almighty only needed ten.'

❦ Protocol

Clemenceau found the British delegates at the Peace of Paris to be stuffy and aloof.

Never a stickler for protocol, Clemenceau attended a grand garden party at the Palace of Versailles in 1919, wearing a bowler hat. Clemenceau met the British Foreign Secretary, Lord Balfour, resplendent in a top hat. Balfour said, 'They told me top hats would be worn.' 'They told me too,' replied Clemenceau.

❦ A waste of time

In Italy politics is the art of the 'impossible'.

Giovanni Giolitti, the Italian prime minister, was once asked by a foreign journalist whether it was very hard to govern Italy. 'Not at all,' said Giolitti. 'It's not hard, it's just useless.'

❦ Now you know why

Life in Stalinist Russia made everyone very careful about what they said and did. When Stalin died in 1953 people felt more willing to express their opinions.

At a public meeting Nikita Khrushchev was criticized by a heckler: 'You were one of Stalin's colleagues. Why didn't you stop him?' 'Who said that?' Khrushchev shouted. There was a sudden painful silence and everyone looked at their neighbours in a guilty way. Then, in a quiet voice, Khrushchev replied, 'Now you know why.'

❦ No mistaking the boss

Under the leadership of Nikita Khrushchev it was believed that conditions would be very different in the USSR from what they had been under Stalin. At least one thing did change – the truth.

During a heated exchange in a Kennedy–Khrushchev Summit meeting in 1961, the American president asked Khrushchev, 'Do you ever admit a mistake?' 'Certainly I do,' said Khrushchev. 'In a speech before the Twentieth Party Congress, I admitted all of Stalin's mistakes.'

❦ Pray take two chairs

Henry Labouchère, in spite of his name, was a member of the British Foreign Service during the nineteenth century. But his skills as a wit may have exceeded his abilities as a diplomat.

While he was working at the British legation in St Petersburg he met a very pompous nobleman, who insisted on meeting the British ambassador forthwith. 'Pray take a chair,' said Labouchère, 'the ambassador will see you shortly.' The visitor was infuriated by what he took to be the young man's incivility. 'Do you know who I am?' he asked, giving Labouchère a full list of his many titles of rank. Unabashed, Labouchère replied, 'Pray take two chairs.'

❧ An expensive gesture

The Marquis de Lafayette was a hero of the American War of Independence and of the early years of the French Revolution.

On one occasion Lafayette's supporters in Paris stopped his coach in the street, unhitched the horses and pulled the vehicle by hand to his destination. It was a heady moment for the young aristocrat and he was later asked if he had been inspired by the actions of the people. Lafayette thought for a moment and then replied: 'Yes, it was delightful, most delightful. But one thing disturbed me though – I never saw any of my horses again.'

❧ Cobbling together an answer

British prime minister Harold Macmillan had a dry wit, which was tested out on many occasions in international diplomacy.

During a stormy scene at the United Nations General Assembly in September 1960, a speech that Macmillan was giving was interrupted by the Soviet leader, Nikita Khrushchev, who took off his shoe and used it to bang loudly on a table. Unperturbed, the British prime minister remarked, 'I would like that translated, if I may.'

❧ No teachers

The Austrian statesman Prince Klemens von Metternich was one of the moving forces in the overthrow of Napoleon and the restoration of autocracy in much of Europe.

Metternich was contemptuous of the English weakness in languages, notably for their inability to speak French. He once told Lord John Dudley that he was the only Englishman he had met who could speak French well. 'The common people of

Vienna speak French better than the educated men of London,' said Metternich. Lord Dudley replied, 'That may be so, but Your Highness will recall that Bonaparte has not been twice in London to teach them.'

❦ Study to deserve

Cecil Rhodes was a self-made man, who rose to become the greatest imperialist of the nineteenth century, conquering large areas of Central and Southern Africa and incorporating them into the British Empire.

Cecil Rhodes died enormously rich and the distribution of his fortune under the terms of his will included a large contribution to academic research. This creation of Rhodes Scholarships caused some resentment among his close family. As his brother Arthur commented on hearing the will, 'Well, there it is. It seems to me I shall have to win a scholarship.'

❦ Turning Dizzy

Lord Odo Russell was the diplomat par excellence, *as this story shows.*

When the Congress of the Powers assembled at Berlin in the summer of 1878, our Ambassador in that city of stucco palaces was the loved and lamented Lord Odo Russell, afterwards Lord Ampthill, a born diplomat if ever there was one . . . On the evening before the formal opening of the Congress, Lord Beaconsfield arrived in all his plenipotentiary glory, and was received with high honours at the British Embassy. In the course of the evening one of his private secretaries came to Lord Odo Russell and said: 'Lord Odo, we are in a frightful mess and we can only turn to you to help us out of it. The old chief has determined to open the proceedings of the Congress in French. He has written out the devil's own long speech in French and learned it by heart, and is going to fire it off at the Congress tomorrow. We shall be the laughing-stock of Europe. He pronounces *épicier* as if it rhymed with 'overseer' and all his pronunciation is to match. It is as much as our places are worth to tell him so. Can you help us?'

Lord Odo listened with amused good humour to this tale of woe, and then replied: 'It is a very delicate mission that you ask me to undertake, but then I am fond of delicate missions. I will see what I can do.'

And so he repaired to the state bedroom, where our venerable Plenipotentiary was beginning those elaborate processes of the toilet with which he prepared for the couch. 'My dear lord,' began Lord Odo, 'a dreadful rumour has reached us.'

'Indeed! Pray what is it?'

'We have heard that you intend to open the proceedings tomorrow in French.'

'Well, Lord Odo, what of that?'

'Why, of course, we all know that there is no one in Europe more competent to do so than yourself. But then, after all, to make a speech in French is a commonplace accomplishment. There will be at least half a dozen men at the Congress who could do it almost, if not quite, as well as yourself. But, on the other hand, who but you can make an English speech? All these Plenipotentiaries have come from the various Courts of Europe expecting the greatest intellectual treat of their lives in hearing English spoken by its greatest living master. The question for you, my dear Lord, is – will you disappoint them?'

Lord Beaconsfield put his glass in his eye, fixed his gaze on Lord Odo, and then said: 'There is much force in what you say. I will consider the point.' And the next day he opened the proceedings in English.

❦ The language of diplomacy

Prince Otto von Bismarck, Chancellor of the German Empire, was a formidable opponent in diplomacy.

Bismarck was once involved in complicated negotiations with two French statesmen, Thiers and Favre. As usual discussions were in French, the accepted language of diplomacy. Suddenly Bismarck switched to German. The Frenchmen were amazed.

'You know we do not understand German,' said Thiers.

'You have heard me accused of being a flatterer,' Disraeli told Arnold. 'It is true. I am a flatterer. I have found it very useful. Everyone likes flattery; and when it comes to Royalty, you should lay it on with a trowel.'

❦ My old dutch

During parliamentary elections in the eighteenth century, prominent politicians frequently called on the support of members of the nobility to help them in their canvassing.

During the Westminster election of 1784, Charles Fox was fortunate in having the beautiful Duchess of Devonshire campaigning on his behalf. With her scarcely less lovely sister, Lady Duncannon, the duchess visited the homes and hovels of even the humblest of the voters, dazzling and enslaving them with her beauty. On more than one occasion she used her own carriage to carry drunken voters to the hustings to win their votes. It is said that she even secured the vote of one stubborn butcher with a kiss. An Irish mechanic paid the duchess the famous compliment, 'I could light my pipe at her eyes.'

❦ Free speech

The free-thinking radical politician Charles Bradlaugh was, on several occasions, elected to parliament but denied his seat because he would not swear on the Bible. At a political meeting in Tottenham Lord George Hamilton encountered the man and his supporters.

I had a most amusing encounter with Mr Bradlaugh at Tottenham. Bradlaugh lived there and was a considerable power amongst the extremists. He had been heavily defeated in a Parliamentary contest at Northampton a day or two before our meeting. This defeat did not improve his temper or that of his followers. As soon as I had spoken, he came from the far end of the hall, where his followers were concentrated, close up to the platform, and he began in a loud and hectoring manner to put to me the catch Radical catechism. Suddenly a man, as much bigger than Bradlaugh as Bradlaugh was than myself, got up with a huge club and said: 'Give me the signal, my lord, and I will crack this infernal scoundrel's skull.'

A perfect pandemonium ensued. Bradlaugh's people tried to come to their hero's rescue, my people keeping them back. Bradlaugh and the big man both remained immovable, but Bradlaugh was furtively watching out of the corner of his eye the big club over his head, and the holder of it was watching intently for me to give the signal for an onslaught. The tension was broken by a big Irish parson who was Rector of Tottenham, and who had had many an encounter with Bradlaugh. He jumped up and began to exorcize Bradlaugh with tongue and fists as if he were the devil. I was afraid he would strike Bradlaugh, so I got hold of one of the very long tails of the parson's frock-coat. One of my uncles seized the end of the other tail, and the result of our combined effort was that the coat split right to the neck, leaving us each with a coat-tail in our hands.

❦ A problem halved

When the unpopular administration of Lord Holland and the Earl of Chatham came under heavy criticism in the mid eighteenth century, one of its greatest critics – the Earl of Bath – was infuriated to hear that although Chatham had been dismissed, Holland was to retain power.

As the Earl of Bath said, 'This half measure is the worst of all, and reminds me of the Gunpowder Plot. The Lord Chamberlain was sent to examine the vaults underneath the Parliament House, and returned with the report that he had found five-and-twenty barrels of gunpowder, but that he had removed ten of them, and hoped the remainder would do no harm.'

❦ Tit for tat

At a diplomatic function, Lady Clanricarde, daughter of Lord Canning, was discussing the Franco-Prussian War of 1870 with the French ambassador.

The Frenchman complained bitterly that England had not intervened on behalf of France. 'But after all,' he said, 'it is only what we might have expected. We always believed that you were a nation of shopkeepers, and now we know you are.'

'And we,' replied Lady Clanricarde, 'always believed that you were a nation of soldiers, and now we know that you are not.'

❦ A wise head

Sir Thomas More was an astute diplomat and one of King Henry VIII's most able ministers.

As More's son-in-law William Roper wrote, 'The king having one day paid him an unexpected visit to dinner, and having afterwards walked with him for an hour in the garden, with his arm round his neck, I took occasion after Henry was gone to congratulate him on his rare good fortune, in being treated by the king with a degree of familiarity never experienced by any other subject.

'"I thank our Lord," replied More, "I find his Grace my very good lord indeed; and I believe he doth as singularly favour me as any subject in this realm. However, son Roper, I may tell thee, I have no cause to be proud thereof; for if my head would win him a castle in France, it would not fail to be struck off."'

❦ Crop ears

During the period of King Charles I's 'Eleven Years' Tyranny', the Puritan pamphleteer, William Prynne, was one of the king's sharpest critics. In 1634, he was sentenced to imprisonment by the Court of Star Chamber and also suffered the cropping of his ears. Nevertheless, he survived the period of civil war and parliamentary rule and by 1660 was numbered a king's man and was appointed Keeper of the Records in the Tower by King Charles II. John Aubrey wrote of William Prynne:

His ears were not quite cut off, only the upper part, his tips were visible ... His manner of study was thus: He wore a long quilt cap which came two or three inches over his eyes, which served him as an umbrella to defend his eyes against the light. About every three hours his man was to bring him a roll and a pot of ale to refocillate his wasted spirits. So he studied and drank and munched some bread, and this maintained him till night, and then he made a good supper...He endured several imprisonments for the King's cause and was very instrumental in his restoration. Upon the opening of the Parliament, viz. letting the secluded members, he girt on his old long rusty sword (longer than ordinary). Sir William Waller, marching behind him (as he went to the House) W Prynne's long sword ran between Sir William's short legs and threw him down which caused laughter.

❦ Jack Robinson

Richard Brinsley Sheridan was not only one of the leading playwrights of his time, author of The Rivals *and* School for Scandal*, but also an able politician, with a sharp wit.*

During a parliamentary debate in 1782, Sheridan accused a member of the government of corruption. His target for criticism was the secretary to the Treasury, John Robinson, but when there were calls for him to be named Sheridan refused, saying, 'Sirs, I shall not name the person. It is an unpleasant and invidious thing to do, and therefore I shall not name him. But don't suppose, Sirs, that I abstain because there is any difficulty in naming him. I could do that, Sirs, as soon as you could say Jack Robinson.'

❦ If I had served God

Cardinal Thomas Wolsey served Henry VIII as chief minister for many years. His fall in 1530, as a result of his failure to secure the king a divorce from Catherine of Aragon, was a dramatic illustration of the ingratitude of kings. A Tudor writer, George Cavendish, recorded the last hours of Wolsey, who died on his way to London to face treason charges.

Master Kyngston bade him good morrow, for it was about 7 of the clock in the morning, and asked him how he did.

'Sir,' quoth he, 'I tarry but the will and the pleasure of God, to render unto him my simple soul into his divine hands.'

'Not yet so, sir,' quoth Master Kyngston, 'with the grace of God, you shall live and do very well, if ye will be of good cheer.'

'Master Kyngston, my disease is such that I cannot live; for I have had some experience in my disease, and thus it is ... '

'Nay, sir, in good faith,' quoth Master Kyngston, 'ye be in such dolour and pensiveness, doubting that thing that ye need not to fear, which maketh you much worse than ye should be.'

'Well, well, Master Kyngston,' quoth he, 'I see the matter against me, how it is framed; but if I had served God as diligently as I have done the king, he would not have given me over in my grey hairs.'

❦ A fat bitch

Horace Walpole, Sir Robert's son, recorded an embarrassing moment his father suffered.

Somebody had told the princess, afterwards Queen Caroline, that Sir Robert Walpole had called her a fat bitch. It was not true. But upon settling her jointure by parliament, when she was Princess of Wales, and £50,000 being proposed, Sir Robert moved and obtained £100,000. The princess, in great good humour, sent word that the 'fat bitch' had forgiven him.

❦ Lord Pumpernickel

The British ambassador at the Congress of Vienna in 1815 was Sir Charles Stewart, the brother-in-law of Lord Castlereagh and later to be the Marquis of Londonderry.

In spite of the fact that the Duke of Wellington had a high opinion of him, Stewart was most eccentric, dressed in yellow boots and was known by the Viennese as 'Lord Pumpernickel'. He was frequently to be seen in the Vienna streets in a drunken condition, with his horse's head covered in lilies of the valley and holding an enormous bunch in his hands. He had brought twenty couples of foxhounds to Vienna with him, to show the Austrians how to hunt properly. His scheme failed, but when he returned to England he took with him 504 gallons of Austrian wine, which he imported without paying any customs dues. On one occasion he caused a diplomatic incident by getting into a brawl with a Viennese cab driver and throwing him into the River Danube.

❦ A hair-raising incident

In Parliament, the deficiency of Lord North's sight was productive to him of many inconveniences. For, even at a distance of a few feet, he saw very imperfectly; and, across the House, he was unable to distinguish persons with any degree of accuracy. In speaking, walking, and every motion, it is enough to say that he wanted grace: he was to the last degree awkward. Sir William Wraxall here records a curious incident that resulted from North's deficient eyesight.

It can hardly obtain belief that, in a full House of Commons, he took off on the point of his sword the wig of Mr Welbore Ellis, and carried it a considerable way across the floor, without ever suspecting or perceiving it. The fact happened in this manner.

Mr Ellis, who was then Treasurer of the Navy, and well advanced towards his seventieth year, always sat in the lowest corner of the Treasury Bench, a few feet removed from Lord North. The latter having occasion to go down the House, previously laid his hand on his sword, holding the chase of the scabbard forward, nearly in a horizontal direction. Mr Ellis, stooping at the same instant that the first Minister rose, the point of the scabbard came exactly in contact with the Treasurer of the Navy's wig, which it completely took off and bore away.

The accident, however ludicrous, was completely unseen by Lord North, who received the first intimation of it from the involuntary bursts of laughter that it occasioned in every quarter of the House. Mr Ellis, however, without altering a muscle of his countenance, and preserving the utmost gravity in the midst of the general convulsion, having received back his wig, readjusted it to his head, and waited patiently till the House had recovered from the effect of so extraordinary, as well as ridiculous, an occurrence.

❦ Overheard listening

Lady Astor was always a notable 'presence' in the House of Commons and was rather too inclined to interrupt other speakers.

On one occasion Lady Astor was warned about this but replied that she had been listening for hours before interrupting. 'Yes, we've *heard* you listening,' said one of her colleagues.

❦ The fair sex

Christabel, the daughter of Emmeline Pankhurst, was the most extreme of all the suffragette leaders.

At a suffragette meeting Christabel Pankhurst found herself facing questions from a very weedy-looking man.

'My question, is this,' he said, 'and will you answer it honestly if you can? At the bottom of your heart, really, don't you think you would like to be a man?'

Christabel flashed back at him, 'Quite honestly, my friend, I don't know. But don't you wish that you were?'

❦ A diplomatic incident

The great French politician Aristide Briand was noted for being rather lazy.

On one occasion a South American diplomat brought him a huge pile of documents for him to read. Briand shook his head sadly, 'You don't suppose I have lost my incapacity for work, do you?'

❦ Arresting death

The politician and playwright Sheridan fought a lifelong battle against extravagance and, losing this, a scarcely less prolonged campaign against his creditors.

The remains of Sheridan were removed from Savile Row to the residence of his kinsman in Great George Street, Westminster. There they lay in state, to indulge the longing grief of the few friends who clung to his bleak and shattered fortunes. On the forenoon of the day fixed for their interment a gentleman dressed in deep mourning entered the house and requested of the attendant, who watched in the chamber of death, to allow him a last look at his departed friend. He professed to have known the deceased early in life; and to have undertaken a long journey in order to seize a parting glance of his pale features. The agony and earnestness with which the application was urged lulled the suspicions of the serving man, if any had arisen in his mind; and after a slight hesitation, it was assented to. The lid of the coffin was removed – the body unshrouded – and the death-chilled frame revealed to view. The gentleman gazed for some minutes upon it; and then fumbling in his waistcoat pocket produced a bailiff's 'wand' with which he touched the face and instantly declared, to the horror and alarm of the servant, that he had arrested the corpse in the king's name for a debt of five hundred pounds. Before the requisite explanations had been gone through, the funeral group had assembled. The circumstance was instantly made known to Mr Canning, who took Lord Sidmouth aside and begged his advice and assistance. Lest the delay might mar the progress of the sorrowful train they generously agreed to discharge the debt; and two cheques for £250 each were given over to the bailiff and accepted by him.

❦ Vested interests

Friedrich Ebert was the first president of the Weimar Republic in Germany. But his attempts to establish democracy in Germany were met by hostility from both left- and right-wing groups.

Once when President Ebert of Germany visited Wilhelmshaven to launch a ship, he was greeted with total silence by the shipyard workers. The problem was that the Germans could not accept Ebert's plebeian origins. One of his colleagues, Gustav Stresemann, observed, 'The truth is that the Germans cannot stand a president in a high hat. They must have a military uniform with plenty of medals. If it is a mere question of wearing a high hat and looking common in it, each member of the public thinks he can do that for himself.' When Ebert visited one town, all along the streets that his car was to travel the shopkeepers hung out underwear from their windows instead of flags.

❦ A diplomatic exchange

The French diplomat Jean Jusserand was once discussing Franco-German relations with the wife of President Theodore Roosevelt.

Mrs Roosevelt told Jusserand, 'Why don't you learn from the United States and Canada? We have a three-thousand-mile unfortified, peaceful frontier. You people arm yourselves to the teeth.'
Jusserand replied, 'Ah, Madame, perhaps we could exchange neighbours.'

❦ A man of straw

Even after their significant victories of 1644, including that at Marston Moor, the Parliamentary leaders were not convinced that victory was in sight in the English Civil War.

As the Earl of Manchester told Oliver Cromwell, 'If we beat the king ninety-nine times, yet he is king still, and so will his posterity be after him; but if the king beat us once we shall all be hanged, and our posterity be made slaves.' Cromwell replied angrily, 'My lord, if this be so, why did we take arms at first? This is against fighting ever hereafter. If so, let us make peace be it never so base.'

Manchester was persuaded to fight on, the battle of Naseby was won the following year and the king forced to sue for peace.

❦ I have sent ships

Apart from Lord Palmerston, earlier in the century, nobody has surpassed Lord Salisbury in his preservation of Britain's national interests in foreign affairs. This story is both true in particular and as a general example of Salisbury's 'gunboat' diplomacy.

At a dinner party given by Lord Salisbury at Hatfield House in 1896, a dispatch box from London was brought to the table and given to the Prime Minister. Salisbury, first asking permission of his exalted guests, opened it and read the short message within. His brow furrowed for a moment and then he scribbled a reply and handed the box back to the courier who had brought it. One of the royal princesses asked him if the matter were a serious one. Salisbury replied that the German emperor had landed troops at Delagoa Bay in Portuguese East Africa. 'What answer have you sent?' the Princess asked. 'I have sent no answer,' said Salisbury, 'I have sent ships.'

❦ Two winners on Derby Day

Preferment in the Church of England was sometimes a process known only to God and the Prime Minister.

At Eton, Lord Rosebery had been friendly with George Kennion, a boy destined for the church. Many years later Kennion, just returned from Australia, where he had been Bishop of Adelaide, happened to be sitting in the Athenaeum Club on Derby Day. For a prank, some of the members told Kennion that returning colonial bishops always had to call on the prime minister when they got back. As a result, Kennion set out for Downing Street and duly reached Number Ten. But Rosebery was not there. Kennion was now directed to Rosebery's magnificent town house in Berkeley Square. There he was told that Lord Rosebery was at Epsom, so Kennion departed, having left his card. As fate would have it, Lord Rosebery's horse won the Derby and he returned in the evening to Berkeley Square in the best of all possible moods. There he found Kennion's card and in the euphoria of the moment, the bishopric of Bath and Wells being conveniently vacant, the prime minister decided to install his Eton chum Kennion as the new bishop.

❦ Leading from behind

During the 1848 Revolution in Paris, the French socialist deputy, Alexandre Ledru-Rollin, found himself blocked by a mob at the barricades. Amidst the confusion he was heard to shout, 'Let me pass, I have to follow them. I am their leader.'

❦ 6. IN THE OVAL OFFICE

❦ Rutherfraud

The election of Rutherford Hayes to the presidency in 1876 was the most controversial in American history.

Many people were convinced that the ballot had been rigged to give Hayes victory over the Democrat Tilden and henceforth Hayes was known to many as 'Rutherfraud B Hayes' or his 'Fraudulency' Hayes.

❦ At home with Queen Victoria

At the end of his presidency, Ulysses Grant and his wife visited England and stayed with Queen Victoria at Windsor Castle.

Unaware that letters to foreign countries always passed through the hands of the American ambassador in that country, some old soldiers from the Army of the Potomac cabled a warm message to General Grant c/o Queen Victoria, Windsor Castle, England. The veterans' message arrived late at night and a messenger set off for the castle, arriving in the early hours and pulling a doorbell at the gate. When challenged by a guard the boy replied, 'Cable for General Grant. Is he staying at this house?'

❦ Lemonade Lucy

After the presidency of Ulysses Grant, when the White House resounded to the sounds of wanton revelry and drunkenness, the period during which Rutherford and Lucy Hayes occupied it was very different.

Under the presidency of Rutherford B Hayes, morning prayers and nightly hymn-singing were common in the White House, and profanity, tobacco and liquor were banished. Mrs Hayes was mostly to blame, earning herself the nickname 'Lemonade Lucy' into the bargain. Wine was never served at official dinners and after one such occasion, Secretary of State William M Evarts remarked, 'It was a brilliant affair. The water flowed like champagne.'

❦ Four Eyes

Theodore Roosevelt, president 1901–9, was almost certainly the toughest and most physically assertive of all American presidents. His famous motto 'Speak softly and carry a big stick' formed the basis for American foreign policy for many years. In his early years, however, Roosevelt had an image to create and he set about doing so with absolute commitment.

In 1883 Theodore Roosevelt travelled to Dakota and decided to buy himself a ranch and become a 'gentleman cowhand'. The cowboys thought Roosevelt was a complete fool and called him 'Four Eyes' on account of his glasses. Amused by his mild curses, 'By Godfrey' being one of his strongest, they fell off their horses with glee when they heard him urging the cattle to 'hasten forward quickly there'. The cowboys only learned to take him seriously when he handed out a thrashing to a bar-room 'tough'. While in a saloon in Mingusville he was accosted by a shabby-looking man with a pistol in each hand, who cried, 'The drinks are on Four Eyes.' Roosevelt tried to ignore him at first but the man persisted until he was forced to get up and knock his assailant unconscious with a single blow to the jaw. One old-timer was heard to say, 'That four-eyed maverick has sand in his craw aplenty.' Roosevelt had been accepted. Years later when he was recruiting to take his 'Rough-Riders' to Cuba during the Spanish–American War, many volunteers came from Mingusville to fight with 'Four Eyes'.

❦ A telling endorsement

During Theodore Roosevelt's campaign for the governorship of New York in 1898, the self-appointed 'hero' of the battle of San Juan toured the state in a special train accompanied by seven of the Rough-Riders who had been with him in the battle. At every stop a bugler would sound the charge and Roosevelt would step forward to give his speech.

On one occasion, ex-Sergeant Buck Taylor was called on to address the crowd at a station. 'I want to talk to you about mah colonel,' Taylor began. 'He kept every promise he made to us and he will to you. When he took us to Cuba he told us ... we would have to lie out in the trenches with the rifle bullets climbing all over us, and we done it ... He told us we might meet wounds and death and we done it. But he was there in the midst of us. And when it came to the great day he led us up San Juan Hill like sheep to the slaughter and so he will lead you.'

❦ The finer points of diplomacy

Jean-Jules Jusserand, the French ambassador to Washington, found President Theodore Roosevelt a physical fitness fanatic. But he was unwilling to admit that he was finding it difficult to keep up with him. After all, the honour of France was at stake. As Jusserand wrote:

President Roosevelt invited me to take a promenade with him this afternoon at three. I arrived at the White House punctually in afternoon dress and silk hat as if we were to stroll in the Tuileries garden or in the Champs Elysées. To my surprise the president soon joined me in a tramping suit with knickerbockers and thick boots and soft felt hat, much worn. Two or three other gentlemen came and we started off at what seemed to me a breakneck pace which soon brought us out of the city. On reaching the country the president went pell-mell over the fields following neither road nor path always on, on, straight ahead! I was much winded but I would not give in nor ask him to slow up because I had the honour of *La Belle France* in my heart. At last we came to the bank of a stream, rather wide and too deep to be forded. I sighed in relief because I thought that now we had reached our goal and would rest a moment and catch our breath before turning homeward. But judge of my horror when I saw the president unbutton his clothes and heard him say, 'We had better strip so as not to wet our things in the Creek.' Then I too, for the honour of France, removed my apparel, everything except my lavender kid gloves. The president cast an enquiring look at these as if they too must come off. But I quickly forestalled any remark by saying, 'With your permission, Mr President, I will keep these on otherwise it would be embarrassing if we should meet ladies.'

❦ The mouth of experience

Just before the end of his presidency, Theodore Roosevelt made plans for a hunting trip to Africa. So that he should be fully prepared he invited an English big-game hunter, who was visiting the United States, to come to Washington and meet him at the White House.

The famous hunter duly arrived and was taken in to meet the president and, presumably, to give him the benefit of his experiences in the Dark Continent. After a two-hour conference the Englishman emerged from the president's office in a daze. 'And what did you tell the president?' asked a curious bystander. 'I told him my name,' said the wearied visitor.

❦ Passing the time

On the death of King Edward VII in 1910, monarchs and heads of government from throughout the world visited London for the state funeral. Theodore Roosevelt, though no longer president, headed the American party. As one White House aide observed, 'With T R and the Kaiser present, it'll be a wonder if the corpse gets a passing thought.'

T R, in fact, was on his best behaviour, until he was introduced to the German emperor. After the funeral ceremony the Kaiser told

111

Roosevelt, 'Call upon me at two o'clock; I have just forty-five minutes to give you.' 'I will be there at two, Your Majesty,' said T R, 'but unfortunately I have but twenty minutes to give you.'

❦ Making waves

President William Howard Taft was – at 350 pounds – the largest of American presidents. He was a model of politeness and in streetcars would always rise to give his place to three women.

One day President Taft was swimming in the sea off the coast of Massachusetts. A young man asked his girl if she wanted to go into the water but she replied, 'Perhaps we had better wait, the president is using the ocean at the moment.'

❦ A large party

Even as a young lawyer Taft was enormously overweight.

Once Taft had occasion to visit a small town on legal business. By the time he had finished he found that there were no more trains stopping at the town that day. After enquiries at the station Taft learned that a fast train was due in an hour but did not stop at this particular town. He therefore wired the divisional rail superintendent, 'Will Number seven stop here for a large party.' When the train duly stopped Taft climbed aboard, telling the astonished conductor, 'You can go ahead. I am the large party.'

❦ America backs off

During his period as governor-general of the Philippines, Taft and his wife were invited to attend the court of the tsar of Russia.

Unfortunately, as Taft and his wife alighted from their carriage there was a loud ripping sound as his trouser seams burst. There was no time to fetch more trousers of the right size and so Mrs Taft borrowed a needle and thread from a lady-in-waiting and proceeded to stitch them as best she could. However, uncertain how long his wife's stitching would last, Taft had to move crabwise towards the tsar and to back away from him after he had been introduced.

❦ Don't quote me

President Calvin Coolidge (1923–9) was a man of few words. Nicknamed 'Silent Cal', his administration did little to combat the problems of the Twenties and 'fiddled' while the country headed towards the Wall Street Crash. His droll sense of humour and deadpan expression gave rise to many anecdotes, few of which were merely apocryphal.

During the 1924 presidential campaign Calvin Coolidge was asked by a reporter, 'Have you any statement on the campaign?' 'No,' replied Coolidge. 'Can you tell us something about the world situation?' 'No.' 'Any information about Prohibition?' 'No.' Then, as the disappointed reporters started to leave, Coolidge said solemnly, 'Now, remember – don't quote me.'

❦ Mystery death

When the death of Calvin Coolidge was announced in 1933, Dorothy Parker exclaimed, 'How can they tell?'

❦ No precedent

While Coolidge was president of the Massachusetts Senate, two senators got involved in a slanging match.

During the row, one senator told the other to 'Go to hell!' The insulted senator was furious and called on Coolidge to do something about it. Coolidge took up a legal book, scanned it for a moment and replied, 'I've looked up the law, Senator, and you don't have to go there.'

❦ SOB OK!

When it was suggested that a well-known industrialist should be given a place in his cabinet, one of Coolidge's advisers complained, 'But Mister President, that fellow's a son-of-a-bitch.' 'Well,' said Coolidge, 'don't you think they ought to be represented too?'

❦ I'm not surprised

President Franklin D Roosevelt, 1933–45, was the only American president to serve more than two terms, the limit set down in the constitution. An attack of polio in 1921 confined him to a wheelchair but he continued in politics and won the election in 1932 on a policy called 'The New Deal', aimed to help the country out of depression. He took the decision to take America into the Second World War in 1941.

During the war Mrs Roosevelt went to visit a Baltimore prison with Maury Maverick from Texas, who was in charge of prison industries and wanted her to see the salvage work being done there. In order to fit the trip into her schedule Mrs Roosevelt had to leave the White House very early that morning without informing her husband. On his way to the office that day Roosevelt called to his wife's secretary and asked where Eleanor was. 'She is in prison, Mr President,' said the secretary. 'I'm not surprised,' said Roosevelt, 'but what for this time?'

❦ Don't shoot, I'm a Republican

President Roosevelt told the story of a conversation he had with a young Marine, just back from the War in the Pacific.

The young man told Roosevelt he had been disappointed not to have got one of the enemy. He had once been told by his officer to shout from the top of a hill, 'To hell with Emperor Hirohito,' on the basis that this was certain to bring the Japanese out into the open. He was right. A Japanese soldier had yelled in reply, 'To hell with Roosevelt.' But the soldier had been unable to fire on the Jap because, as he told the president, 'I couldn't shoot a Republican.'

❦ Hard to please

President Lyndon Johnson, 1963–9, took over on the assassination of John F Kennedy. He extended the war in Vietnam and lost popularity after the Vietnamese Tet offensive in 1968. He was a tough Texan and was particularly hard on his team of advisers. As he once said, 'There are no favourites in my office. I treat them all with the same general degree of inconsideration.'

One day the president went into the White House press office and after glancing at the messy desk of Malcolm Kilduff, his assistant press secretary, said, 'Kilduff, I hope your mind isn't as cluttered as your desk.' Kilduff quickly cleaned up his desk but a day or so later Johnson saw what he had done and said, 'Kilduff, I hope your brain isn't as vacant as your desk.'

❦ Nothing to boast about

President Jimmy Carter, 1977–81, lost popularity in both foreign and domestic affairs. At home his ambitious social policy had to be cut back because of high inflation, while abroad his failed attempt to rescue the Iranian hostages damaged American prestige.

By spring 1979, when Carter visited New Hampshire, his administration was beginning to come under heavy criticism. When a newswoman in Portsmouth asked him whether his daughter Amy ever bragged about her father's being president, Carter said, 'No, she probably apologizes.'

❦ Facing a choice

President Abraham Lincoln, 1861–5, was a self-made man and always retained the simple humour of his background. His achievements in abolishing slavery and maintaining the union during the Civil War make him one of the greatest of American presidents.

During his debates with Senator Stephen A Douglas in 1858, Lincoln replied to Douglas's accusation that he was a 'two-faced man', 'I leave it to my audience,' he said. 'If I had another face, do you think I would wear this one?'

❦ A president helps himself

A foreign diplomat once came upon Lincoln while he was polishing his shoes. 'What, Mr President,' he cried, 'you black your own boots?' 'Yes,' said Lincoln, 'whose do you black?'

❦ Cowardly legs

The problems of cowardice and desertion were considerable in the Union Army during the American Civil War. Yet Lincoln was unwilling to shoot soldiers for these offences, as his generals insisted.

On one occasion, Judge Holt referred a case to Lincoln of a soldier who had thrown down his gun and hidden behind a tree stump. When tried for cowardice the young man had no defence at all and was almost universally unpopular with his comrades. 'Here,' said the judge, 'is a case that comes exactly within your requirements. He does not deny his guilt and will serve the country better dead than living as he has no relations to mourn for him and he is not fit to be in the ranks of patriots.' Lincoln thought about it for a while and then replied, 'Well, after all, Judge, I think I'll have to put this with my leg cases.' 'Leg cases,' said the judge. 'What do you mean by leg cases?' 'Why, Judge,' replied Lincoln, 'do you see those papers crowded into those pigeon-holes? They are cases that you call by that long name Cowardice in the Face of the Enemy. But I call them for short, my leg cases. I put it to you and I leave it for you to decide for yourself; if Almighty God gives a man a cowardly pair of legs, how can he help their running away with him?'

❦ A brief sermon

President Calvin Coolidge attended church alone one Sunday because his wife was unwell. When he returned, she asked whether he had enjoyed the sermon. 'Yes,' he said. 'And what was it about?' 'Sin,' said Coolidge. 'But what did the preacher say?' his wife persisted. 'He was against it,' said Coolidge.

❦ Difficult to remember a harder bargain

When President Ulysses S Grant, 1869–77, was just a young boy a neighbour of his father's owned a colt which young Ulysses wanted very much.

Grant's father offered the neighbour twenty dollars for the horse but the man refused and asked for twenty-five. Grant was so keen that he pestered his father to find the extra five dollars. Eventually he was successful and his father sent him round to the man's house with the instructions to offer twenty, and if he did not accept that to try twenty-two and a half and only twenty-five if that did not work. Young Grant rode round to the neighbour's farm and told the man, 'Papa says I may offer you twenty dollars for the colt. But if you won't take that I'm to offer twenty-two and a half and if you won't take that to give you twenty-five.'

❦ A famous general

When Ulysses Grant was appointed to command the Army of the Potomac by President Lincoln in 1863, he was still something of an unknown figure in the east.

Secretary of State for War Stanton travelled to meet Grant who was arriving by train at Indianapolis. Stanton entered the carriage and shook the hand of Doctor Kitto, a staff surgeon, exclaiming, 'How are you, General Grant? I knew you at sight from your photographs.'

❦ Priorities

President Thomas Jefferson, 1801–9, was one of the Founding Fathers of the United States and was the author of the Declaration of Independence. Like most Americans, in his early days he was a slaveholder.

In February 1770, when Jefferson and his mother were visiting a neighbour one of their slaves rushed after them shouting that their house at Shadwell had caught fire and that everything in it had been burned. 'But were none of my books saved?' cried the distraught Jefferson. 'No, master,' said the slave, 'but we did save the fiddle.'

❦ Revealing all for the press

President John Quincy Adams, 1825–9, was the son of America's second president, John Adams. Something of an intellectual, John Quincy was out of step with the rising power of Western democracy which catapulted Andrew Jackson to the White House in 1829.

On one occasion, when the president was swimming naked in a nearby river, he encountered a newspaper reporter, a woman by the name of Anne Royall. Ms Royall was a most insistent lady who was determined to get an interview with the president. She followed him to the riverbank and sat next to his clothes. 'Come here,' she told him. Adams swam back to the shore and asked what she wanted. 'I'm Anne Royall,' she said, 'and I've been trying to see you to get an interview for months. I've hammered at the White House and they wouldn't let me in... Now I'm sitting on your clothes and you don't get them back until I get the interview. Will you give it to me or do you want to stay in there for the rest of your life?' 'Let me out and dress,' said Adams, 'and I promise to give you the interview.' 'Oh, no, you don't,' replied Royall. 'If you try to get out and get your clothes I'll scream and I just saw three fishermen round the bend. You don't get out ahead of that interview.' She got the interview in the end, with the president still chin-deep in the river.

❦ A match for Jefferson

President John F Kennedy, 1961–3, addressed the following words to the audience on the occasion of a dinner to honour forty-nine Nobel Prize winners in 1962.

'I think this is the most extraordinary collection of human talent, of human knowledge, that has ever been gathered at the White House – with the possible exception of when Thomas Jefferson dined alone.'

❦ Fire alarm

Once when the enormously stout President William Taft visited a cinema he found that he 'overflowed' the very small seat. As he told his son, 'Horace, if this theatre burns, it has got to burn around me.'

❦ Go with the flow

President Lyndon Johnson was keen to get rid of the all-powerful head of the FBI, J Edgar Hoover, but how was it to be done?

Eventually, concluding that it was too difficult a task, Johnson philosophically admitted to an aide, 'It's probably better to have him inside the tent, pissing out, than outside the tent, pissing in.'

❦ A minority interest

The American statesman Adlai Stevenson was one of the founding fathers of the United Nations. He twice stood for president against Eisenhower but lost both times, in 1952 and 1956.

During Adlai Stevenson's campaign for the presidency against Dwight D Eisenhower, one of his female supporters said, 'Every thinking person will be voting for you, Senator.' But Stevenson was not impressed. 'Madam, that is not enough. I need a majority.'

❦ Mistresses mine

President John Adams, 1797–1801, was one of America's aristocrats. His diplomacy helped to smooth peace negotiations with Britain in 1783.

During Adams's presidency his grand style contrasted sharply with the simplicity of his predecessor, George Washington, making him a number of enemies. A scandalous story was circulated which claimed that he had sent General George Pinckney to Britain to select four pretty girls as mistresses, two for himself and two for the general to keep. When he heard about the story Adams complained to a friend, 'I do declare, if this is true, General Pinckney has kept them all for himself and cheated me out of my two.'

❦ Presidential perks

During the 1948 presidential election in the United States, Thomas Dewey led in the opinion polls right up to polling day and everyone was certain that he would defeat his rival, Harry Truman, by a landslide.

On election night Thomas Dewey asked his wife, 'How will it be to sleep with the President of the United States?' She replied, 'A high honour and quite frankly, darling, I'm looking forward to it.' However, by the following morning, the results showed that Dewey had lost and Harry Truman was going to be the next president. At breakfast Mrs Dewey asked her husband, 'Tell me Tom, am I going to Washington or is Harry coming here?'

❦ Mañana

The diplomatic world of the early nineteenth century was far more relaxed than it is today.

While he was president of the United States, Thomas Jefferson once complained that he had not heard from his ambassador to Spain for nearly two years. 'If I don't hear from him next year,' he remarked, 'I will write him a letter.'

❦ Making friends

During the American Civil War, President Abraham Lincoln once referred to the Southern Confederates in polite terms.

Lincoln said that the Southerners were human beings, were they not? An elderly woman in the audience, incensed by this, asked Lincoln how he could speak kindly of his enemies when he should be doing everything to destroy them. Lincoln replied, 'What, madam? Do I not destroy my enemies when I make them my friends?'

❦ Old Hickory gets a choice

General Andrew Jackson – universally known as 'Old Hickory' – was one of America's military heroes, having defeated the British at the battle of New Orleans in 1815. He became president in 1829 and was noted for his strong personality and his tendency to get his own way.

When Andrew Jackson died, someone asked the question, 'Will he go to Heaven?' One of the Tennessee frontiersmen who had known Jackson replied, 'He will if he wants to.'

❦ Washington in the raw

President George Washington, 1789–97, became a legend in his lifetime. Offered the crown by a thankful Congress, Washington refused and retained his essential simplicity throughout his years in office. He always regarded himself as a soldier and not as a politician. When a statue was set up depicting him seated, dressed as an ancient Roman, stripped to the waist and wearing a toga draped over his knees, it prompted Nathaniel Hawthorne to observe:

Did anybody ever see Washington nude? It is inconceivable. He had no nakedness, but I imagine he was born with his clothes on, and his hair powdered and made a stately bow on his first appearance in the world.

❦ A presidential parade

President James Monroe, 1817–25, is perhaps best known for the 'Monroe Doctrine' which was aimed at keeping the European Powers from acquiring any more colonies in the Western hemisphere.

There was a circus at the small town of Haverhill in Massachusetts to celebrate the visit of the president, James Monroe. Haverhill was the home town of the nine-year-old John Greenleaf Whittier and his Quaker parents; the boy wanted to be there when the president came but his strict parents forbade him. Nevertheless, the following day he walked the streets looking for a sign that the president had really been in his home town. Then, in the road, he found the footprint made by the elephant that had led the parade the previous day and, convinced that he had found the footprint of the greatest man in the United States – President Monroe – he happily followed the print for as far as he could make it out.

❦ Sale or return

Before he became President of the United States, Woodrow Wilson was the President of Princeton University.

One day a fussy woman arrived in Woodrow Wilson's office, dragging behind her an apparently unwilling student. She sat down and began to question Wilson concerning the standards at Princeton, about which she admitted she knew nothing as all her relations had attended Harvard. However, she told him, her husband had been to Princeton and wanted their son to do the same. 'William being our only son,' she said, 'we want him to have the very best of everything. We want him to be absolutely outstanding in all his endeavours. We want him to receive an education which will mould him for great things. Can you assure me that William will do well here?'

'Madam,' Wilson replied, 'we guarantee satisfaction or we return the boy.'

❦ There's no such thing as a sure thing

A society woman thought she could get the better of President Calvin Coolidge when she attended a dinner party with him. She even placed a bet with friends.

At the start of the dinner party the woman turned to the president and said, 'I hope you will talk to me, Mr President. I made a bet that I could get more than two words out of you.'

'You lose,' said Coolidge.

🍒 7. THIS REALM OF KINGS

🍒 Who's your fat friend?

'Beau' Brummell was the most famous society figure of the Regency period. As a dandy – his boots were always polished in champagne – and 'friend' of the Prince Regent, Brummell had an influence out of all proportion to his abilities, which were minimal. In 1816 he fled England to escape his creditors and died in France. His 'quarrel' with the Prince Regent has provided numerous collectors of anecdotes with ammunition and his comment, 'Who's your fat friend?' is one of the most famous insults in British history.

A quarrel between the Prince of Wales and Beau Brummell took place in 1812. In April of the following year, the Dandy Club – where Brummell and his friends were members – decided to give a ball at the Argyll Rooms. The main problem was, should the Prince of Wales be invited. The quarrel between the prince and Brummell was common knowledge but it was thought that the ball might provide an opportunity to bring the two men together again as friends. Henry Pierrepoint, who had retained the friendship of the Prince of Wales, was given the job of inviting him to the ball and, to everyone's pleasure and relief, he accepted the invitation. On the evening of the ball the Prince of Wales arrived at the Argyll Rooms and was introduced to the hosts. He shook hands with Lord Alvanley first, and then Pierrepoint, but looked Brummell full in the face and passed on without acknowledging him. The insult was apparent to all. A silence fell over the proceedings. Then Brummell's voice was heard. 'Alvanley,' Brummell said, 'who's your fat friend?' After that there could be no reconciliation.

❦ First impressions

The disastrous marriage between the Prince Regent and Princess Caroline of Brunswick got off to a bad start and headed downhill thereafter. As to which of the two was more to blame, one is thrown back on Samuel Johnson's quip about the louse and the flea.

When George, Prince of Wales, first set eyes on his future wife, at St James's Palace, in April 1795, he was appalled at her appearance. Nevertheless, royal etiquette required him to kiss her. Having done so he stepped back quickly and called to his aide, 'I am unwell. Bring me a glass of brandy.'

❦ Age of innocence

For more than three generations Queen Victoria and her numerous brood set a tone of domestic tranquillity which became the norm for Victorian family life. Some people, however, took it too far.

While playing the part of Cleopatra, in the last years of Queen Victoria's reign, Sarah Bernhardt stabbed the slave who brought her news of Mark Antony's defeat at the battle of Actium, stormed about the stage, raving at the top of her voice, wrecking some of the scenery and finally, as the curtain came down, dropped to the ground in a convulsive heap. As the applause subsided, an elderly British matron was heard to say to her friend, 'How different, how very different from the home life of our own dear Queen.'

❦ Life insurance

Although Charles II was not always popular during his reign, the unpopularity of his Catholic brother, James, Duke of York, made Charles seem a paragon of virtue in comparison. Within three years of coming to the throne in 1685, James was forced to flee to France and was succeeded by King William III and James's daughter Mary II.

King Charles II was notably careless about his personal safety and was content to walk about Hyde Park with just two lords attending him. When his brother, the Duke of York, drove up in his carriage and told Charles that he should not expose himself to danger by travelling without an armed guard, the king replied, 'No danger. For no man in England would take away my life to make *you* king.'

❦ A royal drag

With parents like Queen Victoria and Prince Albert, who set impossibly high standards in behaviour for their children, it is no great surprise that Edward the Prince of Wales grew up to be so permissive.

Disraeli's wife, Lady Beaconsfield, once suggested to the queen that her son must be a great comfort to her, but Victoria replied, 'Comfort! Why, I caught him smoking a fortnight after his dear father died.'

❦ Disgracing the occasion

King Edward VII was no great fan of music, although as leader of society he was often forced to attend concerts.

In 1909 Dame Ethyl Smyth's new opera *The Wreckers* was given its first performance and friends of the composer persuaded the king to grace the occasion. After the opera was over the conductor, Sir Thomas Beecham, asked the king's private secretary what Edward had thought of it. The secretary replied, 'I am not sure.' 'But didn't he say anything?' Sir Thomas persisted. 'Well, yes, he did,' said the secretary. 'He suddenly woke up and said, "Fritz, that's the fourth time that infernal noise has roused me."'

❦ A Flanders mare

Henry VIII's fourth marriage – to the Protestant Anne of Cleves – was a disaster from the start. In order to find out what his future wife looked like, Henry had sent the painter Hans Holbein to Flanders to paint Anne's portrait. Henry had been pleased with what he saw in the picture but the reality was disappointing.

The king no sooner heard that Anne of Cleves had landed at Rochester than he went thither in disguise, to see his future comfort, and found her so different from her picture, which had been drawn by Hans Holbein, that in the impatience of his disappointment he swore they had brought him a Flanders mare.

❦ Street wise

The actress Nell Gwyn was the most popular of Charles II's mistresses, not least because she had the most natural way with ordinary people.

In 1675 Nell Gwyn paid a visit to Oxford with Charles II. The crowd, believing that the king was accompanied by Louis de Keroualle, his unpopular Roman Catholic mistress, angrily shook the coach in which Nell was riding. With an instant appraisal of the situation, she leaned out of the window, calling, 'Pray, good people, be civil; I am the Protestant whore.'

❦ A status symbol

After the English Reformation, Protestant clergymen were allowed to marry. But, enlightened as she was in so many other ways, Queen Elizabeth I could never come to terms with this. Sir John Harington relates an incident that occurred when the queen visited the house of the Archbishop of Canterbury.

Now though this Archbishop [Matthew Parker] dissembled not his Marriage, yet Queen Elizabeth would not dissemble her dislike of it. For whereas it pleased her often to come to his house, in respect of her favour to him (that had been her Mothers Chaplain) being once above the rest greatly seated; at her parting from thence the Archbishop and his Wife being together, she gave him very special thanks, with gratious and honourable terms, and then looking on his Wife, and you (saith she) Madame I may not call you, and Mistress I am ashamed to call you, so I know not what to call you, but yet I do thank you.

Let Them Eat Cake!

❦ Seat of majesty

Queen Elizabeth I was enormously fond of her great minister, William Cecil, Lord Burghley. She had been able to rely on him throughout her reign and knew that he was the only man whose judgement she could always rely on to be impartial. She allowed Burghley concessions that she would have made for no other man.

When the treasurer [Lord Burghley], in the latter part of his life, was much afflicted with gout, the queen always made him sit down in her presence with some obliging expression. 'My Lord,' she would say, 'we make use of you, not for your bad legs, but for your good head.'

❦ He talked to the trees

George III suffered from bouts of insanity, made far worse by the appalling treatment he received from his physicians. His real complaint – porphyria – was beyond treatment at that time.

During the illness of King George III in 1789 it is said that he once ordered his coach to stop in Windsor Park with the words, 'Ah, there he is!' Alighting from the vehicle, he went over to a nearby oak tree and addressed it as the King of Prussia, shaking hands with the tree's lower branches 'with the most apparent cordiality and regard'.

❦ The force of reason

After his defeat in the First Civil War, King Charles I was imprisoned by order of Parliament. Although no decision had been taken to put the king on trial as yet, there were many extremists in the Army who wished to see him deposed and brought to justice.

2 June 1647. The same morning that Cromwell left London, Cornet Joyce, who was one of the agitators in the army, a tailor, a fellow who had two or three years before served in a very inferior employment in Mr Hollis's house, came with a squadron of fifty horse to Holmby, where the king was, about the break of day; and, without any interruption by the guard of horse or foot which waited there, came with two or three more, and knocked at the king's chamber door and said, 'He must presently speak with the king.' His Majesty, surprised at the manner of it, rose out of his bed; and half-dressed, caused the door to be opened, which he knew otherwise would be quickly broken open; they who waited in the chamber being persons of whom he had little knowledge, and less confidence. As soon as the door was opened, Joyce and two or three more came into the chamber, with their hats off and pistols in their hands. Joyce told the king, 'that he must go with him.' His Majesty asked, 'Whither?' He answered, 'to the army.' The king asked him, 'where the army was?' He said, 'they would carry him to the place where it was.' His Majesty asked, 'by what authority they came?' Joyce answered, 'by this' and shewed him his pistol.

❦ Christian festivities

The court of King James I was one of the most dissolute in English history. A visit of Christian IV of Denmark in the summer of 1606

129

was the occasion of astonishing licence. Delighted at the thought of entertaining a king, James set himself to please his royal guest, but in truth entertainment was a simple matter, for Christian's conception of happiness began and ended in the bottle. God forbid, wrote the Earl of Salisbury, that this Dane should think the English did anything but drink. Sir John Harington, a wit of Elizabeth's court, has left a well-known picture of the revels at Theobald's where Salisbury played the host to both sovereigns.

The sport began each day in such a manner as persuades me of Mahomet's paradise. We had women and indeed wine too of such plenty as would have astonished each sober beholder. Our feasts were magnificent, and the two royal guests did most lovingly embrace each other at table; I think the Dane hath strangely wrought on our good English nobles, for those whom I never could get to taste good liquor now followed the fashion and wallow in beastly delights. The ladies abandon their sobriety and roll about in intoxication. There hath been no lack of good living; shows, sights and banquetings from morn to eve. One day a great feast was held, and after dinner the representation of Solomon his Temple and the coming of the Queen of Sheba was made before their Majesties. The lady who did play the queen's part did carry most precious gifts to their Majesties; but forgetting the steps arising to the canopy overset her caskets into his Danish Majesty's lap and fell at his feet, although I rather think it was in his face. Much was hurry and confusion; cloths and napkins were at hand to make all clean. His Majesty then got up and would dance with the Queen of Sheba; but he fell down and humbled himself before her and was carried to an inner chamber and laid on a bed of state, which was not a little defiled with the presents of the queen which had been bestowed on his garments, such as wine, cream, jelly, beverage, cakes, spices and other good matters. The entertainment went forward and most of the presenters went backward or fell down, wine did so occupy their upper chambers. Now did appear Hope, Faith and Charity. Hope did assay to speak but wine rendered her endeavours so feeble that she withdrew and hoped the king would excuse her brevity. Faith was then all alone for I am certain that she was not joined with good works, but left the court in a staggering condition. Charity came to the king's feet and seemed to cover a multitude of sins her sisters had committed. In some sort she made obeisance and brought gifts, but said she would return home again as there was no gift that heaven had not already given His Majesty. She then returned to Hope and Faith who were both sick and spewing in the lower hall. Next came Victory in bright armour and presented a rich sword to the king who did not accept it but put it by with his hand; but Victory did not triumph long, for after much lamentable utterance she was led away like a silly captive and laid to sleep on the outer steps of the antechamber. Now did Peace make entry and strive to get foremost to the king; but I grieve to tell how great wrath she did discover unto her attendants and much contrary to her semblance most rudely made war with her olive branch and laid on the pates of those who did oppose her coming. I did never see such lack of good order, discretion and sobriety as I have now done.

❦ A right royal welcome

On the death of Queen Elizabeth I, James VI of Scotland, son of Mary, Queen of Scots, became King James I of England. But many Englishmen found James crude and uncouth in both manners and speech.

When he travelled south from Scotland in 1603 James was surprised by the enthusiasm of the English people for their new king. Eventually he grew tired of this and asked Sir John Oglander what the people wanted. Oglander replied that they came to see him because they loved him. Then James cried out in Scottish, 'God's wounds! I will pull down my breeches and they shall also see my arse.'

❦ Papal indulgence

Although several Renaissance popes had fathered children, none of them had taken the step suggested by Sixtus V, of marrying a Protestant. Nevertheless, it is an indication of the esteem in which the heretic queen was held by Catholic leaders, including Philip II of Spain, who incidentally also wanted to marry Elizabeth.

When Pope Sixtus V heard of Elizabeth's execution of Mary Queen of Scots in 1587, he commented, 'What a valiant woman. She braves the two greatest kings by land and sea...It is a pity that Elizabeth and I cannot marry; our children would have ruled the whole world.'

❦ A literal truth

The King James Bible is one of the greatest treasures of the English language but as copy editors the world over will know, mistakes do occur, though rarely with the same effect as this one.

Robert Barker and Martin Lucas, the king's printers at London, printed an edition of the Bible of one thousand copies, in which a serious mistake was made by leaving out the word 'not' in the seventh commandment, causing it to read 'Thou shalt commit adultery.' His Majesty, King Charles I, being made acquainted with it by Dr William Laud, Bishop of London, an order was given for calling the printers into the Star Chamber, where, upon the fact being proved, the whole impression was called in, and the printers fined £3,000.

❦ A crowning disaster

On ceremonial occasions the role of the Earl Marshal, responsible for the smooth running of the event, can be a very trying one.

The coronation of George I was not without its hitches. Eventually the king complained about the mistakes to the Deputy Earl-Marshal, Lord Effingham, who replied, 'It is true, sir, that there has been some neglect; but I have taken care that the next coronation shall be regulated in the exactest manner possible.'

❦ We were amused...

The widely held view that Queen Victoria was a humourless monarch who never laughed is not supported by the evidence. In this instance we see a very human side to the little lady.

In order to hear how HMS *Eurydice*, a frigate sunk off Portsmouth, had been salvaged, Queen Victoria invited Admiral Foley to lunch. Having exhausted this melancholy subject, Queen Victoria enquired after her close friend, the admiral's sister. Hard of hearing, Admiral Foley replied in his stentorian voice, 'Well, Ma'am, I'm going to have her turned over, take a good look at her bottom and have it well scraped.' The queen put down her knife and fork, hid her face in her handkerchief, and laughed until the tears ran down her cheeks.

❦ A stud

King Charles II had a reputation as a womanizer and the following story supports this image.

In some of the State Poems, Charles II is ridiculed under the nickname of Old Rowley, which was an ill-favoured stallion kept in the mews, that was remarkable for getting fine colts. Mrs Holford, a young lady much admired by Charles, was sitting in her apartment and singing a satirical ballad upon 'Old Rowley the King', when he knocked at the door. Upon her asking who was there he, with his usual good humour, replied, 'Old Rowley himself, Madame.'

❦ The King meets his Waterloo

King George IV, inheriting some of the eccentricity and insanity of his Hanoverian forebears, suffered from a number of delusions, exacerbated by his over-indulgence in strong drink.

King George IV believed that he was at the battle of Waterloo, and indeed commanded there, and his friends were a little alarmed; but Knighton (his physician), who was a sensible man, said, 'His Majesty has only to leave off curaçao and rest assured he will gain no more victories.'

❦ An ill wind

At the court of Elizabeth I – in the absence of a king or a male consort to the queen – many ambitious young men vied for the royal attention. Sometimes a minor slip could make the difference between royal favour and total ignominy.

On one occasion, as he was bowing low to Queen Elizabeth, Edward de Vere, the Earl of Oxford, audibly broke wind. Deeply embarrassed, the earl withdrew from court and travelled abroad for several years. On his return to court he was greeted by the queen, whose first words were, 'My Lord, I had forgot the fart.'

❦ Faint heart

Walter Ralegh was one of the most brilliant of Queen Elizabeth I's young courtiers. But he was a self-made man, possessing few of the advantages of his aristocratic rivals, and in his efforts to win the queen's favour he had to risk far more than they did.

He was bred in Oriel College in Oxford; and thence coming to court found some hopes of the Queen's favours reflecting upon him. This made him write in a glass window, obvious to the Queen's eye,

'Fain would I climb, yet fear to fall.'

Her Majesty, either espying or being shown it, did underwrite,

'If thy heart fail thee, climb not at all.'

❦ A cure for the gout

King James I was an early disciple of homoeopathic remedies for his ailments, some of which might strike readers today as quite disgusting.

King James I loved hunting but he had a more curious reason for chasing stags than did most monarchs. He suffered a lot from arthritis and gout and had it on good authority that he could gain relief not in the exercise of chasing animals but in paddling in their bloody intestines. He was always in at the kill of each stag so that he could take his treatment 'fresh'. One of his companions described such an incident during a hunt at Eltham. 'On Saturday last the king killed a buck in Eltham Park and so soon as it was opened stood in the belly of it and bathed his bare feet and legs with the warm blood; since which time he has been so nimble that he thinketh this the only remedy for the gout. He hath been of late exceeding merry.'

❦ The unkindest cut of all

The death of Edmund 'Ironside', the last 'English' king, in 1016 resulted from another of history's foul crimes. Edmund had been successfully fighting the Danish invader Canute until an English traitor – one of Edmund's thanes, Edric Streona – hoping to curry favour with Canute, arranged the murder of his great rival. There are several variants on the way the blow was struck but there is complete agreement about the place that Edmund breathed his last.

After feasting one evening Edmund retired to the building which held the privy – little more than a deep hole dug in the ground – in order to relieve the call of nature. Hidden inside the privy was the son of ealdorman Edric. As Edmund sat down Edric's son thrust upwards with his dagger, penetrating Edmund's rectum and leaving the weapon fixed in his bowels. Another version has an even more complex method of killing. A Norman chronicler, Geoffrey Gaimar, wrote that a bow had been fixed in the privy by Edric's son so that as the king sat down he triggered an arrow which flew up and penetrated his body from beneath. Whichever weapon was used, the essential facts are clear: Edmund died by being pierced through the vitals in a privy.

But Edric did not live long to profit from his crime. He presented himself to Canute saying, 'Hail! thou who art sole king of England,' and told the Dane what he had done. To his surprise Canute was angry and replied, 'For this deed I will exalt you, as it merits, higher than all the nobles of England.' He then commanded that Edric should be decapitated and his head placed upon a pole on the highest battlement.

❦ A champion hoaxer

Traditionally at royal coronations, the royal champion challenges anyone to dispute the king or queen's right to the throne. Although the position of champion became an honorary one centuries ago, it is theoretically possible for someone to take up the challenge. What happens next is anyone's guess.

At the coronation banquet of King William III and Queen Mary the Royal Champion's challenge was taken up by an old woman on crutches. Suspecting a hoax, the champion refused the challenge and in theory the monarchs were subsequently dethroned.

At the banquet that followed the coronation of Charles I, the king's champion rode into the great hall, declared his willingness to fight any man who questioned the right of the king to his throne and then fell off his horse.

❦ Foot in the mouth

Queen Anne, daughter of King James II and wife to Prince George of Denmark, was one of history's tragic mothers. When it came to 'trying again', Robert the Bruce's spider just wasn't in it.

At the coronation of Queen Anne the Archbishop of Canterbury made an appalling gaffe. Forgetting that by the time she became queen, Anne had given birth to seventeen children, none of whom had survived infancy, he expressed the hope that she would 'leave a numerous posterity to rule these kingdoms'.

❦ Elevation

Eleanor Gwyn, the actress and mistress of King Charles II, was one of the most popular figures at the royal court. Nevertheless, she was not averse to a bit of social climbing and, like any mother, tried to do the best for her son.

When Nell Gwyn gave birth to a child by Charles II she was very keen to earn the boy a title. When the king refused to grant one she took the desperate step of holding him out of the window by his ankles and threatening to drop him. Charles at last relented and said, 'So be it. Pray, spare the Earl of Burford.'

❦ Misled by the nose

The statue of Queen Anne outside St Paul's Cathedral was desecrated in 1769 by a drunken Lascar, who mistook it for his mother. He broke off its stone nose and then tried to get away carrying the stone orb and sceptre, until arrested by the Watch.

❦ A birthday kiss

Samuel Pepys, like so many people in the past, did not share the modern distaste for and fear of human relics. His natural curiosity took him to places where the more squeamish would fear to tread.

When the Lady Chapel at Westminster Abbey was undergoing renovation in the late seventeenth century, the remains of Henry V's wife, Catherine of Valois, were removed and left alongside the tomb of her husband. Her coffin had been an open one and Samuel Pepys was one of many interested spectators who came to see her remains. Pepys went further than merely looking. 'I had the upper part of her body in my hands and I did kiss her mouth, reflecting upon it that I did kiss a queen and that this was my birthday, thirty six years old, that I did kiss a queen.'

❦ He was a tree

As a young woman, Queen Anne was both short-sighted and obstinate and it was difficult to tell which of these two attributes was the more pronounced.

On one occasion while walking in the park with her sister Mary, the two girls disputed over something they could see in the distance, as to whether it was a tree or a man. Mary insisted it was the latter and Anne the former. As they drew closer to the object it became quite clear that it was a man and the gentleman even tipped his cap to them. 'There, sister,' said Mary, 'I told you it was a man.' But Anne turned away stubbornly, saying, 'Well I say it was a tree.'

❦ A restraining order

After his great victory over the French at the battle of Blenheim in 1704, John Churchill, Duke of Marlborough, was rewarded with the great palace that was to bear the name of his victory. But his wife, the truculent Sarah Jennings, lady-in-waiting and confidante of Queen Anne, was constantly souring relations by bickering with her mistress.

While Sarah, Duchess of Marlborough, was vacating her apartments at St James's Palace, prior to moving to Marlborough House, she sent a message to the queen that she would like to store her furniture in the palace until Marlborough House was completed. Queen Anne, already frustrated by Sarah's financial demands, returned a reply that the duchess could rent storage space for ten shillings a week. Infuriated, Sarah removed all portable fixtures from her apartments in the palace, including fireplaces and doorknobs. In retaliation, Anne ordered a temporary halt to building work at Blenheim, saying that she would not build the duke a house when the duchess was pulling down hers.

❦ The king's hump

The health of King William III was never strong and his perpetual stoop gave him the impression of a hunchback.

On one occasion a doctor from Amsterdam, one Peter Schenk, met the prince while he was dressed in farmer's clothes. Shenk immediately greeted him as 'Your Majesty' and when William asked how he had known it was him, Shenk clumsily replied, 'I know you by your hump.'

❦ Divine right of kings

King William III spent most of his life fighting against France and it was due to him that Louis XIV was prevented from establishing French hegemony in Western Europe. William risked his life on numerous occasions but died, ironically, when his horse fell after stepping in a mole-hole. As this story shows, kings at that time felt their lives were in God's hands, unlike those of lesser men.

During the siege of Namur in 1695 William was annoyed to discover that a civilian, Michael Godfrey, the Deputy Governor of the Bank of England, had made his way into the front line of the fighting. Angrily William ordered him to leave at once but Godfrey replied, 'Sir, I run no more hazard than your Majesty.' 'I'm here where it is my duty to be,' said the king, 'and I may without presumption commit my life to God's keeping, but you. . .' At this point a cannon ball whizzed past and decapitated Godfrey at the king's side.

❦ A royal card: king or knave

King George I, the first of the Hanoverian monarchs, clearly felt no responsibility for the people over whom he reigned. Many thousands of people were ruined by the speculation associated with the fraudulent activities of the South Sea Company. But the king felt no compunction about taking a profit for himself.

At the height of the infamous 'South Sea Bubble' in 1720, many Englishmen were losing everything they had in the Company's crash. But not everyone was so unlucky. As the king explained, 'We had very good luck; for we sold out last week.'

❦ Farmer George

King George III reigned for sixty years – from 1760 to 1820 – and is probably best known for the disastrous policies that led to the loss of the American Colonies and for the fact that he suffered long periods of insanity. In other ways, however, he was a kind man and much loved by the people.

Early one morning the king met a boy in the stables at Windsor and asked him, 'Well, boy! What do you do? What do they pay you?' 'I help in the stable,' said the lad, 'but they only give me victuals and clothes.' 'Be content,' said the king, 'I have no more.'

❦ Giving offence

King Edward VII was the son of Queen Victoria, while Kaiser Wilhelm II of Germany was her grandson. Yet the two men had no sense of family friendship and the Kaiser in particular was jealous of his uncle. Their sense of rivalry contributed to the arms race between Britain and Germany in the first decade of the twentieth century.

On one of the numerous state occasions where King Edward VII and his nephew, Kaiser Wilhelm II of Germany, were forced to share a state carriage, one of the carriage horses passed wind and made an offensive smell. Edward found the incident embarrassing but when it happened a second time he felt obliged to apologize. 'My dear Uncle Bertie,' the Kaiser replied, 'please don't mention it – I really thought it was one of the horses.'

❦ Dizzy declines to play Mercury

The relationship between Queen Victoria and the Conservative party leader, Benjamin Disraeli, Lord Beaconsfield, was particularly good. Disraeli knew how to flatter the old lady, as he said 'to lay it on with a trowel', but on his deathbed he felt not up to the task of taking a message to the long-deceased Prince Regent.

When Disraeli was on his deathbed it was suggested to him that Queen Victoria might pay him a visit. But he refused, saying, 'No, it is better not. She would only ask me to take a message to Albert.'

❦ Mama's spirit gives a sign

During her lifetime, Queen Victoria's influence on all around her was so great that few could imagine life without her.

Not long after the death of Queen Victoria, the royal family were at prayers in the chapel at Frogmore when a dove was observed to enter. 'That's Mama's spirit,' some of the younger ones agreed. 'No, I'm sure it is not,' said Princess Louise. 'Dear Mama's spirit would never have ruined Beatrice's hat.'

❦ A wild chase

Fanny Burney, who had been appointed to the position of Keeper of the Queen's Robes in 1786, wrote in her diary the best account of the onset of George III's insanity. Fanny herself had numerous encounters with the mad king, commenting that on occasions his eyes looked like blackberries and he foamed at the mouth. Yet, although she was afraid of him in his fits, she also liked the poor old man and pitied him his harsh treatment.

I had proceeded, in my quick way, nearly half the round, when I suddenly perceived, through some trees, two or three figures. Relying on the instructions of Dr John Willis I concluded them to be workmen and gardeners; yet tried to look sharp, and in so doing, as they were less shaded, I thought I saw the person of his Majesty! Alarmed past all possible expression, I waited not to know more, but turning back, ran off with all my might. But what was my terror to hear myself pursued! – to hear the voice of the King himself loudly and hoarsely calling after me 'Miss Burney! Miss Burney!'

I protest I was ready to die. I knew not in what state he might be at the time; I only knew the orders to keep out of his way were universal...

The steps still pursued me, and still the poor hoarse and altered voice rang in my ears: more and more footsteps resounded frightfully behind me – the attendants all running to catch their eager master, and the voices of the two Doctors Willises loudly exhorting him not to heat himself so unmercifully.

Heavens, how I ran! I do not think I should have felt the hot lava from Vesuvius – at least not the hot cinders – had I so run during its eruption. My feet were not sensible that they even touched the ground.

Soon after, I heard other voices, shriller, though less nervous, call out, 'Stop! Stop! Stop!'

I could by no means consent: I knew not what was purported, but I recollected fully my agreement with Dr John that very morning, that I should decamp if surprised and not be named...Still, therefore, on I fly; and such was my speed, so almost incredible to relate or recollect, that I fairly believe no one of the whole party could have overtaken me, if these words, from one of the attendants, had not reached me, 'Doctor Willis begs you to stop!'

'I cannot!' I answered, still flying on, when he called out, 'You must, Ma'am; it hurts the King to run...'

When they were within a few yards of me, the king called out 'Why did you run away?'

Shocked at a question impossible to answer, yet a little assured by the mild tone of his voice, I instantly forced myself forward, to meet him...

The effort answered: I looked up, and met all his wonted benignity of countenance, though something still of wildness in his eyes. Think, however, of my surprise, to feel him put both his hands round my two shoulders, and then kiss my cheek!

I wonder I did not really sink, so exquisite was my affright when I saw him spread out his arms! Involuntarily, I concluded he meant to crush me: but the Willises, who had never seen him till this fatal illness, not knowing how very extraordinary an action this was from him, simply smiled and looked pleased, supposing, perhaps, it was his customary salutation!

I believe, however, it was but the joy of a heart unbridled, now, by the forms and proprieties of established custom and sober reason. To see any of his household thus by accident, seemed such a near approach to liberty and recovery, that who can wonder it should serve rather to elate than lessen what yet remains of his disorder!

❦ The kingfisher

Queen Victoria's husband, Prince Albert, was not noted for his wit. This may be one of the few examples.

A picture at Balmoral portrayed all the royal children, and various birds and animals. Someone asked which was Princess Helena. 'There, with the kingfisher,' said Prince Albert, adding, 'a very proper bird for a princess.'

❦ Grounded

The following story about Queen Alexandra rejects not bitterness but tiredness. Edward VII had led his wife a 'merry dance' and at last it had ended.

On 10 May 1910, King Edward VII died. At first, as he lay on his deathbed, his long-suffering wife Alexandra, who had turned a blind eye to his infidelities on so many occasions, was stricken with grief. But it was not long before her sense of humour returned. She remarked to Lord Esher, 'Now at least I know where he is.'

❦ No room for Bacon

At the end of her reign, all the men Elizabeth had grown up with – Leicester, Burghley, Walsingham and so on – had died, leaving her feeling old and lonely. A new generation of courtiers had replaced the men of her youth, among them the brilliant lawyer, Francis Bacon.

Once when Queen Elizabeth I visited Bacon, her lord chancellor, at his home at Gorhambury, in Hertfordshire, she was surprised at how modest his house was when compared with the palaces of her other ministers. 'What a little house you have got,' she told him. Bacon replied with his usual tact, 'The house is well, but it is you, Your Majesty, who have made me too great for it.'

❦ Nothing much upstairs

Francis Bacon was the most brilliant intellect in England during the reign of King James I. In addition to his acuity he had a ready wit.

When a new ambassador was sent by the French king to the court of King James I of England, the king was disappointed by the poor impression the Frenchman made, being tall, ungainly and poorly attired. When the Frenchman had presented his credentials and retired, the king asked Bacon what he thought of him. 'Your Majesty,' replied Bacon, 'people of such dimensions are like four- or five-storey houses – the upper rooms are the most poorly furnished.'

❦ A royal reminder

Oliver Cromwell, Lord Protector of England, holds with his son Richard the distinction of being the only rulers of England in a thousand years not to be of royal blood.

Queen Caroline attended an exhibition of royal portraits by Jonathan Richardson. Observing the picture of Oliver Cromwell, hung between Charles I and Charles II, she asked the artist, 'Surely that person is not a king?' 'No, Madame,' replied Richardson. 'He is not a king, but it is good for kings to have him among them as a memento.'

❦ Rationing

Value and price are not always the same thing. The value of the unpopular George II had a startling effect on the price of the services he was offered, as in this case.

King George once stopped at a village inn and was served a light meal. He was charged a guinea for an egg, which even a king felt was rather steep. 'Eggs must be very scarce in this area,' he said to the innkeeper. 'Not half as scarce as kings are,' the man replied.

❦ A convenient smoking room

As we have seen, Queen Victoria heartily disapproved of smoking and so her sons, who smoked a great deal, had to do so in constant fear of being discovered.

At Windsor Castle they found a suitable room to be used as a smoking room, but their mother, who suspected what was going on, said she would personally inspect all the rooms to make certain that her instructions were being carried out. Panic ensued among the boys until Edward, Prince of Wales, thought of a solution: he fixed the letters WC on the door.

❦ Victoria rules the waves

Deprived of normal experiences by the closeted life she led, Queen Victoria could be remarkably naïve.

Queen Victoria was crossing to Ireland in the royal yacht, when the ship encountered very rough weather. A huge wave caused the ship to lurch, almost knocking the queen off her feet. Recovering herself, she sent one of her attendants to the bridge. 'Give the admiral my compliments,' she said, 'and tell him that he's not to let that happen again.'

❦ The conqueror stoops

Queen Elizabeth I could be a harsh taskmaster, notably when dealing with foreign princes or those who questioned her authority. But there was another gentler side to her character.

Queen Elizabeth I had the greatest respect and affection for her minister of state, Lord Burghley. While he was sick with gout at his house, in the Strand the queen visited him there. Finding that her head attire made her too tall to pass through the front door easily, Lord Burghley's servant asked her if she would be pleased to stoop. Elizabeth replied, 'For your master's sake I will stoop, but not for the king of Spain's.'

❦ The birds are flown

The king's attempt to arrest the 'five members' in the House of Commons, on the advice of his wife Henrietta Maria, was one of his greatest blunders, and made civil war almost inevitable. Edmund Ludlow was present that day.

The king, finding his instruments thus discouraged, and being resolved to remove all obstructions in his way, went in person to the House of Commons, attended not only with his ordinary Guard of Pensioners, but also with those desperadoes that for some time he had entertained at Whitehall, to the number of three or four hundred, armed with partizans, sword and pistol. At the door of the House he left his Guard commanded by Lord Roxberry, entering accompanied only by the Prince Palatine; where, taking possession of the Speaker's Chair, and not seeing those that he looked for, he said: 'The birds are flown.'

For, upon being given notice by a lady of the Court of the King's intention, they were retired into the City. The King then demanded of the Speaker where such and such were, naming the five Members: to which he answered in these words: 'I have neither eyes to see, ears to hear, nor tongue to speak, save what this House gives me.'

The King replied: 'I think you are in the right.'

❦ No greater man

It is doubtful if even a modern headmaster would disagree with Dr Busby.

When King Charles had occasion to visit Westminster School, he was shown around the premises by its famous headmaster, Dr Busby. The headmaster apologized to the king for not removing his hat in the royal presence but explained, 'It would not do for my boys to suppose that there existed in the world a greater man than Dr Busby.'

❦ Royal embarrassment

During the eleven years – 1629 to 1640 – when King Charles II tried to rule England without summoning a parliament, he tried to raise revenue in many ways, like Ship Money and Forced Loans, which earned him the hatred of his subjects. Clearly the king felt this personally.

Charles II once demanded of Dr Stillingfleet, who was a preacher at the court, why he read his sermons before him, when on every other occasion his sermons were delivered without notes. The doctor answered that, overawed by so many and noble personages, and in the presence of his sovereign, he dared not trust his powers of memory.

'And now,' said the preacher, 'will Your Majesty permit me to ask a question? Why does Your Majesty read your speeches, when it may be presumed that you can have no such fear?'

'Why, truly,' said the king, 'I have asked my subjects so often for money that I am ashamed to look them in the face.'

❦ The cough of a leviathan

During her time as Lady of the Queen's Robes, Fanny Burney made friends with a number of the royal family, notably the young Princess Charlotte Augusta. Her accounts of her experiences provide a unique glimpse of the home life of eighteenth-century royals.

Fanny Burney recorded an amusing conversation she had with the young Princess Charlotte:

Afterwards I happened to be alone with this charming princess and her sister Elizabeth, in the queen's dressing-room. She then came up to me and said:

'Now will you excuse me, Miss Burney, if I ask you the truth of something I have heard about you?'

'Certainly, ma'am,' I replied.

'It's such an odd thing, I don't know how to mention it; but I have wished to ask you about it this great while. Pray is it really true that, in your illness last year, you coughed so violently that you broke the whalebone of your stays in two?'

'As nearly true as possible, ma'am; it actually split with the force of the convulsive motion of a cough that seemed loud and powerful enough for a giant. I could hardly believe it was little I that had made so formidable a noise.'

❦ A queen in bloom

Queen Charlotte, wife to King George III, was never noted for her good looks. Yet, as she grew older, it was generally felt that her appearance was improving.

One day someone suggested this to her chamberlain, Colonel Disbrowe, who replied, 'Yes. I do think that the bloom of her ugliness is going off.'

❦ Profits up in smoke

Sir Walter Ralegh, poet, courtier, soldier, explorer and historian, is – with the possible exception of Sir Philip Sidney – the closest the Elizabethans ever came to a true Renaissance man. Among the so-called 'discoveries' that Ralegh made in the New World were tobacco and potatoes, but the evidence that Ralegh discovered them is far from strong. Nevertheless, he exploited them for profit on their arrival in England.

Sir Walter Ralegh was conversing with his royal mistress upon the singular properties of this new and extraordinary herb tobacco. He assured her that he had so well experienced the nature of it that he could tell her the exact weight of the smoke in any quantity proposed to be consumed.

Her Majesty immediately fixed her thoughts upon the most impracticable part of the experiment, that of bounding the smoke in a balance ... and laying a wager that he could not solve the doubt.

Upon this Ralegh selected the quantity agreed on, and having thoroughly smoked it, set himself to weighing – but it was of the ashes; and, in conclusion, demonstrating to the queen the difference between the weight of the ashes and the original weight of the tobacco, her majesty did not deny that this must be the weight of what was evaporated in smoke.

Upon this Elizabeth, paying down the money, remarked that she had heard of many labourers in the fire who had turned their gold into smoke, but that Ralegh was certainly the first who had turned his smoke into gold.

❦ The merry widow

Edward IV was a remarkably handsome man, almost certainly the best-looking monarch in English history. However, like every other English ruler, he was always short of money and looking for ways to raise new revenue to finance his wars.

On one occasion he sent for a rich widow and asked her with a smile how much she would be willing to pay in taxes.

'For thy lovely face,' said the old lady, 'thou shalt have twenty pounds.'

The king was delighted. He had expected only half as much. In thanks he gave the lady a kiss, which delighted her so much, that she doubled her offer and left him with forty pounds.

❦ A box on the ears

Queen Elizabeth I's relationship with Robert Devereux, Earl of Essex, was very stormy. She tolerated from him more than from any of her other courtiers but occasionally she lost patience and then she would strike. William Camden records the most famous such incident.

There followed a pretty warm dispute between the Queen and Essex, about the choice of some fit and able persons to superintend the affairs of Ireland...

The Queen looked upon Sir William Knollys, uncle to Essex, as the most proper person for that charge; and Essex contended, on the other side, that Sir George Carew would much better become that post... and when the Queen could by no means be persuaded to approve his choice, he quite forgot himself and his duty, and turned his back upon his Sovereign in a kind of contempt. The queen was not able to bear this insolence, and so bestowed on him a box on the ear, and bade him 'go and be hanged'.

He immediately clapped his hand on his sword, and the Lord Admiral stepping in between, he swore a great oath that he neither could nor would put up with an affront of that nature, nor would he have taken it at the hands of Henry VIII himself; and, in a great passion, he immediately withdrew from the Court.

❦ Uneasy lies the head

The queen's godson, Sir John Harington, who, incidentally, is credited with the invention of the water closet, described Elizabeth in her last years, obsessed with the fear of rebellion or assassination.

149

The many evil plots have overcome all her Highness's sweet temper. She walks much in her Privy Chamber, and stamps with her feet at ill news, and thrusts her trusty sword at times into the arras in a great rage. The dangers are over and yet she always keeps a sword by her table.

❦ HM or HM?

Mr H K Marsden was a housemaster at Eton, who was noted not only for his eccentricity but for his stern discipline.

A boy in his house was once invited to tea at Windsor castle, with King George VI and Queen Elizabeth. As a result he was late arriving back at Eton and was sent for by Marsden to explain his late return. The boy told his story but Marsden was unimpressed and demanded written proof of the boy's story.

As a result the lad was sent back to the castle the next day. King George entered into the spirit of the occasion and duly wrote the boy a note on Windsor Castle notepaper: 'Please excuse_____. He was having tea with me and it was my fault that he was late returning to Eton. George, RI.'

The boy took the note to Marsden, who glanced at it and then tore it into little pieces and put them in the wastepaper basket. Then, turning to the lad, he said sternly, 'Don't ever be late again.'

❦ Prince charming

Frederick, Prince of Wales, son of George II and Queen Caroline, was a disappointment to his parents. Not to mince words, they hated him. Nevertheless, he would have to be found a wife, at whatever the cost.

When George II was trying to find a wife for his son Frederick from among the German princesses, he was warned that there were strains of madness in some of them. This prompted him to remark, 'I did not think ingrafting my half-witted coxcomb upon a madwoman would mend the breed.' Queen Caroline added about her son, 'My dear firstborn is the greatest ass, and the greatest liar, and the greatest *canaille*, and the greatest beast in the whole world, and I most heartily wish he was out of it.'

❦ A royal visit

King George III was not known as 'Farmer George' for nothing.

Once at harvest time, when passing a field where only one woman was at work, George III stopped to ask her where the other labourers were. The woman said, 'They have gone to see the king,' adding, 'I wouldn't give a pin to see him. Besides, the fools will lose a day's work by it, and that is more than I can afford to do. I have five children to work for.'

'Well then,' said the king, putting some money in her hand, 'You may tell your companions who are gone to see the king, that the king came to see you.'

❦ The king of beasts

Horace Walpole records a curious incident that occurred when a new ambassador, Omar Effendi, arrived at King George II's court from the North African kingdom of Algiers.

The ambassador brought over as a present twenty four fine horses, a lion, two tigers, and some curious sheep. He was very desirous of having the lions and tigers led before the king in procession, such being the custom, he declared, in his own country; his request, however, could not be granted; the fine horses and sheep were, however, admitted into the procession. But here he wished that the animals might actually be driven into the presence of the king, that he might report to his master that he had delivered them with his own hand. On being informed that this could not be granted, as the horses could not ascend the stairs, he wished to be informed whether, as the horses could not ascend to the king, the king could not descend to them. The animals were then driven into the royal gardens and his majesty viewed them from the window of the palace. The ambassador was then admitted into the royal presence and he apologized to his majesty for his not being attended with the lion and tigers.

151

❦ A lot to see

When the extremely portly George IV visited Scotland in 1822, Lady Jane Hamilton Dalrymple described an amusing incident that occurred.

The king, it will be remembered, appeared in full Highland costume and begged the ladies to tell him how he looked. They all assured him nothing could be better. At that moment appeared the portly alderman, Sir William Curtis – also in full Highland costume – a most ridiculous figure. The king bit his lip and said, 'I hope I do not look like that; at all events, that my kilt is not so short.' Lady Jane made him a low curtsy and said: 'As Your Majesty stays so short a time in Scotland, the more we see of you the better.'

❦ Trading names

When war broke out against Germany in 1914 there was a wave of anti-German feeling in Britain. Even Dachshunds – German 'sausage-dogs' – were attacked in the streets and one owner decked hers out in a union jack coat, with the inscription 'I am fully naturalized'.

In 1914 anti-German feeling reached as far as the royal family, which felt obliged to change its name from Saxe-Coburg-Gotha to something more intrinsically English. The choice of alternative was a difficult one and the College of Heralds were consulted. They were convinced that the correct name could not be Stewart, or Guelph. Some helpful people suggested Wipper or Wettin but the king was determined that the name must be obviously British. The Duke of Connaught suggested that Tudor should be used. Others said York, Lancaster, Plantagenet, England, Fitzroy and many others. Eventually, the best alternative came from the king's private secretary – Windsor. As he said, Edward III had been known as Edward of Windsor, so there was really no need to look any further. And so the name was adopted, much to the annoyance of the German Kaiser. Wilhelm retaliated by ordering a performance of one of Shakespeare's lesser-known plays, 'The Merry Wives of Saxe-Coburg-Gotha'.

❦ The price of hospitality

During the English Civil War, King Charles I's wife Henrietta Maria worked tirelessly on the continent, obtaining arms and equipment for the royal armies.

In 1643, Queen Henrietta Maria landed at Bridlington in Yorkshire, bringing munitions for the king from France. Before advancing on York, Henrietta Maria quartered herself on a Parliamentarian family, at the house of Lady Strickland of Boynton Hall. Half honoured and half embarrassed by her royal visitor, Lady Strickland did the best she could to entertain the queen, bringing out all the best family silver for dinner. Unfortunately, the sight of the silver was too much for the queen, who thought of all the munitions it could buy for her husband.

'I am afraid,' said the queen, 'I may be accused of ill appreciating the courtesy you have shown me. But unhappily the affairs of the king, thanks to the disaffection and evil conduct of those who should show themselves his most loyal defenders, have arrived at a point where he has need of money. Parliament having refused the subsidies necessary to sustain the honour of the Crown, it is incumbent to obtain it by other methods, and it is with real regret that I find myself compelled to take possession of the silver which I have seen during my stay here.'

Lady Strickland was astounded at such ingratitude, but could only bow in submission, while the queen hastened to explain that it was just a loan, which would soon be repaid, because she had no doubt of the early pacifying of the country. The silver would then be returned, she assured her hostess, or at least its value. Meanwhile, all she could do was to leave Lady Strickland a portrait of herself as much as a pledge as a souvenir of her visit.

❦ Holding his head above water

King John, 1167–1216, was one of the most unpopular of English sovereigns. Nevertheless, his reign produced a number of curious anecdotes, of which this is one.

King John gave several lands, at Kepperton and Atterton, in Kent, to Solomon Attefeld, to be held by this singular service – that as often as the king should be pleased to cross the sea, the said Solomon, or his heirs, should be obliged to go with him *to hold his majesty's head*, if there should be occasion for it, 'that is if he should be sea-sick'; and it appears, by the record in the Tower, the same office of head-holding was actually performed in the reign of Edward I.

❦ Mrs Morley and Mrs Freeman

Sarah Churchill, friend and confidante of Queen Anne, enjoyed a relationship with the queen that nobody else could match. Sarah explains.

As Queen Anne said, 'She grew uneasy to be treated by me with the form and ceremony due to her rank; nor could she hear from me the sound of words which implied in them distance and superiority. It was this turn of mind that made her one day propose to me, that whenever I should happen to be absent from her, we might in all our letters write ourselves by feigned names, such as would import nothing of distinction of rank between us. Morley and Freeman were the names her fancy hit upon; and she left me to choose by which of them I would be called. My frank, open temper, naturally led me to pitch upon Freeman, and so the princess took the other; and from this time Mrs Morley and Mrs Freeman began to converse as equals, made so by affection and friendship.

❧ An immovable object

Queen Victoria's personal conservatism preserved the institution of monarchy in Britain at a time when it had fallen into disrepute. On the sixtieth anniversary of her accession she was still prepared to fight to preserve the status quo.

During preparations for Queen Victoria's Diamond Jubilee in 1897, it was decided that the queen should attend a service on the steps of St Paul's Cathedral. In arranging for the royal carriage and the procession of horsemen it was found that the statue of Queen Anne would not only block the way, but obscure the view of the crowds of onlookers. It was therefore proposed to temporarily move the statue. But the queen would not hear of it. 'What a ridiculous idea! Move Queen Anne? Most certainly not! Why, it might some day be suggested that my statue should be moved, which I should much dislike!'

❧ The turn of the screw

The accession of King William III in 1688 marked the triumph of the Protestant religion in Britain.

In 1684 William Carstairs, later Principal of Edinburgh University, was implicated in a treason trial and subjected to torture with a device named the thumbiken. After the 'Glorious Revolution' of 1688, Carstairs, no longer under suspicion, was presented with the very device that was used to torture him as a souvenir. When King William III was visiting Edinburgh he said to Carstairs, 'I have heard, principal, that you were tortured with something they call the thumbiken; pray what sort of instrument of torture is that?'

'I will show it to you,' replied Carstairs.

'I must try it,' said the king, 'I must put in my thumbs here – now, principal, turn the screw. O, not so gently – another turn – another. Stop! Stop! No more. Another turn, I'm afraid, would make me confess anything.'

❦ Paradise regained

King Edward VIII enjoyed a social life that would have left most ordinary people gasping. Yet even he had moments when solitude seemed attractive.

After the American explorer Mr Lincoln Elsworth had returned from his flight across the Antarctic he was introduced to King Edward VIII. The king asked him if it was true that the entire continent was uninhabited. Elsworth replied that it was.

'Not even Eskimos?' asked the king.

'Not one at all, sir,' said Elsworth, with an air of authority.

'Then, Mr Elsworth,' said His Majesty, 'if there are no people there, there are no politics.'

'I am not sure, sir, that I quite understand,' Elsworth said.

'Ah,' said the king, 'To think of a whole continent with no Prime Minister, no Archbishop, no Chancellor of the Exchequer – not even a king. It must be paradise.'

❦ Crowned with fire

According to Orderic Vitalis, the only case on record of William the Conqueror showing fear was during his coronation at Westminster Abbey in 1066.

At the prompting of the devil, who hates everything good, a sudden disaster and portent of future catastrophes occurred. For when Archbishop Ealdred asked the English and Geoffrey, bishop of Coutances, asked the Normans, if they would accept William as their king, all of them gladly shouted out with one voice if not in one language that they would. The armed guard outside, hearing the tumult of the joyful crowd in the church and the harsh accents of a foreign tongue, imagined that some treachery was on foot, and rashly set fire to some of the buildings. The fire spread rapidly from house to house; the crowd who had been rejoicing in the church took fright and throngs of men and women of every rank and condition rushed out of the church in frantic haste. Only the bishops and a few clergy and monks remained, terrified, in the sanctuary, and with difficulty completed the consecration of the king, who was trembling from head to foot. Almost all the rest made for the scene of the conflagration; some to fight the flames, and many others hoping to find loot for themselves in the general confusion. The English, after hearing of the perpetration of such misdeeds, never again trusted the Normans who seemed to have betrayed them but nursed their anger and bided their time for revenge.

❦ My pretty whore

Queen Mary Tudor had enjoyed a very sheltered upbringing and was very ignorant of the ways of the world.

One day Queen Mary overheard her Lord Chamberlain say to one of her ladies-in-waiting, Frances Neville, as he tickled her under the chin, 'My pretty whore, how dost thou?'

A few minutes afterwards, Mary summoned Frances to her and said, 'God a'mercy, my pretty whore.'

Lady Neville stood as if thunderstruck. Mary explained that she had only used the same expression that she had heard the Lord Chamberlain use. Frances then replied, 'My Lord Chamberlain is an idle gentleman, and we respect not what he sayeth or doth; but Your Majesty doth amaze me either in jest or earnest to be called so by you. A whore is a wicked, misliving woman.'

❦ A false crown and a true subject

The execution of Mary Stuart at Fotheringay Castle in 1587 was accompanied by a number of affecting stories. In the first, Mary's crowning glory – her thick red hair – was found to be false.

Once the executioner had severed Mary's head from her body he bent down to take up the head and hold it up for all to see, saying the time honoured words, 'Behold the head of a traitor.' But as the masked figure grasped the hair on Mary's head it came away in his hand. He found himself holding just a ribbon, attached to an auburn wig. Everyone looked down at the head of the Queen of Scots, which was nearly bald and covered only in a thin stubble of grey hair.

The executioner was in for a second surprise.

As he 'went about to pluck off her stockings he found her little dog crept under her coat, which being put from thence, went and laid himself down between her head and body, and being besmeared with her blood, was caused to be washed as were other things whereon any blood was. The executioners were dismissed with fees, not having anything that was hers. Her body, with the head, was conveyed into the great chamber by the Sheriff, where it was by the chirurgeons embalmed until its interment.'

❦ Banqueting blunder

At the coronation of King George III, the Lord Steward of the Royal Household, Earl Talbot – a swaggering bully of a man, who patronized prize fighters – was responsible for the royal banquet that followed the ceremony of crowning. Unfortunately, Talbot was a blunderer and many of the guests found themselves without places at the dining tables or without food to eat. Talbot listened to all the complaints but finally lost patience.

Among those who were unable to find seats were the Knights of the Bath, the aldermen of the City of London and the Barons of the Cinque Ports. Sir William Stanhope angrily told Talbot, 'To us it is an affront for some of us are gentlemen.' One of the London aldermen complained, 'We have invited the king to a banquet which will cost ten thousand pounds, and yet, when we come to court, we are to be given nothing to eat.' By the time the Barons of the Cinque Ports began to complain, Talbot had had enough. Far from finding them food or seats he offered to fight them one at a time, saying, 'I'm a match for any of you.' The barons had the last laugh, however. As Lord Steward, Talbot had to ride his horse to the royal table, bow to the king and queen, and then back the animal out of the hall. Everything went wrong. In spite of its training the horse insisted on coming into the hall in reverse, backing towards the royal table and whisking its tail all over the royal food. Talbot was so humiliated that when the incident was reported by John Wilkes in the newspaper the *North Briton*, Talbot challenged him to a duel, which took place by moonlight near Bagshot. Both men missed.

❦ The privy seal

During his illness, King George III was very harshly treated by his physicians. Sometimes he responded in kind.

On one occasion, Dr Baker released the king's arms from his strait-jacket in order to feel his pulse. The king promptly punched him in the head, knocking him to the ground, and then poured the contents of his chamber pot over the doctor's head. Sitting down, the king said to the distraught physician, 'Rise, Sir George, knight of the most ancient, most puissant Order of Cloacina – the Goddess of Privies.' He then laughed himself to sleep and was no further trouble.

❦ A royal satyr

King George II had a reputation as a 'randy old stag'. But some ladies of his court were resistant to both his charms and his purse.

Once at a court ball the king's eye fell on the lovely Mary Bellenden, who was widely regarded as the most agreeable and likeable woman of her time. Mary was seated on a settee when the king came and sat down beside her. Without saying a word, he took out his purse and began counting out gold coins, over and over again, clearly indicating to the girl that he was planning to make her an offer she could not refuse. But Mary was not to be purchased in this way. 'Sir,' she said, 'if you count

159

your money once more I shall leave the room.' For a few minutes there was silence and then the king began counting the coins again. Mary leapt to her feet, kicked the money out of the king's hands and fled from the room, her reputation intact.

❦ Splitting your sides

King George II was notoriously unfaithful to his wife, Caroline of Ansbach, yet the two retained affection for each other. On her deathbed Caroline told him to marry again and he replied with the immortal – though redundant, one suspects – comment, 'No, I shall have mistresses.' Caroline's death from stomach cancer was a gruesome one and yet she retained her sense of humour to the end.

In November 1737, Caroline's sickness took a turn for the worse when 'her diseased innards burst'. An immediate operation was necessary, without anaesthetics, and the queen must have been in unbearable agony when a ridiculous incident took place. The operation was taking place by candlelight and as one of the surgeons leaned forward to probe her stomach with a scalpel his wig brushed against the candle and burst into flame. Caroline called on the surgeons to stop the operation for a moment while she laughed heartily.

❦ A belly full

After the death of Queen Victoria on 22 January 1901, Edward, the Prince of Wales, became king. Unfortunately, at the last moment his coronation had to be postponed for seven weeks as he was struck by a severe bout of appendicitis. The postponement was a disaster for the royal caterers but proved a windfall for the poor of London's East End.

When the news of the postponement of the king's coronation reached the cooks responsible for the catering, they had no alternative but to find a use for the huge quantities of food that had been prepared. The decision was eventually reached to distribute it among London's poor, and so 2,500 quails, 300 legs of mutton, *consommé de faisan aux quenelles*, sole poached in Chablis, oysters, prawns and snipe were served out by London's soup-kitchens.

❦ The king's loose box

Prince Edward was a lover of fast horses and fast women, and had been a notorious womanizer in his youth – and later. So, when it came to allocating places at Westminster Abbey for his coronation in 1901, he did not forget his old friends.

For his coronation, at the express command of the king, a special pew at Westminster Abbey was set aside for Sarah Bernhardt, Mrs Alice Keppel, Lady Kilmorey, Mrs Arthur Paget, Mrs Hartmann, and others of his former mistresses. One observer referred to the pew as 'the king's loose box'.

❦ Jumping to conclusions

The affair between King Edward VIII and the American Mrs Simpson was the most famous royal love affair in British history. It finally resulted in the king abdicating in 1936 rather than giving up the woman he loved. The British Establishment were united in preventing the divorced Wallis Simpson from ever becoming the king's wife. The king took the title of the Duke of Windsor and was the governor of the Bahamas during the Second World War.

Shortly after the Windsors took up residence at Nassau, in the Bahamas, one American businesswoman, who was there on vacation, had an extraordinary experience. The woman was walking along a road in Nassau when she saw a blue coupé, which she knew to be one of the cars the royals used, driving towards her. There was a chauffeur in the front seat, but from the back seats she could hear moaning and groaning, and a female voice crying, 'No, darling! No more, no more.' The American lady was almost too embarrassed to look at what was going on in the back seat. It was the Duchess of Windsor pleading with the duke to stop playing the bagpipes.

❦ No flies on him

King George V much enjoyed the story Lord Mountbatten had told him of his sister's visit to Uppsala Cathedral in Sweden.

The archbishop, trying to impress his visitor with his excellent command of the English language, approached a large chest of drawers in the sacristy and said to her, 'I will now open these trousers and reveal some even more precious treasures to Your Royal Highness.'

❦ A family likeness

Intermarriage between royal houses was so frequent during the nineteenth century that it was not surprising that members of royal families in different countries came to resemble each other. This was truest of the future Tsar Nicholas II of Russia and King George V of Britain. As a result, diplomatic gaffes were likely.

In 1893, Tsar Nicholas II of Russia, at that time the tsarevitch, came to London to attend the wedding of Prince George, Duke of York and later King George V. Unfortunately, Prince George was mistaken for Nicholas by one of the diplomats, who asked him if he had come over specially for the Duke of York's wedding. Prince George replied, 'Well, as I am the Duke of York, I suppose I had better attend my own wedding.'

❦ Tum-Tum

Edward VII, while Prince of Wales, was inclined to allow some of his friends to adopt an over-familiar approach towards him and on some occasions this got out of hand.

Once, Sir Frederick Johnstone, somewhat the worse for drink, was behaving rather badly in the billiard room at Sandringham. Edward, the Prince of Wales, tried to calm him down, saying, 'Freddy, Freddy, you're very drunk!' Johnstone replied by patting the prince's stomach and saying, 'Tum-Tum, you're verrrrrry fat!' There was a shocked silence and the prince turned away and summoned one of his equerries, ordering him to pack Sir Frederick's bags before breakfast.

❦ Limbing about

Queen Alexandra was a woman of spirit and possessed a notable sense of humour. Marriage to King Edward VII must have required both qualities.

When Queen Alexandra was visiting a hospital on one occasion she was shown a patient who had been wounded in the leg and had only just realized that his knee would be permanently stiff and useless. Alexandra went straight to his bedside, saying, 'My dear, dear man, I hear you have a stiff leg; so have I. Now just watch what I can do with it.' At which she lifted up her skirt and swept her lame leg right over the top of his bedside table.

❦ A soldier's life is terrible 'ard

More proof that Queen Victoria did have a sense of humour.

Queen Victoria wrote to tell her grandson, Prince George, of an unusual encounter she once had at Windsor Castle. It was a warm, moonlit night and as she was leaning out of her bedroom window to get some air, she heard a voice calling out to her from below. It was a sentry who was obviously feeling amorous and had mistaken the queen for a housemaid.

❦ Traitor's Gate

During the reign of her sister, Queen Mary, Princess Elizabeth's life was in constant danger. Mary's Catholic advisers pressed her to execute Elizabeth, who was a focus for discontent with the queen's re-imposition of Roman Catholicism in England. But Elizabeth insisted on remaining loyal to Mary and resisted becoming associated with any attempts to place her on the throne at the expense of her sister. Elizabeth's delaying tactics proved justified and she succeeded to the throne peacefully on Mary's death.

When Princess Elizabeth was taken to the Tower of London on the orders of her sister, Queen Mary, she was forced by her guards to land at the Traitor's Gate. She showed herself full of courage in spite of her desperate plight, declaring, 'Here lands as true a subject, being prisoner, as ever landed at these stairs. Before thee, O God, I speak it, having no other friend but thee alone.'

❦ The Queen of Hearts

When dealing with foreign princes or arrogant diplomats Queen Elizabeth I could be as hard as Medusa, but when handling the petty follies and foibles of little men she had a lightness of touch that made every man who met her love her.

On her way to visit the Earl of Leicester at Kenilworth, Queen Elizabeth passed through the town of Warwick. She was greeted by the Recorder, who made a long speech of welcome, in which he had given her what he felt to be much good advice. She replied, 'Come hither, little Recorder; it was told to me that you would be afraid to look upon me, or to speak boldly; but you were not so afraid of me as I was of you, and I now thank you for putting me in mind of my duty and what should be in me.'

❦ The fairest footcloth

Sir Walter Ralegh was a self-made man who lived beyond his means and gambled on his capacity to ensnare a queen with his dazzling good looks and his casual gallantry.

This Captain Ralegh, coming out of Ireland to the English court in good habit – his clothes then being a considerable part of his estate – found the queen walking, till meeting with a plashy place, she seemed to scruple going thereon. Presently, Ralegh cast and spread his new plush cloak on the ground, whereon the queen trod gently, rewarding him afterwards with many suits, for his so free and seasonable tender of so fair a footcloth.

❦ A marriage of interests

Immediately after Queen Victoria's wedding to Prince Albert, the subject of the young queen's sex life briefly became tied up in the public mind with the ongoing struggle over the Corn Laws. The laws had been created to keep foreign grain out of England and to please British farmers with high prices for their homegrown corn. But government subsidies kept food prices high and there was pressure in Parliament to repeal the legislation. The MP Dillon Browne summed up the arguments for repeal by linking the subject to the newly wed royals.

'What is the use of all this botheration about the Corn Laws?' Dillon Browne asked. 'Has not the little Queen – the saints preserve her – settled the question by opening up her port for the reception of foreign seed?'

❦ A resounding silence

The coronation of King Charles I in 1626 was accompanied by a mysterious absence of popular acclamation. The following account is taken from a letter written by an eyewitness, Symonds D'Ewes, to Sir Martin Stuteville.

My expectation was soon answered with His Majesty's approach: who, presenting himself bare-headed to the people (all the doors being then opened for their entrance), the Archbishop on the right hand and Earl Marshal on his left, the Bishop said in my articulate hearing:

'My masters and friends, I am here come to present unto you your King, King Charles, to whom the crown of his ancestors and predecessors is now devolved by lineal right, and he himself come hither to be settled in that Throne which God and his birth have appointed for him: and therefore I desire you by your general acclamation to testify your consent and willingness thereunto.'

Upon which, whether some expected he should have spoken more, others, not hearing well what he said, hindered those by questioning which might have heard... or the presence of so dear a King drew admiring silence, so that those which were nearest doubted what to do; but not one word followed, till my Lord of Arundel told them they should cry out:

'God save King Charles!'

Upon which, as ashamed of their first oversight, a little shouting followed.

❦ The queen is a woman

However forceful Queen Elizabeth I was in a court that was dominated by men, she never pretended that she was anything other than a woman. At times she could be difficult, even cantankerous, as this anecdote suggests. But it was a brave man who dared to hint at any feminine weakness.

The remove of the court from Windsor is still constantly put off. The carter that three times came to Windsor with his cart to carry away some of the stuff of the Queen's wardrobe, when he repaired there for the third time and was told by those of the wardrobe that the remove held not, clapping his hand on his thigh cried out, 'Now I see that the Queen is a woman as well as my wife.' These words being overheard by Her Majesty, who then stood at the window, she said, 'What a villain is this!' and so sends him three angels [coins to the value of ten shillings] to stop his mouth.

❦ Tongue-tied

As a woman in a world dominated by men, Elizabeth never allowed herself to betray any sign of weakness. This made her feared by many men who had dealings with her, as here when she met the Speaker of the House of Commons.

Mr Popham, when he was Speaker, and the Lower House had sat long, and done in effect nothing, coming one day to Queen Elizabeth, she said to him: 'Now, Mr Speaker, what hath passed in the Lower House?' He answered: 'If it please Your Majesty, seven weeks.'

❦ The lady surprised

This famous incident marked the first step in the catastrophic fall of the Earl of Essex. Sent to Ireland at his own request by Elizabeth, Essex feared that his enemies at court were blackening his name to the queen. Failing to subdue the Irish rebels, Essex abandoned his command and hurried back to England. Bursting in on the queen, and finding the old lady unprepared, he hoped to win her support before news of his failure should reach England. Instead, by seeing her unmade-up and in her night attire, he humiliated an old woman for whom her appearance still meant so much. Essex blundered and in a way that Elizabeth could never forgive.

This morning, about 10 o'clock, he lighted at the court gate at Nonsuch in post and made all haste up to the Presence and so to the Privy Chamber, and stayed not till he came to the Queen's bedchamber, where he found the Queen newly up, her hair about her face. He kneeled unto her, kissed her hands and her neck and had some private speech with her, which seemed to give him great contentment, for coming from Her Majesty for to shift himself in his chamber, he was very pleasant and thanked God that though he had suffered much trouble and storms abroad he found a sweet calm at home. Tis much wondered at that he went so boldly to Her Majesty's presence, she not being ready, and he so full of dirt and mire that his very face was full of it. About 11 he was ready and went up again to the Queen and conferred with her till half an hour after 12. He went to dinner and during all that time discoursed merely about his travels and journies in Ireland ... He was visited frankly by all sorts of lords, ladies and gentlemen; only a strangeness was observed between him and Mr Secretary and that party. Then he went up to the Queen but found her much changed in that small time, for she began to call him to question for his return and was not satisfied in the manner of his coming away, and leaving all things at so great hazard ...

29 September: Late last night, between 10 and 11 o'clock, a commandment came from the Queen to my Lord of Essex that he should keep his chamber ... Afterwards my Lord of Essex was commanded from Court and committed to my Lord keeper's; he

is now come to London to York House in my Lord of Worcester's coach. At his going from Court few or none of his friends accompanied him.

❧ Take your seats

Horace Walpole tells the story of high jinks at a royal card party.

There has been a great fracas at Kensington: one of the mesdames (the king's daughters) pulled the chair from under the Countess Deloraine (the king's favourite) at cards, who, being provoked that her Monarch was diverted with her disgrace, with the malice of a hobbyhorse, gave him just such another fall. But alas! The Monarch, like Louis XIV, is mortal in the part that touched the ground and was so hurt and so angry that the countess is disgraced and her German rival remains in sole and quiet possession of her royal master's favour.

❧ Corruption in high places

The funeral service of William the Conqueror was held on a very hot day and the inadequacies of the embalming procedures were soon revealed.

When the body of the bulky king was lifted from its bier to be fitted into its sarcophagus it was found to have swelled so much that it would not fit in properly. The priests who attended the body then tried to squeeze it into its container by pressing on the abdomen, but still the lid would not shut. Eventually they pressed too hard on the swollen cadaver and the stomach suddenly burst, emitting pus and putrefaction all over the king's funeral robes, as well as such a terrible smell that the priests all fled, and the congregation assembled in the church ran to open the doors to let out the dreadful stench.

❧ Something fishy going on

There is no law that says that kings need to be intellectuals. Sport has frequently played a greater part in the good government of the country than reading books or reciting poetry. Even so, there was something fishy about this story.

King George V was far fonder of fishing than reading. When the prime minister telephoned the Palace and asked if the king would care to send a telegram to congratulate 'Old Hardy' (Thomas Hardy the novelist) on his birthday, His Majesty got the wrong idea. A few hours later a Mr Hardy of Alnwick in Northumberland – the esteemed maker of fishing rods – received a telegram from the king congratulating him on reaching an age he had not yet reached and on a day that was not even his birthday.

❦ A packed lunch

The coronation of Queen Elizabeth II in 1953 was an event of worldwide importance and heads of state from many foreign countries came to London to participate. Prominent among those who came were the leaders of the recently created Commonwealth of Nations.

The first head of state to arrive at Westminster Abbey was the very large and immensely popular Queen Salote of Tonga. Opposite

her in her carriage sat a diminutive man in white, whom nobody seemed to recognize. Someone asked Noël Coward, 'Who is that with the Queen of Tonga?' 'I expect it's her lunch,' he replied.

❦ The voice of reason

The British philanthropist and chocolate-manufacturer, George Cadbury, was as stubborn as he was generous.

When King George V and Queen Mary visited his chocolate works, George Cadbury led the way around the buildings with Her Majesty at his side. It was very cold and George had removed his hat as a mark of respect. But he had only just recovered from illness and the queen was concerned in case he caught a chill. She asked him to put on his hat but he would not. 'Please Mr Cadbury,' said the queen, 'put on your hat or else I shall have to ask the king to command you.' Even now George hesitated, until a loud voice from behind was heard: 'George, put your hat on!' It was his wife Elizabeth Cadbury. George jumped to it and replaced his hat.

❦ Dey-dreaming

The extended divorce proceedings between the Prince Regent and Caroline of Brunswick involved revelations of a humiliating kind.

During the trial of Queen Caroline in 1820, details of the queen's improper behaviour were made public for the first time. It was widely believed that she had conducted an affair with the Muslim Dey of Algiers. The Chief Justice, Lord Norbury, remarked, 'She was happy as the dey was long.'

❦ The Iron Duke's strategic retreat

Caroline of Brunswick was popular with the common people, who believed that the Prince Regent was a blackguard, who had treated her badly. They were probably right, but the bulk of the establishment had never liked the vulgar German princess and stood four-square behind the new king, George IV.

Caroline of Brunswick returned to England in 1820 on the death of King George III, determined to assert her claim to be the queen. She was intensely popular with the common people but treated almost as a pariah by the wealthy classes. Her husband, George IV, and his ministers were determined to prevent Caroline ever being crowned, but they were attacked in the streets by angry mobs who took her side. The Duke of Wellington's coach was stopped by a gang of ruffians wielding pick-axes, who demanded that he express his support for Caroline. The Duke replied laconically as usual: 'Well, gentlemen, since you will have it so, God save the Queen. And may all your wives be like her!'

❦ Final victory

King George IV's hatred of his wife, Caroline of Brunswick, blinded him to everything else, even to the greatest enemy his country had ever known.

On the death of Napoleon at St Helena, one of King George IV's servants congratulated him, saying, 'Sir, your bitterest enemy is dead.'

'Is she, by God!' replied the king.

❦ Of cabbages and kings

When preaching to kings a subtle tongue is the first essential.

Dr South, when once preaching before King Charles II, observed that the monarch and his attendants began to nod. And as nobles are common men when they are asleep, some of them soon after snored; on which he broke off his sermon and called, 'Lord Lauderdale, let me entreat you to rouse yourself; you snore so loud that you will wake the king.'

❦ A loyal Englishman

Negotiations between England and France for the marriage of Queen Elizabeth I to the Duc d'Alençon, youngest son of Queen Catherine de

Medici, were intensely unpopular among Protestants in England, who feared that the Catholic duke might threaten their religious settlement. Puritan pamphleteers were foremost in the criticism of the queen who reacted with uncharacteristic severity. William Camden described what happened to the author, John Stubbes.

Her Majesty...burned with choler that there was a book published in print inveighing against the marriage, as fearing the alteration of religion, which was entitled *A gaping gulf to swallow England by a French marriage.* Neither would Queen Elizabeth be persuaded that the author of the book had any other purpose but to bring her into hatred with her subjects, and to open a gap to some prodigious innovation...

She began to be the more displeased with Puritans than she had been beforetime, persuading herself that such a thing had not passed without their privity; and within a few days after, John Stubbes of Lincoln's Inn, a zealous professor of religion, the author of this relative pamphlet (whose sister Thomas Cartwright the arch Puritan had married), William Page the disperser of the copies, and Singleton the printer were apprehended: against whom sentence was given that their right hands should be cut off by a law in the time of Philip and Mary against the authors of seditious writings, and those that dispersed them...

Not long after, upon a stage set up in the market place at Westminster, Stubbes and Page had their right hands cut off by the blow of a butcher's knife with a mallet struck through their wrists. The printer had his pardon. I can remember that, standing by John Stubbes, so soon as his right hand was cut off he put off his hat with the left and cried aloud, 'God save the Queen.' The people round him stood mute, whether stricken with fear at the first sight of this strange kind of punishment or for commiseration of the man whom they reputed honest, or out of a secret inward repining they had at this marriage, which they suspected would be dangerous to religion.

❦ An unhappy childhood

In the crowded nurseries of England's royal courts in the

eighteenth century, childish sensibilities were rarely respected.

William Henry, Duke of Gloucester, was not much loved by his parents. His mother in particular thought him a stupid and dull child and told him as much in front of his brothers and sisters. Once she told them all to laugh at 'the fool' and the highly strung boy hung his head in shame. His mother told him not to sulk but he replied that he was not sulking, only thinking. When she asked him what he was thinking, he said, 'I was thinking what I should feel if I had a son as unhappy as you make me.'

❦ An apprentice butcher

William, Duke of Cumberland – later to be known as the 'Butcher' after his victory over the Scots at Culloden – was a surprisingly precocious boy, who was much indulged by his parents.

One day the queen shut the nine-year-old Duke of Cumberland in his room after a display of temper. When she let him out later in the day she asked him what he had been doing.

'Reading,' he said.

'Reading what?' asked the Queen.

'The Bible.'

'And what did you read there?'

'About Jesus and Mary,' said the boy.

'And what about them?'

'Why, that Jesus said to Mary, "Woman what hast thou to do with me?"'

On another occasion the king jokingly asked the young duke whether he would rather be king or queen.

'Sir, I have never yet tried,' he said pertly. 'Let me be one of them a month and I will tell you.'

❦ When his back was turned

King George II suffered from piles and travelling long distances by horse or in an uncomfortable carriage only made the condition worse. Although the king believed that his ailment was unknown to the court, he was wrong: it had become a matter for humorous comment.

Everyone at court suffered equally from King George II's terrible temper and far from feeling ashamed at the frequent abuse that they received, his courtiers openly boasted about it. Those on whom he had rudely turned his back were said to have been 'rumped' and they formed themselves into the 'Rumpsteak Club'.

❦ With a bang and a whimper

The death of King George II in 1760 was the subject for much merriment among those who liked him least.

Having risen at six o'clock, and having first partaken of his chocolate, King George then retired to the privy. His valet, hearing a noise far louder 'than the royal wind' followed by a groan, became alarmed. The valet ran into the room where the king was attending to the call of nature and found him lying on the floor, having cut his face in falling. He was carried to his bed and the doctors tried to bleed him, but no blood flowed. Apparently the ventricle of his heart had burst and he had died instantly.

❦ Not knowing his place

Elizabeth I had a ready wit and enjoyed a joke, as long as it was at someone else's expense.

Queen Elizabeth I once visited Oxford in order to give an address to the scholars there, but before she could begin she had to endure a welcoming speech by Dr Westphaling. She suffered in silence for a while and then became exasperated, sending the good doctor the following message: 'Make an end of your discourse without delay.' But the doctor did not stop for a further thirty minutes, the fact being that he had so committed his speech to memory that he knew that if he omitted any of it he would forget the rest. The result was that there was no time at all for the queen to do her speech. Elizabeth now sent him another message: 'How dared you presume to go on with your discourse to so unreasonable a length after I had sent my command to you to bring it briefly to a close?' The poor doctor was brought before the queen and admitted his fault, telling her that if he had stopped he might never have started again. Elizabeth burst out laughing, but to show him what a mere woman, who had not been to Oxford, could do, in the midst of her own oration the following morning at the same place, she stopped upon seeing Lord Burghley, who was suffering from gout, standing and did not proceed until her order to bring him a seat was carried out.

❦ Ahead of the Times

The wedding of Edward, Prince of Wales, to Princess Alexandra of Denmark in 1863 was the social event of the decade and nobody who was anybody could bear to miss out on it.

In the weeks before the wedding there was much competition for securing viewing places along the proposed procession route, and large sums were paid for prime sites. Ten days before the wedding *The Times*, the most prestigious newspaper in the country if not the whole world, was hoaxed by an advertiser. The advert read, 'ROYAL PROCESSION. First floor, with two large windows, to be let in the best part of Cockspur Street, with entrance accessible behind. For cards apply to Mr Lindley, Number 19, Catherine Street, Strand, WC.' However, 19 Catherine Street was a 'house of ill repute'. When the truth came out the 'Thunderer's' lapse was the subject of much hilarity and copies of the edition which carried the advert soon fetched seven shillings and sixpence among collectors.

❦ An unfortunate misconception

In the early years of Queen Victoria's reign, the queen earned much unpopularity over a scandal involving one of her maids of honour, Lady Flora Hastings.

Victoria had taken an early dislike to Lady Flora, who had once lightly mocked the queen's passion for caraway seeds. When Lady

Flora's shape began to change noticeably and she seemed to be thickening around the waist, tongues began to wag. It was remembered that she had shared a coach from Scotland with Sir John Conroy, the confidential secretary of the Duchess of Kent. Everyone began to suspect the worst, including the queen. Lady Flora, hearing what was being said of her, submitted herself to a medical examination, which completely exonerated her. However, even this did not satisfy some people and Lady Flora remained highly unpopular among the ladies at court. Infuriated by the unfairness of the queen and her ladies, Lady Flora's brother leaked the whole matter to the press and *The Times* took up the case on her behalf. The newspaper said that she was an innocent victim of a depraved court. Matters grew worse when the true reason for Lady Flora's swollen condition became known: she was dying of a stomach tumour. The Prime Minister, Lord Melbourne, prevailed on the queen to visit Lady Flora, and it is possible – though it would have been somewhat out of character – that Victoria apologized to the dying woman. Lady Flora's subsequent death inflamed hostility to the monarchy and to the royal court. Queen Victoria was hissed in public by the Duchess of Montrose and Lady Sarah Ingestre, to which offence she replied, 'Those two abominable women ought to be flogged.'

8. ARTS AND SCIENCES

❦ Dramatic licence

Richard Burbage was the most famous actor at the time that Shakespeare lived and gave the first performances of a number of Shakespeare's leading roles.

Upon a time when Burbage played Richard III, there was a citizen grew so far in liking with him that before she went from the play she appointed him to come that night unto her by the name of Richard the Third. Shakespeare, overhearing their conclusion, went before, was entertained and at his game ere Burbage came. Then message being brought that Richard the Third was at the door, Shakespeare caused return to be made that William the Conqueror was before Richard the Third.

❦ The price of fame

In the sixteenth century poets, unless they had private means, were dependent on aristocratic patrons.

When Spenser first showed portions of 'The Faerie Queene' to the Earl of Southampton, that great connoisseur of literature was enchanted by what he read. 'Go bear Master Spenser a gift of twenty pounds,' he commanded his attendants. He read on and again the charms of the poetry encouraged him to further generosity: 'Go bear Master Spenser another twenty pounds.' Still he went on reading and then cried out a third time, 'Go turn that fellow out of my house, for I shall be ruined if I read further.'

❧ His room was a picture

Necessity is the mother of invention ...

The artist Capit Soldi was so poor that he came up with an ingenious way of furnishing his apartment. He painted chairs, pictures and window curtains on the walls and by adding a real table and two real chairs he was able to entertain guests in his well-appointed rooms.

❧ A sting in the tale

The great poet and dramatist Ben Jonson was also something of a lovable rogue when it came to wine and women.

At the Cheshire Cheese tavern in London one evening, a curious poetic duel took place between Joshua Sylvester and Ben Jonson. The chosen weapons were to be rhyming couplets. Sylvester went first and said, 'I Sylvester, kissed your sister.' Jonson, unimpressed, replied with, 'I Ben Jonson, kissed your wife.' Sylvester complained that this was not a rhyming couplet, to which Jonson replied, 'No, but it is true.'

❧ They also serve ...

Female gravediggers must have been as unusual in the eighteenth century as female entrepreneurs. Elizabeth, in this story, was both and even managed to put one over the established church.

The tomb of the great poet John Milton in St Giles Church, Cripplegate, was disturbed in 1790. During extensive renovations to the church, the poet's coffin was removed from the crypt by the local gravedigger, a woman named Elizabeth. She prised off the lead from the coffin, exposing the poet's corpse. She ripped off the shroud and clumsily crushed the rib cage. Milton's five remaining upper teeth, still firmly embedded after some 116 years in the tomb, were ripped out and taken as souvenirs by a local innkeeper. A pawnbroker took a tuft of Milton's hair and a tooth from the lower jaw. Other parts of the poet's body were investigated but thrown back into the coffin. Noticing that the coffin was being rifled by souvenir-hunters, Elizabeth decided to charge people to see Milton's corpse. She employed two burly 'bouncers' to bar the door to those unwilling or unable to pay, and set up the coffin in a darkened corner of the church, lit by a single tinder. Viewers then paid threepence to light up the area so that they could see what was left of Milton. After a while business dropped off and Elizabeth reduced the fee, first to twopence and then just a penny. On the third day, Elizabeth reinterred the corpse, having made a handy profit. When the local vicar heard what Elizabeth had been doing he was furious, not on account of the desecration of Milton's tomb but because he had not thought of the idea himself and had consequently allowed someone else to make a profit. Only with great difficulty was he prevented from suing Elizabeth for a tithe of her earnings.

❦ A reward from on high

Leonardo da Vinci tells the tale of a clash between Art and Religion.

A priest while going the round of his parish on the Saturday before Easter in order to sprinkle the houses with holy water as was his custom, coming to the studio of a painter and there beginning to sprinkle the water upon some of his pictures the painter turning round with some annoyance asked him why he sprinkled the pictures in this manner. The priest replied that it was the custom and that it was his duty to act thus, that he was doing a good deed and that whoever did a good deed might expect a recompense as great or even greater; for so God had promised that for every good deed which we do on the earth we shall be rewarded a hundred fold from on high. Then the painter, having waited until the priest had made his exit, stepped to the window and threw a large bucket of water down onto his head calling out to him, 'See, there is the reward that comes to you a hundred fold from on high as you said it would, on account of the good deed you did me with your holy water with which you have half-ruined my pictures.'

❦ An exercise in declension

Edward Gibbon was the greatest British historian of the eighteenth century. His The Decline and Fall of the Roman Empire *was marked not only by its attention to detail but by the magnificence of its style. Richard Porson, the classical scholar, was a friend of Edward Gibbon.*

Porson thought Gibbon's *Decline and Fall* beyond all comparison the greatest literary production of the eighteenth century, and was in the habit of repeating long passages from it. Yet I have heard him say that 'There could not be a better exercise for a schoolboy than to turn a page of it into English.'

❦ The unseeing eye of the artist

Apart from being an artist and critic, John Ruskin was also a social reformer in his later years. This shows him at a stage where reality and art are still locked in battle.

Yesterday, I came on a poor little child lying flat on the pavement in Bologna – sleeping like a corpse – possibly from too little food. I pulled up immediately – not in pity but in delight at the folds of its poor little ragged chemise over the thin bosom – and gave the mother money – not in charity, but to keep the flies off it while I made a sketch. I don't see how this is to be avoided, but it is very hardening.

❦ A critic

Prince William of Gloucester, like so many of the royal progeny of King George II, was a philistine who did much to undermine the reputation of the monarchy in Great Britain.

Edward Gibbon dedicated the second volume of his great book, *The Decline and Fall of the Roman Empire*, to Prince William of Gloucester, who was not, in fact, a very learned man. On receiving a copy of the book the duke said to Gibbon, 'Another damned, thick, square book! Always scribble, scribble, scribble, eh, Mr Gibbon?'

❦ Standing room only

One wonders if King Charles I was reserving one final prank to play on the man who graced his court and that of his father as the acknowledged first poet laureate of the realm. Jonson may well have been the first to laugh at the jest.

The great poet and playwright Ben Jonson hoped to be buried in Westminster Abbey and asked his benefactor, King Charles I, for just a square foot of the abbey grounds. Jonson might have been surprised to find that the king took him so literally. When he died, Jonson was buried in an upright position so that he took up not an inch more than the square foot he had asked for.

❦ Nom de plume

The English essayist and critic Charles Lamb was a notable failure when he tried to write plays. In this instance he seems to be pre-echoing the saying, 'Don't shoot me, I'm only the pianist.'

When Charles Lamb's farce *Mr H—* was a complete failure on its first night at the Drury Lane Theatre, the author joined in the hissing and booing from the pit. As he later explained to friends, 'I was damnably afraid to be taken for the author.'

❦ The prodigy

Wolfgang Amadeus Mozart may have been a musical prodigy but this story seems to indicate that he was just as precocious in the amatory stakes. Significantly, had the princess accepted his offer she might have lived to a ripe old age, rather than ending her days at the guillotine.

In 1762, the child-prodigy, the six-year-old Mozart, was visiting the Austrian royal palace of Schönbrunn. The little boy slipped over on the polished floor while playing with the young princesses. He was picked up and comforted by the seven-year-old Marie Antoinette, later to be Queen of France. At once Mozart kissed her and said, 'You are good. I will marry you.'

❦ Seven years' bad luck

The American painter, James Whistler, spent much of his later life in London.

James Whistler once accosted a particularly filthy street urchin who was selling newspapers and asked him how long he had been doing the work.

'Three years, sir,' said the boy.

'And how old are you?' asked Whistler.

'Seven, sir.'

'Oh, come now, you must be older than that.'

'No, I ain't, sir.'

Whistler turned to a friend and said, 'I don't think he could get that dirty in seven years. Do you?'

❦ Wilde about Columbus

British writer and wit, Oscar Wilde, had no penchant for suffering fools gladly.

Wilde was once talking to an American visitor, who was anxious to impress him. 'Wonderful man, Columbus,' said the American.

'Why is that?' asked Wilde.

'He discovered America,' replied the man.

'Oh, no,' said Wilde. 'It had often been discovered before, but it had always been hushed up.'

❦ A louse and a flea

The English critic and writer Doctor Samuel Johnson had the sharpest wit of an age noted for its satire and comedy. Like Wilde, Johnson was particularly critical of cant and humbug.

Doctor Johnson, for sport perhaps, or from the spirit of contradiction, eagerly maintained that Derrick had merit as a writer. Mr Morgann argued with him directly, but in vain. At length he had recourse to this device.

'Pray, sir,' said he, 'do you reckon Derrick or Smart the best poet?'

Johnson at once felt himself roused, and answered, 'Sir, there is no settling the point of precedency between a louse and a flea.'

❦ Railing at age and infirmity

Dr Samuel Johnson had a sense of fun which astonished his more self-important colleagues.

A gentleman of Lichfield meeting the doctor returning from a walk, enquired how far he had been. The doctor replied that he had gone round Mr Levet's field (the place where the scholars play) in search of a rail that he used to jump over when a boy. 'And,' said the doctor, in a transport of joy, 'I have been so fortunate as to find it. I stood gazing upon it some time with a degree of rapture, for it brought to my mind all my juvenile sports and pastimes, and at length I determined to try my skill and dexterity; I laid aside my hat and wig, pulled off my coat, and leapt over it twice.' Thus the great Doctor Johnson, only three years before his death was, without hat, wig or coat, jumping over a rail that he had used to fly over when a schoolboy.

❦ The joys of banishment

Boswell wrote of a story that Samuel Johnson had told him of his meeting with the Mayor of Windsor.

I was dining with the Mayor of Windsor, who gave me a very hearty dinner; but, not satisfied with feeding my body, he would also feed my understanding. So, after he had spoke a great deal of clumsy nonsense, he told me that at the last Sessions he had transported three people to the Plantations. I was so provoked with the fellow's dullness and impertinence that I exclaimed, 'I wish to God, Sir, I was the fourth.' Nothing could more strongly express his dissatisfaction.

❦ Last words

The French poet and critic François de Malherbe found it difficult to keep his private and public life entirely separate. His obsession with maintaining the standards of French classical poetry spilled over into his relations with ordinary folk, making him an intolerant companion.

François de Malherbe,was so critical of the misuse of grammar that it even concerned him on his deathbed. Having slumped into unconsciousness, and seeming to be very close to death, Malherbe suddenly woke up and told off his landlady, who was waiting on him, for using a word that was not good French. When his priest told him to concentrate on less worldly things, Malherbe replied that he would defend the purity of the French language until death. The priest then tried to paint the joys of Paradise for him, but Malherbe told him, 'Speak no more of it; your bad style disgusts me.'

❦ A dry wit

The poet Alexander Pope once wrote of a meeting he had with his friend, the eccentric Dean Swift, a man whose sense of humour was so dry that it often appeared scarcely distinguishable from disapproval.

Dr Swift had an odd, blunt way, that is mistaken by strangers for ill-nature. 'Tis so odd that there is no describing it but by facts. I'll tell you one that just comes into my head.

'Hey-dey gentlemen,' says the doctor, 'what's the meaning of this visit? How come you to leave all the great lords that you are so fond of, to come hither to see a poor dean?'

'Because we would rather see you than any of them.'

'Ay, anyone that did not know you as well as I do might believe you. But since you are come, I must get some supper for you, I suppose?'

'No, doctor, we have supped already.'

'Supped already! That's impossible: why 'tis not eight o'clock yet.'

'Indeed we have.'

'That's very strange: but if you had not supped, I must have got something for you. Let me see, what should I have had? A couple of lobsters? Ay, that would have done very well – two shillings; tarts – a shilling. But you'll drink a glass of wine with me, though you supped so much before your usual time, only to spare my pocket?'

'No, we had rather talk with you than drink with you.'

'But if you had supped with me, as in all reason you ought to have done, you must have drank with me. A bottle of wine – two shillings. Two and two is four, and one is five: just two and sixpence a piece. There, Pope, there's half a crown for you and there's another for you, sir; for I won't save anything by you, I am determined.'

This was all said and done with his usual seriousness on such occasions; and in spite of everything we could say to the contrary he actually obliged us to take the money.

❦ A frothy head on his shoulders

Sarah Siddons was the most famous British actress of the late eighteenth and early nineteenth centuries. She excelled in tragic roles, making the following story even more ridiculous.

Once during her engagement to play Lady Macbeth, the evening being hot, Mrs Siddons was tempted by a torturing thirst to avail herself of the only relief to be obtained at the moment. Her dresser, therefore, dispatched a boy in great haste to 'fetch a pint of beer for Mrs Siddons'.

Meanwhile, the play proceeded, and on the boy's return with the frothed pitcher, he looked about for the person who had sent him on his errand, and not seeing her, enquired, 'Where is Mrs Siddons?'

The scene shifter whom he questioned, pointing his finger to the stage, where she was performing the sleeping scene of Lady Macbeth, replied, 'There she is.'

To the horror of the performers, the boy promptly walked onto the stage close up to Mrs Siddons. Her distress may be imagined; she waved the boy away in her grand manner several times without effect. At last the people behind the scenes, by dint of beckoning, stamping, etc., succeeded in getting him off with the beer, while the audience were in an uproar of laughter which the dignity of the actress was unable to quell for several minutes.

❦ A music critic

Dr Samuel Johnson was no lover of music, as this example from James Boswell shows.

Upon hearing a celebrated performer go through a hard composition, and hearing it remarked that it was very difficult, Dr Johnson said, 'I would it had been impossible.'

❦ The magic flute

During his imprisonment in Bedford Gaol, John Bunyan was forced to improvise when seeking entertainment.

To pass away the gloomy hours in prison, Bunyan took a rail out of the stool belonging to his cell and, with his knife, fashioned it into a flute. The keeper, hearing music, followed the sound to Bunyan's cell; but, while they were unlocking the door, the ingenious prisoner replaced the rail in the stool, so that the searchers were unable to solve the mystery; nor, during the remainder of Bunyan's residence in the jail, did they ever discover how the music had been produced.

❦ Adam and Eve and a visitor

Nudism was not a common activity in nineteenth-century England but William Blake and his wife were determined to let life imitate art when reading Milton's Paradise Lost.

William Blake and his wife, Catherine, were once sitting naked in their garden at Lambeth, reading extracts from Milton's *Paradise Lost*, when a visitor – a Mr Butts – called on them. Blake invited him into the garden saying, 'Come in! It's only Adam and Eve, you know!'

Some years later, when Lady Stuart de Rothesay heard the story, she remarked: 'It could not have been so with the real Adam and Eve, for they could never dread any droppers-in!'

❦ The power of money

'Neither a borrower nor a lender be'... as the British writer and politician Joseph Addison found out.

Joseph Addison once lent some money to a friend who hitherto had debated many subjects with the politician and had always held his own. But Addison noticed that once his friend had borrowed the money he became subservient, agreeing with everything Addison said. On one occasion the two men were debating a point and Addison, noting that his friend no longer even supported the view that he had once, was so incensed that he exclaimed: 'Either contradict me, sir, or pay me my money.'

❦ Staël writing

Anne Louise Germaine, Baronne de Staël, daughter of King Louis XVI's finance minister Jacques Necker, was a writer and political commentator during the Napoleonic period. Her salon was the centre of a circle of politicians and she later became an opponent of the Emperor Napoleon. He eventually suppressed her writings and exiled her from France. She had many lovers, including Prince Talleyrand.

When Madame de Staël published her celebrated novel *Delphine*, she was supposed to have painted herself in the person of the heroine, and Monsieur Talleyrand in that of an elderly lady, who is one of the principal characters. 'They tell me,' said he, the first time he met her, 'that we are both of us in your novel, in the disguise of women.'

❦ Second Thoughts

Samuel Foote was a witty man, and a good actor, both of which accomplishments must have proved useful in this situation.

Charles Howard of Greystock published a silly book he called 'Thoughts'. He met Samuel Foote at a coffee house. 'And have you read my *Thoughts?*' said he. 'No,' replied Foote, 'I wait for the second volume.' 'And why so?' asked Howard. 'Because,' said Foote, 'I have heard that Second Thoughts are best.'

❦ A conspiracy revealed

Wilde was either the best or the worst man to consult in Sir Lewis Morris's predicament, depending on whether you took seriously a word he said.

Oscar Wilde once encountered a distraught Sir Lewis Morris, who was complaining about what he called the studied neglect of his claims to the poet laureateship after the death of Lord Tennyson. Morris, author of *The Epic of Hades*, said, 'It is a complete conspiracy of silence against me – a conspiracy of silence! What ought I to do, Oscar?' 'Join it,' replied Wilde readily.

❦ Con brio

The British conductor Sir Thomas Beecham was very fashionable as a young man and very attentive to his dress.

One warm summer's evening, he was walking in London and felt himself overdressed. He therefore summoned a cab, tossed his overcoat inside and told the driver, 'Follow me!'

❦ The tools of genius

The German-born physicist Albert Einstein revolutionized the study of his subject and extended man's knowledge of the universe.

Albert Einstein's wife was once shown around the giant telescope at the Mount Wilson observatory. She was very interested at first and asked what it was used for. When she was told that it was being used to discover the shape of the universe she scornfully commented, 'Oh, my husband does that on the back of an old envelope.'

❦ Grave humour

Sir William Shwenck Gilbert was the brilliant librettist who, with Sir Arthur Sullivan, created a series of enormously successful light operas. Gilbert was also a writer of humorous verse.

Soon after the death of a well-known composer, someone who did not keep pace with events asked Sir W S Gilbert what the maestro in question was doing.

'He is doing nothing,' remarked Gilbert soberly.

'Surely he is composing,' persisted the other man.

'On the contrary,' said Gilbert, 'he is decomposing.'

❦ A big new penny

Marie Curie and her husband Pierre were awarded the Nobel Prize for physics for their discovery of radioactivity. Marie eventually died in 1934 as a result of the radiation to which she had exposed herself during her experiments.

In 1903 Pierre and Marie Curie were awarded the highest accolade by the Royal Society: the Davy Medal. Although Marie was too ill to attend the presentation ceremony, her husband went and returned from England with a large gold medal, on which their names were engraved. Unfortunately Pierre Curie could not find a safe place to keep it. Eventually, he reached the eccentric decision to give it to his six-year-old daughter Irene for safety, assuming that she would love her 'big new penny' far too much ever to lose it.

❦ I belong to Glasgee...

The meeting between Adam Smith and Samuel Johnson, both ardent nationalists and both intolerant of opinions other than their own, must have been something to witness – at a distance.

The economist Adam Smith was once extolling the virtues of his beloved Glasgow in the company of Dr Samuel Johnson. The good doctor put up with it as long as he could and then said, 'Pray, Sir, have you ever seen Brentford?'

❦ A dispute over a woman

James Boswell was a Scottish lawyer who wrote the biography of Dr Samuel Johnson. Boswell and Johnson undertook a famous tour of Scotland and the Isles of the Hebrides which included a number of extraordinary incidents.

When we advanced a good way by the side of Loch Ness, I perceived a little hut with an old-looking woman at the door of it. I thought here might be a scene that would amuse Dr Johnson; so I mentioned it to him. 'Let's go in,' said he. We dismounted, and we and our guides entered the hut. It was a wretched little hovel of earth only, I think, and for a window had only a small hole, which was stopped with a piece of turf, that was taken out occasionally to let in light. In the middle of the room or space which we entered was a fire of peat, the smoke going out at a hole in the roof. She had a pot upon it, with goat's flesh boiling. There was at one end under the same roof, but divided by a kind of partition made of wattles, a pen or fold in which we saw a good many kids.

Dr Johnson was curious to know where she slept. I asked one of the guides, who questioned her in Erse. She answered with a tone of emotion, saying (as he told us) she was afraid we wanted to go to bed with her. This coquetry or whatever it may be called of so wretched a being was truly ludicrous. Dr Johnson and I afterwards were merry upon it. I said, it was he who alarmed the poor woman's virtue – 'No, sir,' said he, 'she'll say, "There came a wicked young fellow, a wild dog who I believe would have ravished me, had there not been with him a grave old gentleman who repressed him: but when he gets out of sight of his tutor, I'll warrant you he'll spare no woman he meets, young or old." 'No, sir,' I replied. 'She'll say, "There was a terrible ruffian who would have forced me, had it not been for a civil decent young man, who, I take it, was an angel sent from heaven to protect me."'

❦ Inspired silences

Thomas Babington, 1st Baron Macaulay, was a Scottish statesman and historian. Noted as a supreme stylist and a great orator, he became a target for the sharp wit of Sydney Smith.

Yes, I take great credit to myself; I always prophesied his greatness from the first moment I saw him, then a very young and unknown man, on the Northern Circuit. There are no limits to his knowledge, on small subjects as well as great; he is like a book in breeches... Yes, I agree, he is certainly more agreeable since his return from India. His enemies might perhaps have said before (though I never did so) that he talked rather too much; but now he has occasional flashes of silence that make his conversation perfectly delightful.

❦ No arms just thumbs

English clergyman Sydney Smith was the most noted wit of the early nineteenth century in Britain.

He was writing one morning in his favourite bay window, when a pompous little man in rusty black was ushered in. 'May I ask what procures me the honour of this visit,' said my father. 'Oh,' said the little man, 'I am compounding a history of the distinguished families in Somersetshire and have called to obtain the Smith arms.' 'I regret, sir,' said my father, 'not to be able to contribute to so valuable a work; but the Smiths never had any arms and have invariably sealed their letters with their thumbs.'

❦ The price of fame

Like Charles Dickens, the British novelist William Makepeace Thackeray also undertook a tour of the United States to popularize his works. The following story might suggest that he was less successful in this aim.

During Thackeray's visit to St Louis, Missouri, on his American tour, the following exchange was heard between two Irish waiters.

'Do you know who that is?'
'No,' was the answer.
'That,' said the first, 'is the celebrated Thacker.'
'What's he done?'
'Damned if I know.'

❦ An aggregate of minds

The Irish writer and satirist Dean Jonathan Swift, author of Gulliver's Travels, *was one of a group of brilliant literary figures in the early eighteenth century who frequented London coffee houses.*

Dean Swift and Dr Arbuthnot once met in a coffee house. The doctor had been scribbling a letter in great haste, which was much blotted; and seeing this odd parson near him, with a design to play upon him said, 'Pray, sir, have you any sand about you?' 'No,' replied Swift, 'but I have the gravel, and if you will give me your letter I'll piss upon it.' Thus singularly commenced an acquaintance between those two great wits, which afterwards ripened into the closest friendship.

❦ A bombast fellow

King George II was lamentably ignorant when it came to intellectual pursuits. He was the last British monarch to lead an army into battle and was famous more for the number of his mistresses than for anything else.

'Who is this Pope that I hear so much about?' asked George II. 'I cannot discover what is his merit. Why will not my subjects write in prose? I hear a great deal too of Shakespeare, but I cannot read him, he is such a *bombast* fellow.'

❦ Dr Hash

Dr Samuel Johnson's Dictionary *was one of the great books of the eighteenth century and it was much imitated, often far from effectively.*

Johnson received from some unknown source a letter deriving the word 'curmudgeon' from *coeur méchant* or wicked heart – a wild enough guess, which pleased the doctor so much that he adopted it in his dictionary giving due credit to 'unknown correspondent'. Twenty years later, Dr Ash, preparing a dictionary of his own, was struck by this gem and transferred it to his own pages. But, wishing all the glory of the discovery for himself, he gave no credit to Johnson, and informed a wondering world that curmudgeon was formed from *coeur*, unknown, and *méchant*, correspondent.

❦ La bête humaine

Dr Samuel Johnson became so popular that he was frequently invited out to be exhibited rather than entertained. Johnson's wit generally rose or fell to the occasion as appropriate.

A very accomplished young lady who became in process of time the Hon. Mrs Digby, related to her former tutor the following anecdote. This lady was present at the introduction of Dr Johnson at one of the late Mrs Montagu's literary parties, when Mrs Digby herself, with several still younger ladies, almost immediately surrounded our colossus of literature (an odd figure sure enough) with more wonder than politeness. And while contemplating him, as if he had been some monster from the deserts of Africa, Johnson said to them, 'Ladies, I am tame; you may stroke me.'

❦ The wrong sign

Aaron Copland was one of the most famous American composers of the twentieth century.

One day Copland was browsing in a New York bookshop. He was pleased to see a woman buy a copy of his new book *What to Listen for in Music* as well as a paperback edition of a Shakespeare play. As she went to leave the shop Copland stopped her and asked if she would like him to autograph the book. The woman looked blankly at his beaming face and asked, 'Which one?'

❦ Judging by appearances

The painter Stanley Spencer never took much care about his appearance. Once when he was going to collect the Nettleship Prize for his work entitled Nativity *he had an unusual encounter.*

'As I stepped out of the station an elderly man with a beard put his bag down, whistled and called, "I say, boy, just carry this bag for me." I picked it up and walked by his side down Gower Street. When we got to the Slade porter's lodge he told me to put the bag down and began to fumble in his pockets. I said I was going inside myself so we walked across the quadrangle to the door on the left which leads to the office and theatre where the award was to be made. Here he told me again to put the bag down and fished out some coins. "Oh, no," I said, "that's all right," and began going towards the theatre door. "You can't go in there," he said disapproving and, pointing to the office, "that's where you deliver messages." I then explained I had come for the Nettleship Prize.'

❦ Critics!

The Mexican painter, José Orozco, decided to go to live in the United States in 1917 because he did not find in Mexico an atmosphere favourable to artists.

In passing through Laredo, Texas, Orozco was detained in an American Customs House and his baggage was inspected. The pictures that he carried were spread over the entire office in an 'official' exhibition and carefully examined by all members of the staff. After the 'examination' they were separated and some sixty were torn into bits. They told him that it was against the law to bring immoral prints into the United States.

🎇 9. KINGS AND KAISERS, PRINCES AND POTENTATES

🎇 Pause for cheers

The stolid Emperor Franz Joseph was a Habsburg to his fingertips, yet behind all the pomp and ceremony the emperor was an uncertain and lonely man.

The Habsburg emperor Franz Joseph was not noted as a public speaker and went through agonies every time he had to give a public address. Halfway through one speech – at birthday celebrations for Kaiser Wilhelm II – Franz Joseph assured his mistress, Katherina Schratt, that he was excelling himself, and all 'without a prompter and without getting stuck'. Unfortunately, as he drew to the end of his speech he read from his notes, 'And now, ladies and gentlemen, I ask you to join me in a triple salute: Kaiser Wilhelm, hurrah! hurrah!' – there now followed a long pause while he struggled to turn over the page – 'hurrah!'

🎇 Safe sex

Catherine the Great was a German princess who was brought to Russia in 1745 to marry Grand Duke Peter, the heir to the throne. But Peter was a lunatic and the marriage proved just the first step in Catherine's seizing power for herself.

Catherine the Great's marriage to Grand Duke Peter was unusual to say the least. Peter had a passion for military life and spent much of their early married life drilling Catherine in the use of the military manual of arms. It is said that on their wedding night Peter ordered his wife to stand guard at their door.

❦ The truth hurts

King Frederick William of Prussia – known ever afterwards as the 'Sergeant-Major' king because of his obsession with marching his army up and down like toy soldiers on the parade ground – was a cruel and ruthless man whose subjects feared rather than loved him.

One day a Jew saw the royal cavalcade approaching in the street and ran away to avoid it, but the king had spied him and sent after him. He was caught and brought trembling into the royal presence. 'Why did you run away from me?' demanded the king. 'Because I was afraid,' replied the Jew truthfully. 'But you ought to love me,' proclaimed the king in injured tones and immediately set about the poor Jew and beat him mercilessly.

❦ The convenient victim

The assassination of the Empress Elizabeth of Austria was a tragic end to a wasted life that had brought her nothing but bitterness and isolation.

The beautiful and tragic empress Elizabeth of Austria was assassinated at Geneva in 1898 by an Italian anarchist named Luigi Lucheni. It appears that Lucheni's real target had been King Umberto of Italy but he could not afford to pay the 50 lire fare to Rome and so made do with Elizabeth instead.

❦ Find the lady

Catherine the Great often felt more at ease with the servants at her court than with the Russian nobles, who resented her as a German intruder.

At one of her private parties, when she was as usual walking about from card table to card table looking at the players, she suddenly rang the bell for her page, but he did not come; she looked agitated and impatient. At length she left the room and did not again return; and conjecture was of course busy as to what might be the fate of the inattentive page. Shortly after, however, someone having occasion to go into the antechamber of the pages found a party of them at cards and the empress seated playing cards with them. Evidently, she had found that the page she rang for was so interested in the game he was engaged in that he could not leave it to attend to her summons; and accordingly she had quietly taken his hand for him to play it out.

❦ Cutting down on the crowds

On his Grand Tour to Western Europe between 1696 and 1698, Tsar Peter often found that his dictatorial behaviour was inappropriate in the more democratic states of Western Europe.

When Peter the Great, Tsar of Russia, visited Holland, William invited him to a grand dinner at the Hague. A huge crowd assembled to watch the two kings dining but so great was the congestion that Peter offered to decapitate a few of them for William to make more space. It was what he would have done in Russia, he added. William politely declined his offer.

❦ A king on the roof

The 'culture-shock' that Peter the Great experienced when visiting England and Holland on his western tour made him uneasy, particularly when confronted with large crowds of people.

So great were the crowds that assembled wherever the tsar went on his tour that he became quite paranoid and feared that he would be assassinated. When Peter wanted to see parliament in session but refused to go inside the building he was 'put in a gutter upon the house top, to peep in at the window, where he made so ridiculous a figure that neither king nor people could forbear laughing'. As one observer remarked, 'Today, I have seen the rarest thing in the world: one monarch on the throne and another on the roof.'

❦ Leaving in style

What Tsar Peter I lacked in style he made up for in generosity.

When Peter left England in 1697 he thanked King William III and gave his host a fabulous ruby, valued at £10,000, 'wrapp'd up in a piece of brown paper'.

❦ The wanderer's return

Peter the Great returned to Russia fired up with many new ideas he had picked up in his travels. But one thing he had not learned abroad was how to curb his ferocious temper.

When Peter arrived back in Russia, only just in time to punish the Streltszi who had rebelled against him, he gave a magnificent feast for the imperial ambassador in Moscow, which lasted for three days. As entertainment for the diners, on the first day 1,500 men were beheaded; on the second day 700 were strangled and on the third day 400 men had their ears and noses cut off.

❦ The spoils of office

The dismissal of Prince Bismarck by the Kaiser in 1890 had a disastrous effect on German policy in the next two decades. Bismarck left very much 'encumbered with the past'.

When Kaiser Wilhelm II 'dropped his pilot', by accepting Bismarck's resignation, the chancellor moved his personal belongings from the chancellery building in Berlin. Along with 300 packing cases filled with state papers, Bismarck also had 13,000 bottles of wine shifted from the cellars there to his private residence at Friedrichsruh.

❦ A disturbing experience

Exhausted by the burden of earthly power, the Holy Roman Emperor Charles V retired to a monastery in 1555. However, he sometimes found it difficult to adapt to the slower pace of life.

On one occasion the emperor, going in his turn to awaken the other monks, found a young man, who was but a novice, so fast asleep that he would hardly awaken. The novice getting up at last against his will, and being yet half asleep, could not forbear saying to Charles that he ought to be satisfied to have disturbed the quiet of the world as long as he had been in it without coming again to disturb the quiet of those who had left it.

❦ The crown falls

The wedding of Napoleon III and the Empress Eugénie in 1853 contained at least one moment of misfortune that boded ill for all concerned.

The emperor and empress – he in full uniform and again wearing the collar of the Legion of Honour and the Golden Fleece – went together in a great coach, surmounted by an imperial crown and elaborately gilded and adorned with paintings, which had been built for the wedding of Napoleon I and Marie Louise of Austria. But at the outset a curious and ominous mishap occurred. The bridal pair had taken their seats and the vehicle was passing from under the vaulted entrance of the Tuileries into the courtyard, when the imperial crown suddenly fell from the coach to the ground. The eight horses were at once halted, the crown was picked up, and in some fashion or other set in place again. Meantime, as the emperor, surprised at the delay, enquired the cause of it, Fleury, approaching the coach, quietly informed him, whereupon the emperor replied that he would tell him an anecdote some other time. But the first equerry knew it already. A virtually identical accident had occurred with the same coach and the same crown at the marriage of Napoleon I and Marie Louise.

❦ A faithful friend

Napoleon III and the Empress Eugénie visited England on a state visit in 1855 but their transport arrangements were chaotic.

Members of the royal party were separated from each other and

199

Eugénie's hairdresser was left behind. As the royal couple were reaching London, some of their attendants were only just landing at Dover. As the Comte de Fleury was getting into the court landau which was to carry him to London, he was accosted by an individual with a greenish hue and woebegone expression whom he did not recognize, but who earnestly entreated permission to get up behind with the footmen. 'But who may you be?' Fleury somewhat sharply enquired. 'I am Felix, Her Majesty the Empress's hairdresser,' was the reply. 'And I am in despair at being left behind! What Her Majesty will do without me I cannot tell, but I feel like cutting my throat!' The position was indeed serious: the empress already at Windsor and no coiffeur to dress her hair for dinner! What a disaster! 'Quick, then, get up behind,' said Fleury, and away the party went. When they arrived at Windsor Fleury hastened to inform the empress of the incident. 'Tell Felix not to distress himself,' said she, laughing. 'He must on no account commit suicide. We want no *affaire Vatel* here. My maids have done their best for me in his absence.' The empress's reference to the Vatel affair would have reminded Fleury and Felix of the Prince of Condé's cook, who had committed suicide after the fish arrived late on the occasion of Louis XIV's famous visit to the Prince of Condé's castle at Chantilly.

❦ No crocodile tears

In 1855 Queen Victoria and Prince Albert arrived in Paris on a state visit, hoping to improve relations with England's traditional enemy – France. But they found there were still many painful memories to overcome.

Queen Victoria expressed a wish to visit the tomb of Napoleon at the Invalides, of which old Prince Jérôme – Napoleon's brother – was the governor. At that time Jérôme was staying at Le Hâvre and when the emperor requested him to return to Paris in order that he might do the honours of the Invalides to the queen, he feigned illness to avoid obeying the command. Unfortunately, he could not control his tongue, and the truth leaked out. 'He had fought at Waterloo,' said he, 'and he was not going to exhibit his brother's tomb to the descendants of those who had sent the great man to perish on the rock of St Helena. He had no fancy for crocodile's tears such as those English royalties would doubtless shed.' Meanwhile, the emperor had suggested to Marshal Vaillant that he, in default of Prince Jérôme, should receive the queen at the Invalides; but that old soldier of the first empire, though frequently in contact with the royal visitors, was apparently influenced by feelings akin to Jérôme's. At all events, he eluded the duty by pleading that it was surely one which a prince of the Imperial House ought to discharge.

❦ Son of a gun

The birth of the Prince Imperial was an important event for all Frenchmen, offering the hope that the blood of the great Napoleon would be extended into another generation. At the time most Frenchmen were still Bonapartist at heart.

During the first confinement of the Empress Eugénie, it was decreed that the people of Paris would learn the sex of the new baby by means of an artillery salute. Twenty-one guns would be fired if the baby were a girl and one hundred and one if it were a boy. It seemed a foolproof system.

At last the guns of the Invalides began booming and the multitude gathered around the Tuileries began counting the shots. The tension rose as the number approached twenty-one. Then the twenty-first shot was fired, followed by a silence. For a moment the listeners felt grievously disappointed. The baby was a girl. They would have to wait again for a boy to be born. Suddenly a twenty-second report was heard and then the salute continued, right up to one hundred and one. The pregnant pause had been the result of human error. An old wooden-legged artilleryman, wounded at some Napoleonic battle, but brought out of retirement for this unique occasion, had stumbled and fallen while in the process of loading the twenty-second shot. And this had been the cause of the brief delay that had disappointed – temporarily at least – the waiting multitude.

❦ The new nobility

Still subject to democratic tendencies, the Emperor Napoleon III wanted to open up France's aristocracy to men of talent rather than simply men of birth and breeding.

During the early 1860s, Napoleon III was presented with a plan for a new nobility, by which ministers, judges, senators, prefects and other bureaucrats would be offered titles in recognition of their services. Some of these titles would have been clearly absurd and the Empress Eugénie was quick to point out the folly of the proposed idea, telling Napoleon of some of the absurd titles that existed in her home country of Spain, like the Marquis of the Lover's Rock, the Marquis of Eggshell, the Marquis of the Calves' Grotto, the Count of the Castle of Sparks and the Viscount of the Deep Bay of Royal Fidelity. Napoleon III – convinced – dropped the idea.

❦ Diplomacy

Kaiser Wilhelm II of Germany was renowned for the volatility of his temperament.

One of the Kaiser's advisers was once asked how he managed to keep the emperor in such a good humour. He replied, 'His Majesty delights in explaining mechanical contrivances, such as a clock, or a compass, or a barometer. I keep a special barometer, and when the emperor comes in I ask him to explain how it works, telling him I have forgotten what he told me last time. He gives an admirable exposition; this puts him in an excellent temper, and he signs the documents I put before him.'

❦ Holy water for inner cleanliness

Prince Napoleon – 'Plon-Plon' – was the nephew of Napoleon I and the cousin of the Emperor Napoleon III. Known also as 'the greatest scamp in Europe', Plon-Plon could not have done anything ordinary if he had tried.

When Prince Napoleon's chosen wife – Princess Clothilde of Savoy – arrived from Turin, she brought with her 'holy water' to sanctify the rooms of the heathen French. Clothilde even sprinkled the holy water over her bedroom on her marriage night with Plon-Plon. Before going to bed, Clothilde sent to her chaplain for more holy water and two whole carafes were supplied, one of which Clothilde placed on the mantelpiece for later use. During the night, however, Plon-Plon got up feeling thirsty and drank the whole carafe of the holy water, which had a miraculous effect on him, purging him more thoroughly than his pharmacist had been able to do for many days.

❦ Military discipline

Catherine the Great's husband, the Grand Duke Peter, heir to the throne of Russia, was insane and impotent into the bargain, and Catherine's marriage to him was nothing but a mockery.

While the grand duke lived, Catherine had to indulge his bizarre activities. One day when she entered their bedroom Catherine found a large rat hanging from the ceiling, bearing all the marks of having been tortured. When she asked Peter to explain the reason for this capital punishment, he told her that the rat was guilty, according to military law, of having eaten two soldiers made of starch and that he had been hanged after 'having his kidneys broken by a dog' and that he would remain exposed to the public eye 'for three days to set an example'. Catherine thought he was joking but when she laughed Peter's face darkened menacingly.

❦ The smallest office

Catherine the Great worked prodigiously hard and liked to oversee most of the activities of her government. She has been called by historians an 'enlightened despot'.

On one occasion Catherine the Great explained to the Prince de Ligne, 'I am working like a horse and my four secretaries are not enough.' She liked to take all decisions herself and she often felt that the weight of all Russian policy – domestic and foreign – was on her shoulders. She spoke to the prince about her 'St Petersburg office' and the prince replied, 'I don't know of a smaller office, as it is only a few inches large: it extends from one temple to the other, and from the root of the nose to the roots of the hair.'

❦ The privileges of youth

As a young man Tsar Alexander I of Russia was said to have had an irresistible attraction for women. However, not every woman lost her senses in his presence, as this story shows.

When Alexander was visiting Paris following the defeat of Napoleon in 1815, he attended anniversary celebrations at one of the hospitals. The ladies who had organized the event passed collecting plates round for contributions. One particularly attractive girl was given the job of approaching the tsar for a contribution. Alexander dropped some gold onto her plate, saying, 'That is for your beautiful, bright eyes.' The girl curtsied but stood her ground, holding out the plate again. 'What? More?' said the tsar. 'Yes, sire,' she replied. 'Now I want something for the poor people.'

❦ The land of opportunity

Life in Romania under King Carol, 1930–40, was particularly hard. Given the chance to leave the country, some chose to do so.

While in exile, King Carol told the British diplomat Bruce Lockhart that he had once selected fourteen of the brightest of his subjects for special training in the government service. Seven of them had been sent to England and seven to the United States, to study politics and economics. The seven who had been sent to England were very smart, returning and achieving high office in the Romanian diplomatic service in Bucharest. 'What about the seven you sent to the United States?' asked Lockhart. 'They were even smarter,' said the king, 'they stayed there.'

❦ A cynical bricklayer

Joseph II of Austria and Catherine the Great of Russia are both accounted 'enlightened despots' of the eighteenth century. Joseph was noted more for his unrealizable ambitions than for his common sense and yet in this instance a degree of cynicism is present, quite untypical of this ruler. In fact, cynical or otherwise, Joseph's prediction proved to be correct.

Catherine the Great constantly dreamed of establishing great cities, to match her predecessor Peter the Great, who had set up St Petersburg on the Baltic coast. During the state visit of the Emperor Joseph II of Austria, the two rulers proceeded to lay the foundation stones of one of Catherine's proposed new cities. Catherine laid the first stone and Joseph laid the second. Afterwards, Joseph commented, 'I have finished in a single day a most important business with the empress of Russia; she has laid the first stone of a city and I have laid the last.'

❦ A royal understanding

The Habsburg–Valois struggle of the sixteenth century led to a complex series of wars known overall by the title, the Italian Wars. Significantly, the Habsburg emperor, Charles V, showed no obvious hostility towards his French rival, Francis I. For both of them war was merely an affair of state, the lives of people being viewed as irrelevant.

In 1521, when the Holy Roman Emperor Charles renewed his struggle with King Francis I of France for control of northern Italy, the emperor remarked, 'My cousin Francis and I are in perfect agreement – he wants Milan and so do I.'

❦ Masquerades

The royal court under Tsar Peter I of Russia lacked the sophistication of those he had visited in London and Vienna on his 'Great Embassy' to Western Europe. In fact, the sort of entertainment that Peter enjoyed was far closer to that of the peasantry than to the aristocracy, though in Russia it was sometimes hard to tell one group from the other.

On 27 and 28 January 1715, the whole court joined in a two-day masquerade, preparations for which had been underway for three months. The occasion was the wedding of Nikita Zotov, who forty years before had been Peter's tutor, and now was in his eighty-fourth year. The bride was a buxom widow of thirty-four.

'The nuptials of this extraordinary couple was solemnized by the court in masks,' reported Weber. 'The four persons appointed to invite the guests were the greatest stammerers that could be found in all Russia. Old decrepit men who were not able to walk or stand had been picked out to serve for bridesmen, stewards and waiters. There were four running footmen, the most unwieldy fellows who had been troubled with gout most of their lifetime, and were so fat and bulky they needed others to lead them. The Mock-Tsar of Moscow, who represented King David in his dress, instead of a harp had a lyre covered with a bearskin to play upon. He was carried on a sort of pageant [float], placed on a sled, to the four corners of which were tied bears, which, being pricked with goads by fellows purposely appointed for it, made such a frightful roaring as well suited the confused and horrible din raised by the disagreeing instruments of the rest of the company. The tsar himself was dressed like a Boor of Frizeland, and skilfully beat a drum in company with three generals. In this manner, bells ringing everywhere the ill-matched couple were attended by the maskers to the altar of the great church, where they were joined in matrimony by a priest a hundred years old who had lost his eyesight and memory, to supply which defect a pair of spectacles were put on his nose, two candles held before his eyes and the words sounded into his ears so that he was able to pronounce them. From the church the procession went to the tsar's palace, where the diversions lasted some days.'

❦ Lager louts

When Tsar Peter the Great of Russia visited England in 1697 he was given the use of Sayes Court, the magnificent home of the celebrated diarist John Evelyn. Evelyn had spent forty-five years beautifying his house and was quite unprepared for what was to happen when the Russian party took over his property. At the end of their three-months' stay Evelyn came to inspect his house again.

Appalled by what he saw, Evelyn hurried off to the Royal Surveyor, Sir Christopher Wren, and the Royal Gardener, Mr London, to ask them to estimate the cost of the repairs. They found floors and carpets so stained and smeared with ink and grease that new floors had to be installed. Tiles had been pulled from the Dutch stoves and brass doorlocks prised open. The paintwork was battered and filthy. Windows were broken, and more than fifty chairs – every one in the house – had simply disappeared, probably into the stoves. Feather beds, sheets and canopies were ripped and torn as if by wild animals. Twenty pictures and portraits were torn, probably used for target practice. Outside, the garden was ruined. The lawn was trampled into mud and dust, 'as if a regiment of soldiers in iron shoes had drilled on it'. The magnificent holly hedge, 400 feet long, 9 feet high and 5 feet thick, had been flattened by wheelbarrows rammed through it. The bowling green, the gravel paths, the bushes and trees, all were ravaged. Neighbours reported that the Russians had found three wheelbarrows, unknown in Russia, and had developed a game with one man, sometimes the tsar, inside the wheelbarrow and another racing him into the hedges. Wren and his companions noted all this and made a recommendation which resulted in a recompense to Evelyn of 350 pounds and nine pence. An enormous sum for that day.

❧ Hedging your bets

The role of Prince Talleyrand in the July revolution of 1830, which brought Louis Philippe to the throne of France, remains as obscure now as it was to his contemporaries.

A widely told story relates how the elderly statesman, sitting in his house in Paris during the three days of riots, heard the pealing of the bells and remarked, 'Ah, the tocsin! We're winning.'

'Who's we, mon prince?' asked a friend.

Talleyrand gestured for silence. 'Not a word. I'll tell you who we are tomorrow.'

❦ Paris is worth a mass

During the French Wars of Religion Catholics and Huguenots (Protestants) fought for more than forty years to control the kingdom of France. The Huguenot leader, Henry of Navarre, finally emerged victorious and became King Henry IV, one of France's greatest kings. But he was forced to compromise to do so.

Paris was one of the centres that held out most stubbornly against the Protestant forces during the French Wars of Religion. The Protestant leader, King Henry IV, who had made a feigned abjuration of his faith to escape the Massacre of the Protestants in 1572, decided once again that a lasting peace between the warring religious groups was more important than his personal religious inclinations. In July 1593 he solemnly converted to Roman Catholicism. All opposition collapsed and Paris opened its gates to him. As he rode into his capital city he is said to have remarked, 'Paris is well worth a mass.'

❦ An unexpected welcome

King Henry IV of France was a man with a strong sense of humour.

As the king passed through a small town, a deputation of burgesses was drawn up at the gates to receive him. Just as the leading dignitary began his speech of welcome a donkey near by started to bray. The king turned toward the noisy creature and said with great gravity, 'Gentlemen, one at a time please.'

❦ A date to remember

The revolution in 1789 came as a surprise to the French king, Louis XVI, showing just how out of touch he had become with the aspirations of his people.

On 14 July 1789, a Paris mob stormed and captured the Bastille, the old royal prison in Paris. That day Louis XVI, who had been out hunting, returned to Versailles and entered a note in his diary, 'July 14: nothing'. Then the Duc de la Rochefoucauld-Liancourt hurried in from Paris to tell the king of the successful attack. 'Why, this is a revolt!' said the monarch. 'No, sire,' replied the Duc. 'It is a revolution.'

❦ The price of virtue

The French emperor, Napoleon III, presided over the brilliant but corrupt Second Empire.

The emperor was once implored by a lady to forbid all smoking on the grounds that it was a great vice. Laying aside his cigar, he replied, 'This vice brings in one hundred million francs in taxes every year. I will certainly forbid it at once – as soon as you can name a virtue that brings in as much revenue.'

❦ L'État c'est moi

King Louis XIV of France was an absolute monarch, taking advice from everyone but accepting no limits to his authority.

On 13 April 1661, Louis tried to impose himself on his opponents in the Parlement de Paris. The king was at Vincennes and, learning that the Parlement was preparing to debate the edicts that he had made, rode directly to the Palais in his hunting clothes, riding crop in his hand, fuming angrily. And when the president Pomponne de Bellièvre referred to the interest of the state, Louis replied angrily, 'L'État c'est moi.'

❦ A fussy patient

The royal court at Vienna, even in the nineteenth century, was run according to principles established centuries before in Spain. Its formality was claustrophobic and proved too much for free-spirits like the Empress Elizabeth, wife of Franz Joseph, who fled the court and lived abroad.

Franz Joseph was a stickler for court protocol. Even in moments of extreme urgency he could not forget the importance of correct procedure. One night he fell ill and his personal physician was summoned. The doctor just put on his dressing gown and rushed to the bedside of the sick man, only for the emperor to choke out the words, 'Full dress suit', forcing the physician to retire to his room to prepare himself appropriately with sashes, orders and medals.

❦ A good-natured emperor

In the Habsburg Empire blood meant everything, ability nothing. This was seen most clearly in the tragic case of the Emperor Ferdinand I.

The Emperor Ferdinand of Habsburg was one of the most unfortunate of men, incredibly ugly and a moron into the bargain. He came to the throne in 1835 but was quite incapable of ruling the country, a task that was left to Count Metternich. The kinder people referred to him as Ferdinand the 'good-natured'. However, he was an epileptic and an idiot, and could hardly speak two words in succession. His favourite activity was climbing into waste-paper baskets and rolling about the floor in them, or catching flies with his hands. Ferdinand had a grossly enlarged head from encephalitis and could not lift a glass to his lips or open a door with one hand. When the Tsarina Alexandra first met him, she wrote in her diary, 'Great God, I had heard so much about him, about his small, ugly shrunken figure and his huge head, void of any expression except that of stupidity – but the reality beggared all description.' Ferdinand reigned for thirteen years during which Metternich ran the country, referring to his emperor as 'a lump of putty'. Amazingly, Ferdinand's physicians allowed him to marry a twenty-eight-year-old princess, Maria Anna of Sardinia. There were no children. On his wedding night Ferdinand had five epileptic fits.

❦ An honest penny

The beautiful Elizabeth of Bavaria was one of the tragic wives of the nineteenth century. A wild, free-spirited girl, she was married to the dull and worthy Austrian emperor Franz Joseph, and expected to suppress her vitality and adapt to strict court protocol.

When the future Empress Elizabeth of Austria was a young girl she would accompany her eccentric father, Maximilian of Bavaria, who used to dress in torn garments and strum a guitar at peasant weddings, where Elizabeth would dance and catch the coins that were thrown to them. She saved the money, later saying that it was the only money she had ever earned honestly.

❦ Crowning glory

The Empress Elizabeth of Austria was the most beautiful woman of her age, but with her beauty went a fragile personality, constantly seeking to escape from the burdens of her office.

For the dressing of the beautiful hair of the Empress Elizabeth, special precautions were taken. At each washing twenty bottles of the best brandy were mixed with huge quantities of raw egg yolks. 'The dressing room would be covered for the occasion with a white cloth spread over the carpet. The empress seated herself on a low chair in the centre. The hairdresser, clad completely in white, would begin to brush and comb. After the hair was arranged, the hairdresser would carefully gather up all the stray hairs from the floor, the clothes, the brush and comb. Then they would be counted and the empress would be told how many hairs had fallen out. If in her opinion there were too many, she would become perturbed.

❦ The red and the black

Austrian rule in Lombardy was much resented by Italian patriots. They longed to be free to join a united Italy.

When the Empress Elizabeth visited Milan, which was the capital of the Austrian province of Lombardy, it was feared that there might be displays of discontent due to her unpopularity. When she was due to visit the opera all the rich Milanese families who owned the boxes were told that they must attend and that the boxes must be filled. On the night that the empress attended, they were filled with the servants of the rich Milanese, and the servants were wearing red and black gloves, which were local symbols of mourning.

❦ The equestrienne

Bored with court protocol, Elizabeth of Austria took every chance to indulge her passion for physical pursuits.

Escape from the claustrophobic world of the court enabled Elizabeth to show off her undoubted skills as an equestrienne. She took lessons from a circus rider, a girl named Elise Renz, who she assured Franz Joseph was a perfectly respectable girl. Soon she could perform complicated stunts on horseback. She purchased four fully trained circus ponies and kept a red notebook in which she criticized her own performances. The only spectators were her dogs.

❦ Absolute confidence

Louis XIV was perhaps the most absolute of all absolutists during the seventeenth and eighteenth centuries. He ruled rather than reigned and acknowledged no superior authority under God.

Louis XIV was one day explaining to his courtiers the powers that an absolute monarch has over the lives of his subjects. Then the Comte de Guiche interjected that such power must have its limits, Louis replied, 'If I commanded you to throw yourself into the sea, you would be the first to obey me.' The count did not reply but turned on his heel and walked rapidly out of the room. Louis was astonished at his discourtesy and asked him where he was going. 'To learn to swim, sire,' replied de Guiche.

❦ The wrong conclusion

The courtiers who surrounded Louis XIV at Versailles were notoriously ambitious. They lived on the job and for the job and were intensely competitive.

When one of Louis XIV's courtiers was asked by the king if he knew Spanish, he concluded that it must mean that Louis intended him for an ambassadorial role in the future. He hurried away and devoted himself night and day to learning the Spanish language and finally he was able to report to the king that he did indeed now speak Spanish. 'I congratulate you,' said Louis. 'Now you can read *Don Quixote* in the original.'

❦ Down on her ass

Marie Antoinette, daughter of the Austrian Empress Maria Theresa and wife to King Louis XVI of France, was sometimes a bad influence on her husband as a result of her feather-brained personality.

The stultifying etiquette at the court of Louis XVI sometimes proved too much for the young Marie Antoinette. To escape she sometimes enjoyed taking donkey rides in the Bois de Boulogne, to the evident disgust of her ladies-in-waiting. On one occasion her donkey rolled over on its back, tipping her off onto the grass. She lay there laughing for a while and then remembered where she was and with whom. She summoned the grand mistress of ceremonies and asked her, 'Madame, I have sent for you to ask you to instruct me regarding the etiquette to be followed when the Queen of France and her donkey have both fallen. Which of them is to get up first?'

❦ Fed up with the Bible

Emperor Menelik II of Ethiopia maintained his country's independence against Italian aggression, winning the decisive battle of Adowa over the Italians in 1896.

Menelik had one particular quirk. When he felt unwell he had convinced himself that if he ate a few pages from the Bible he would immediately feel better. This strange behaviour appeared to do him no harm until in December 1913, when he was recovering from the effects of a stroke, he decided to dose himself with the complete Book of Kings, from the Old Testament. His doctors fed the text to him page by page but he found it difficult to consume more than a few chapters before dying.

❦ Poorly executed

Tsar Nicholas I, 1796–1855, was a cruel and dictatorial ruler of Russia, who stamped out freedom movements in Poland and Hungary.

One of the Decembrist conspirators, who had been condemned to be hanged, fell from the scaffold uninjured when the rope broke.

Picking himself up, he sneered, 'In Russia they do not know how to do anything properly, not even how to make a rope.' Normally, in such an instance, the condemned man would be reprieved. So a messenger was sent to inform the tsar what had happened. When Nicholas I asked what the condemned man had said, he was told that he had said that in Russia they did not even know how to make a rope. Nicholas replied, 'Well, let the contrary be proved.'

❦ Remarkably modest

Few rulers would have matched King Oscar II of Sweden, 1829–1907, in self-effacement. Oscar was also king of Norway until 1905 but willingly renounced his title when the Norwegians chose the path of independence from Sweden.

The king was visiting a village school one day and asked the pupils if they could name the greatest kings in Swedish history. One child said Gustavus Vasa. Another said Gustavus Adolphus, while a third added Charles XII. Then the teacher leaned over to one little boy and whispered something in his ear. At once the boy called out, 'King Oscar II.' 'Really?' said the king. 'And what has king Oscar done that is so remarkable?' 'I – I – don't know,' stammered the little boy. 'That's all right,' said the king, 'neither do I.'

❦ Dancing master

Being a tsar called for fewer diplomatic skills than being a princess.

While attending a ball at Wiesbaden, Tsar Alexander danced with a German cousin who, strictly adhering to the conventions of the occasion, thanked him for 'the great pleasure of the dance'. But Alexander cut her short: 'Why can't you be honest?' he said. 'It was just a duty neither of us can have relished. I have ruined your slippers and you have made me nearly sick with the scent you use.'

❦ Spring's eternal

Though a German, Catherine the Great understood the deep sentimentality of the Russian people and came to share it.

While Bismarck was staying in St Petersburg as Prussian

ambassador in 1859, he encountered a curious Russian custom. In the first days of spring everyone at the court promenaded in the palace gardens along the River Neva and on such an occasion the tsar noticed one of his sentries standing in the middle of a grass plot, apparently doing nothing. He called the man over and asked him what he was doing there. The soldier could only reply, 'Those are my orders.' The tsar sent one of his equerries to the guardroom to find out who had given the order, but nobody seemed to know, except that a sentry had to stand there day and night, winter and summer. The matter was widely discussed at court and eventually an old servant heard of it. He was brought before the tsar and explained that his father had told him that 'on that spot the Empress Catherine once noticed a snowdrop in bloom unusually early, and gave orders that it was not to be plucked'. The flower was immediately placed under guard and nobody ever cancelled the order. And so, for more than eighty years, winter and summer, the spot where the flower had bloomed was assiduously guarded.

❦ The judgement of Solomon

There was more to being a king than some people supposed.

Two ladies were constantly striving for precedence at the court of King Charles V of France. Eventually, they asked the king to decide the matter. Which of them should go before the other? Charles thought for a moment and then, like Solomon, he reached a solution.

'Let the elder go first,' he said.

Afterwards the two women were never seen together.

❦ No regrets

After the death of her husband in 1873 and the tragic loss of her son, the Prince Imperial, during the Zulu War in 1879, Empress Eugénie lived the rest of her years (she died in 1920) in England, alone with her memories .

In her old age the Empress Eugénie returned to France for occasional visits. When she passed through Paris she liked to visit the Tuileries and sit in the gardens, having paid the entrance fee of a *sou*, like all the other visitors.

❦ A telling blow

The death of the French king Henry II in a jousting accident seemingly confirmed a prediction by the French seer Nostradamus, thereby establishing his reputation as history's greatest fortune-teller. More important still, however, the early death of Henry condemned France to nearly fifty years of religious turmoil and civil war.

Even as late as 1559, the tournament was still a popular activity in France and, to celebrate peace with Spain and the marriage of his daughter to King Philip II of Spain, King Henry II engaged in numerous brilliant passages of arms in the lists. Just as the sports were due to end, Henry called for one final joust against the captain of his Scottish Guard, the young Protestant knight Count Montgomery. The two lances broke on contact, but Montgomery's shattered weapon struck the king's golden helmet and pieces penetrated his eye and entered his brain, so that he fell from his saddle seriously wounded, to die in agony ten days later. As Nostradamus had predicted four years before, 'The young lion will overcome the elder, in a field of combat in a single fight, he will pierce his eyes in their golden helm, two wounds in one, then dies a cruel death.'

❦ Almost

As we have seen, King Louis XIV of France was an absolutist, who believed that everything that took place in the state revolved around him.

Louis XIV made a fetish of time-keeping, expecting all visitors to arrive a few minutes early so that their appointments could begin exactly on time. When one of his ministers arrived not early but on time he remarked coldly, 'I almost had to wait.'

❦ A mark of distinction

Court etiquette under Louis XIV reached new heights of absurdity, particularly when it came to the apparently disguised distinctions that courtiers were able to detect in the way they were treated by the king.

It was one of the tasks of the Master of the Household in seventeenth-century France under Louis XIV to mark with chalk on the doors of the palace bedrooms the names of the occupants. For most people this meant simply their names, but for those who were being specially honoured the word *pour* was added. On visiting Marly once, the Princesse des Ursins fainted with joy when she found that her bedroom door was marked '*Pour Mme des Ursins*' rather than '*Princesse des Ursins*', as she had expected.

❦ Belated forgiveness

The King of Prussia detested his brother-in-law, the English monarch George II.

When Frederick William I was dying, the Lutheran pastor who attended him said that he would not go to Paradise unless he forgave all his enemies.

'Is that certain?' asked the king.

'Most certain,' replied the pastor.

'In that case,' said Frederick William to his wife, who was standing near by, 'write to your brother and tell him that I forgive him, but be sure not to do it until after my death.'

❦ Uniformly naked

King Frederick William I of Prussia was known as the 'Sergeant-Major king' on account of his obsession with military matters.

On his deathbed the pastor tried to console him by reading from the book of Job: 'Naked came I out of my mother's womb and naked shall I return thither.'

'No,' interrupted the king, 'not quite naked. I shall have my uniform on.'

❦ Quick thinking

King Louis XI of France, 1423–83, was known as the 'Spider King' as a result of his cunning diplomacy.

A quack doctor once told King Louis that one of his favourite ladies at court would die in eight days. When the prediction proved correct, Louis was infuriated and ordered his servants to fetch the man and be ready to throw him out of the window when he gave the order. When the quack arrived, Louis said to him, 'You pretend to understand astrology as well as medicine, and to know exactly the fate of others. Tell me then, what will be your fate? How long will you live?' The quack, sensing his danger, replied boldly, 'Sire, I shall die just three days before your Majesty.'

❦ The Cyrano of Bulgaria

In 1886 Prince Ferdinand of Coburg took up the vacant throne of Bulgaria in succession to Prince Alexander of Battenburg, who had abdicated after a reign of seven years. Ferdinand had not liked Alexander, a fact that was made quite clear when he first arrived at the royal palace in Sofia.

When Ferdinand first met his Bulgarian tutor, Dobri Gancheff. Gancheff asked the prince if he would be comfortable in his new accommodation. 'Do you know, Mr Gancheff,' Ferdinand replied, 'that the moment I entered the palace I noticed Prince Alexander's smell?' Ferdinand then told him that he had first encountered his predecessor at the coronation of the tsar of Russia where he noticed the unpleasant smell of his body. Gancheff was simply amazed and wrote, 'I had heard it said that a Chinaman can notice the smell of a European in a closed room. But that one German prince should be especially able to detect the smell of another one, amazed me. I tried to believe it, not because Prince

Ferdinand tried to assure me that it was true with all the appearance of sincerity, but because I was looking at his huge nose. A veritable chimney. It particularly reminded me of a chimney when he picked it. Wide, long and voluminous, it was often left out in the cold. He poked about inside it with the calm and patience of a chimney sweep. Why should I not admit to myself that the enormous intake of air of which this gigantic nose was capable might not contain odours which would remain undetected by other, ordinary noses?'

❦ A cold outlook

Tsar Ferdinand of Bulgaria's marriage to Princess Marie-Louise of Bourbon-Parma was a very unhappy one.

Ferdinand treated his wife so badly that he even forbade her to eat at the same table as himself, ordering her to take her meals in her own apartments. One day, Ferdinand's enormous nose detected the smell of cooking in one of the palace corridors. On investigation he learned that the smell came from his wife's meal. He therefore ordered, 'In future, if the queen dines in her apartments she is to be brought cold meals.'

❦ A royal prankster

In December 1909, Tsar Ferdinand of Bulgaria undertook a state visit to Germany. Combining business with pleasure, he was looking for arms suppliers and intended to deal with Krupp of Essen. However, all did not go according to plan.

At a banquet in his honour, held by Kaiser Wilhelm II in the New Palace at Potsdam, Tsar Ferdinand of Bulgaria was standing by a window talking to some other guests. Seeing something that interested him, Ferdinand leant out of the window and as he bent forward, the Kaiser – unable to resist the large area of royal buttock, with stretched uniform breeches – came up quickly and slapped Ferdinand's bottom with a laugh. Ferdinand swung round as if he had been shot and demanded an apology in front of everyone present. The Kaiser said it was just a joke and refused to apologize. Without another word, Ferdinand stormed out of the palace and immediately transferred his military contracts from Krupp to the French company of Schneider-Creusot. Relations between the Kaiser and the Tsar of Bulgaria remained strained for some time. At the funeral in London of King Edward VII in 1910, Ferdinand found himself snubbed by the German emperor. Ferdinand had been talking to ex-President Theodore Roosevelt of the United States, when Wilhelm swept up, put his arm round Roosevelt's shoulders and said, with a furious glance at Ferdinand, 'Roosevelt, my friend, I want to introduce you to the king of Spain. He *is* worth talking to.'

❦ A royal pachyderm

It is sometimes said that owners come to resemble the pets they keep.

Tsar Ferdinand of Bulgaria loved to have wild animals wandering about the grounds of his palace. He kept three elephants, whom he visited regularly, staring at them in silence for long periods. As he once said, 'I enjoy studying their heads – they bear such a strong resemblance to my own.'

❦ Handbags at dawn

Queen Anne continued the anti-French policy of her predecessors, William III and Mary.

Shortly after the accession to the throne of Queen Anne, England declared war on France. King Louis XIV commented sardonically, 'It means I'm growing old when ladies declare war on me.'

❦ In debt but defiant

At the Congress of Vienna in 1814 enormous sums of money were spent by the most prominent Viennese hostesses to entertain the galaxy of visiting notables.

To help finance the entertainments, Tsar Alexander I had willingly provided interest-free loans. The dazzling Molly Zichy-Ferraris had borrowed a million roubles from the tsar on the assumption that he would never ask to be repaid. Unfortunately, on the death of Alexander in 1825, his son, Tsar Nicholas I, demanded repayment of his father's loans. When the ebullient Molly received a final demand she wrote back to the tsar, 'If Your Majesty wants the million back you only need to declare war on me.'

🐾 Spies under the bed – and in it

Catherine de Medici, wife of Henry II and mother of the next three monarchs – Francis II, Charles IX and Henry III – had a reputation as a machiavellian ruler. She was willing to use any means available to keep herself in power, even as far as arranging the massacre of the French Protestants on St Bartholomew's Day in 1571.

During the religious turmoil in France in the mid-sixteenth century, the Regent, Catherine de Medici, had her own band of spies. She selected a number of beautiful and ambitious young women to join her 'Flying Squadron' and used them to entice prominent politicians and diplomats to their beds to learn their secrets.

🐾 The machinery of state

During the French Wars of Religion, Queen Catherine de Medici even resorted to magic to combat her enemies.

Catherine wanted, above all, to destroy the Prince of Condé, Admiral Coligny and his brother, so she engaged an Italian who made 'three bronze figures, of the shape of Condé, the Admiral and Ancelot, full of screws in the joints and the breast to open and shut them and to rivet the arms and the thighs, with the face upturned. Every day the Italian scanned the nativities of these three persons and consulted his astrolabe and screwed and unscrewed the joints.'

❦ A royal lifesaver

In 1571, during the French Wars of Religion, the wedding of King Charles IX's sister, Margaret of Valois, to the Huguenot leader, Henry of Navarre, was used by the Catholics as a ruse to draw all the prominent Protestant leaders into Paris, where they would be killed. The killing began on the evening of St Bartholomew's Day and it took some time for the news of what was happening in the streets to reach the royal palace.

At dawn, Henry of Navarre left his new wife asleep in her room and went off with the Prince of Condé to play tennis. Suddenly, Margaret was awoken by a tremendous banging on her door and a voice shouting, 'Navarre! Navarre!' Margaret's nurse, thinking it was the Prince of Navarre returning, opened the door and a man dashed in, streaming with blood and with two deep gashes in his arms. He threw himself onto the bed and clung to the terrified Margaret. As she rolled onto the floor he clamped his arms around her. As Margaret later said, 'This man was a total stranger to me, and I did not know whether he came there to rape me, or whether the archers were against me or him. We were both of us screaming, and one was just as much alarmed as the other. At last God willed that Monsieur de Nançay, captain of the guard, should come upon the scene who, perceiving me in this plight, could not refrain from laughing in spite of the compassion he felt for me.'

Margaret now learned what was happening outside the palace. The man was one of her husband's captains, who had been set on by the Catholics and had run to warn his lord. She ordered de Nançay to leave, bandaged the man's wounds and hid him under her bed. Quickly changing from her bloodstained nightgown, she tried to reach her sister Claude's bedroom, but as she opened her door, 'a gentleman named Bourse was run through by a pike within three paces of me. I fell to one side, half-fainting, into Monsieur de Nançay's arms, thinking that this thrust was about to impale us both.' But Margaret survived, and later saved the lives of two more of her husband's Huguenot followers.

❦ A professional interest

During the massacre of the Huguenots on St Bartholomew's Day, the girls of Catherine de Medici's 'Flying Squadron' were temporarily redundant.

Many of Catherine's young ladies assembled at the palace to inspect the bodies of the slaughtered Huguenots, some of whom they remembered from having taken them to their beds. With a professional, almost proprietorial air, they requested the king's Swiss guards to let them make very personal inspections of the corpses, including that of the Sieur de Beauvois, who had been in the process of being divorced by his wife for non-consummation of marriage.

❦ Worshipping idols

Tsar Peter the Great of Russia made so many reforms to the everyday lives of Russians that the people began to fear that he would eventually change everything. This resulted in some absurd rumours gaining credence, including one that Peter had been killed by his foreign experts, nailed up in a barrel and thrown into the sea. The man who sat on the throne now was not Peter but Antichrist. It was in this atmosphere that an extraordinary revolt broke out in 1705.

The people listened to a rumour to the effect that Russian men had been forbidden to marry Russian women, who were instead being married off to foreigners arriving in Russia by sea. The result was that, in Astrakhan, mass marriages took place to prevent the foreigners getting the local women. The local people then rushed from the marriage celebrations, beheaded the local governor, and outlawed the worship of idols in Astrakhan. They sent a letter to Moscow telling the tsar that they had killed their governor because he and his ministers kept idols in their houses and were trying to force the people to worship them. Now, the people wrote, the idols had been taken out and destroyed. When Peter sent officials to investigate the insurrection they discovered that the 'idols' had been wig-stands shaped like human heads, which Peter's westernized officials had used to keep their wigs in shape.

❦ A night journey

King Ludwig II of Bavaria was the eccentric patron of Richard Wagner and the builder of a number of fairy-tale castles. In his later years his odd behaviour verged on insanity. One of his courtiers, Graf Trauttmansdorf, describes his nocturnal rides.

The king likes to imagine that he is riding to some particular place. He calculates the distances according to the circumference of the riding school, and then, night after night, rides round and round from 8 o'clock in the evening until 2 or 3 o'clock in the morning, followed by a groom, and changing horses when necessary. After several hours he dismounts and has a picnic supper brought to him on the spot, then remounts and rides on until he calculates that he has reached his goal … The groom who recently rode with him 'from Munich to Innsbruck' received in reward a gold watch and chain.

❦ A game of skittles

King Ludwig suffered from insomnia and often wandered the countryside by night with just a single companion, a young trooper named Thomas Osterauer. On one occasion Ludwig and Osterauer wandered into the mountains and came to a small village inn, which had a skittle-alley. By the light of the moon Ludwig decided to have a game. Osterauer described what happened next.

I set up the skittles and rolled the ball to him. The king had had three or four shots when I suddenly heard the sound of swearing, and the inn-keeper appeared on the scene; he was dressed in his pants and carried a hefty stick, and he was making a fearful shindy. The king sprang out of the alley and ran off across country while I leaped forward, ball in hand. When the inn-keeper found himself face to face with me – I was in full uniform, which we had to wear on Sundays and holidays – he opened his eyes and mouth wide, dropped his stick, turned on his heels and ran into the house, bolting the door after him. I went in pursuit of the king, who imagined that the inn-keeper was at my heels; but after I had called to him a number of times he calmed down. Two days later came a letter from the inn-keeper, begging forgiveness.

❦ Mummy's boy

King Ludwig of Bavaria was obsessed with court etiquette and treated his mother with cold correctness.

Ludwig found it difficult to address his mother directly, usually referring to her as 'the widow of my predecessor' or – curiously – by the honorary title of 'the Colonel of the 3rd Artillery Regiment'. He once told one of her ladies-in-waiting, 'I shall never cease to revere her because she has the honour of being the mother of the King. But there are times when she rather overdoes the mother and rather underdoes the King. I am the Sovereign; she is simply my mother; and at the same time My subject.'

❦ The way to go

King Augustus the Strong of Poland was a larger-than-life character in every way. A huge man in size, and with an enormous appetite for food and for women, he sired 354 bastards and enjoyed snapping horseshoes with his bare hands. He once picked up a trumpeter with each hand and held them while the men kept playing. Even in his old age his appetites remained strong.

When Augustus was told that the Duc d'Orléans had died in the arms of one of his mistresses, he replied, 'Ah, that I may die in this way.'

❦ Barberism

After his return from the West, Peter the Great immediately began to introduce reforms designed to modernize Russia. One of the first was his order forbidding his nobles to wear beards.

Peter was met on his return by hundreds of his leading noblemen, all eager to express their support for him. But Peter was soon to test their resolve. At his first meeting with them he produced a long and very sharp barber's razor, seized them by the beards, one after another, and shaved them very roughly. He began with his leading general, Count Alexis Shein, who was too shocked to offer any resistance. In fact, nobody dared to resist the demon barber, and soon all of his boyars were clean shaven, so that none could laugh at any other. Alone Peter spared the beard of the Orthodox Patriarch.

Peter had a personal hatred of beards, regarding them as useless and uncivilized, making his country and his people a subject for ridicule in the West. Whenever he attended a banquet or a ceremonial occasion, he took his razor with him and those who came with full beards left without them. Within a week of his return from his visit to the West, Peter attended a banquet to which he took his fool – Jacob Turgenev – who acted as impromptu barber. Turgenev had little skill and many faces were left sore and bloodied after he had shaved them. Ridiculous as they felt, none of the boyars dared to object. Any who showed even the slightest reluctance had their ears boxed by the tsar's far from gentle hands.

Eventually, those who were willing to pay heavily for the privilege were allowed to keep their beards but while in the company of the tsar they always risked Peter tearing them out by the roots, with his bare hands.

Yet few Russians parted willingly with their beards. In one case, as John Perry, an English carpenter who had returned under contract to Peter relates, an old Russian carpenter had just had his beard shaved off because the tsar was visiting his town. Perry joked with the man, telling him that he had become young again, and asking him what he had done with his beard. The old man put his hand inside his coat and pulled out the beard, saying that he would keep it at home so that it could be placed in his coffin and buried with him. He did this, he said, so that he would be able to show it to Saint Nicholas when he went to the other world. He added that all his brothers intended to do the same thing with their beards.

♥ Muzzy Capel's dentist

After the abdication of Napoleon in 1814, Tsar Alexander I visited London. He was an enormous success with the common people but not everyone was so impressed.

The Channel crossing had been a rough one and the tsar had been seasick for much of the voyage. One seventeen-year-old English girl, who had been waiting with her family at Dover to witness the arrival of the Russian royal party, was disappointed with what she saw. Muzzy Capel commented, 'I was near enough to touch them and think Alexander not the least handsome – horridly pink and pudding-like. He looked like our dentist.'

♥ A poor prince

When Tsar Alexander I arrived in London on 7 June, 1814, he travelled straight to the Pulteney Hotel where he was staying and where he met his sister, the Grand Duchess Catherine. He was surprised that the Prince Regent did not welcome him to his capital city.

The tsar waited patiently to meet Prince George but he did not turn up. Eventually a message arrived at the hotel explaining that the Prince Regent had been 'threatened with annoyance' if he appeared in the streets and that he dared not drive to meet the tsar for fear of being hissed by the mob and pelted with eggs. The message therefore asked the tsar if he would drive to Carlton House where the Prince Regent would be waiting to meet him. Alexander drove through the London streets to the cheers of the crowds but spent only a short time at Carlton House, commenting as he left that the Prince Regent was 'a poor prince'.

♥ A stage whisper

Relations between the British royal family and their Russian visitors remained strained in 1814. The Prince Regent felt that Tsar Alexander was deliberately snubbing him. At a palace banquet George introduced his latest mistress to the tsar.

Prince George took his current mistress, Lady Hertford, to present her to the tsar. Alexander, at that moment, was ogling an attractive lady through his spyglass and hardly heard the Prince Regent's introduction: 'This is Lady Hertford.' The tsar bowed in his cold fashion but half-turned away to continue viewing the other lady. The Prince Regent, knowing that the tsar was hard of hearing and assuming that he had not heard what he said, repeated in a very loud voice, 'This is Lady Hertford.' The tsar bowed again and then turned to his sister and said in a stage whisper, 'She looks mighty old.'

❦ Love and marriage

The disastrous marriage between George, the Prince Regent, and Princess Caroline of Brunswick was one of the great scandals of the age. During their visit to London in June 1814 the Russian royal family, notably the tsar's sister Catherine, made frequent reference to the fact that the prince and his wife were living apart, thereby embarrassing Prince George. At a dinner party given by the prime minister, Lord Liverpool, the Russian Grand Duchess and the Prince Regent were seated next to each other and the following exchange took place about the prince's daughter, Charlotte.

Catherine: Why then, Your Highness, do you keep your daughter under lock and key? Why does she go nowhere with you?

Regent: My daughter is too young, Madame, to go into the world.

Catherine: She is not too young for you to have fixed on a husband for her.

Regent: She will not marry for two years.

Catherine: When she does marry, I do hope she will manage to make up to herself for her present prison.

Regent: When she is married, Madame, she will do as her husband pleases. For the present she does as I wish.

Catherine: Your Highness is right. Between husband and wife there can only be one will.

Regent: (turning purple with rage) This is intolerable.

❦ 'Well, let them bawl, then.'

Since her arrival in England on the tsar's royal visit of June, 1814, the Grand Duchess Catherine had proved to be a very difficult guest. She found fault with almost everything and made it known that music of any kind made her physically sick. When the City of London staged a great banquet for the tsar at the Guildhall – an occasion normally for men only – Catherine insisted on attending and making her presence felt.

As soon as the guests were seated, the Italian singers, who had been hired for the occasion, began their programme of songs. Scarcely had a note passed their lips when the grand duchess leaned over to warn the prince regent, 'If the music goes on I'm going to be sick.' In alarm, Prince George stood up and ordered the music to stop, much to the annoyance of the rest of the audience. As the musicians put away their instruments, people began to remonstrate with the regent, one telling him, 'This won't do in England.' The regent was caught between a rock and a hard place. He pleaded with the grand duchess that the orchestra might at least play 'God save the King'. But Catherine was adamant. At this point an anonymous note was passed to the regent saying, 'If your duchess does not allow the music, we won't answer for the royal table.' When she heard the threat Catherine shrugged her shoulders, 'Well, let them bawl, then!' The national anthem was played but the popularity of the tsar and his sister – and incidentally of the prince regent – sank even lower.

❦ Back to the womb

Prince Napoleon, nephew of Napoleon I and cousin of Napoleon III, was known by the nickname Plon-Plon. Before the birth of the Prince Imperial to Napoleon III and the Empress Eugénie, he was the heir to the French throne, and he was bitterly disappointed when a baby was born. His behaviour on that occasion was most extraordinary. When called on to sign the baby's birth certificate he refused, at first, on the grounds that he had not been in the room at the moment the baby was born and had not seen it emerge from the womb. Only when his sister, Princess Mathilde, criticized him for his behaviour would he agree to sign. Matters were even worse at the baby's christening.

Plon-Plon was the godfather to the new Prince Imperial but during the christening ceremony at the cathedral of Notre Dame, he was so choked with anger at the thought of what he had lost that he could not pronounce the names of the baby. His sister, Mathilde, angrily told him to do his duty, observing that the baby was a fact and he must get used to it. 'You can't get him to go back in,' said Mathilde.

❦ The almost queen of France

A fortune teller once prophesied that the pretty little daughter of Jeanne-Antoinette Poisson and his wife would become the – almost – Queen of France. She was right. The girl grew up to become Madame de Pompadour.

Jeanne-Antoinette Poisson regarded the prophecy as ridiculous but his wife took it more seriously. From that moment she began to prepare her daughter for greatness. She set aside as much money as possible to see that the girl got the best education and was always impeccably dressed. At an early age she was introduced to the great salons of Paris, meeting there such luminaries as Montesquieu, Fontenelle and Marivaux. Although she was married early to a Monsieur d'Etoiles, this was not intended to present any obstacle to her rise towards greatness. Ignoring her husband, Madame d'Etoiles now took up the running from her mother and herself began the pursuit of Louis XV. She became a leader of Parisian society, arriving at the royal hunt on successive days, first wearing a light blue costume in a pink phaeton, then a pink costume in a blue phaeton. The king found it difficult to resist this dazzling young woman. The next step was for Madame d'Etoiles to be introduced at court. Through a family contact she was introduced to Louis XV at Versailles on 27 February 1745. It was a masked ball and the king's attention was immediately taken up by one young lady who, when passing by him, dropped her handkerchief (everyone but he saw that it was thrown) and as Louis stooped to pick it up he asked if the mysterious lady would unmask herself. She did so and Louis was smitten. With her husband moved to a far-off province, Madame d'Etoiles was free to install herself at Versailles and become the – almost – Queen of France, as the Marquise de Pompadour.

❦ A royal benefactor

The Prussian king, Frederick William I, was noted for his parsimony.

When the court physician managed to save Frederick William's son from a virulent attack of smallpox, the king in his intense gratitude ordered the successful doctor to be paid with two bottles of beer and a dinner which was not to exceed the value of nine pence. Later, when his favourite stallion was taken seriously ill, to his evident distress, he placed the animal in the care of General Schwarin who, after devoting many hours of his time to the animal, succeeded in curing it and triumphantly returned it to the king in the bloom of health. Frederick William was so delighted that he awarded the general's nephew, who had brought the horse back, a full breakfast and sent him back to his uncle with a royal reward of one florin.

❦ The next generation

Prince Rudolf of Habsburg, son of the Emperor Franz Joseph and the Empress Elizabeth, indulged in many youthful pranks. In this he was led astray by his cousin Archduke Otto. On one occasion, Archduke Otto had emerged from a bedroom at the Hotel Sacher wearing a cap, gloves and his sabre, but otherwise completely naked.

Otto, Rudolf and another cousin, Franz Ferdinand, were riding in the Prater woods when they encountered a funeral procession. The three young officers ordered it to halt and then took it in turns to jump their horses over the coffin. The incident was taken so seriously that it was taken up in Parliament by Deputy

Engelbert Pernersdorfer. In retaliation, the royal officers arranged for some of their friends to administer a sound thrashing to Pernersdorfer. The police were called and the young royals were summoned to account for their actions, but as Rudolf told his wife, the men responsible had been 'spirited away, one to Hungary and the other to Herzegovina'.

❦ The Emperor of the Peasants

Napoleon III, like his uncle the great Napoleon, never lost touch with his simple origins.

One evening, on turning up at a village dance near Vichy, the Emperor Napoleon III singled out a good-looking girl and asked her to be his partner. It was by no means the first time he had done such a thing, but it aroused all the customary enthusiasm. While the dance proceeded, however, an old peasant among the onlookers remarked to the orderly in mufti, who was in attendance on the emperor: 'Think of that now! Do you see how pleased Marie Boilon looks at having the emperor for her partner? She's my niece, you know.'

'Ah,' said the officer. 'She certainly does look pleased, as you say.'

'Yes,' continued the old man, 'she won't forget it, not if she lives for a hundred years. *Voyez-vous, Monsieur*, I am getting old and I have seen a few things in my time. We had Charles X, he was the King of the Nobility. Then we had Louis Philippe, he was the King of the Bourgeois. But Napoleon – you can't say the contrary – he's the Emperor of the Peasants.'

❦ An air of dread

King Henry IV of France survived the appalling killing of Huguenots during the Massacre of St Bartholomew's Day, but it left its mark on him. For years afterwards he related a dreadful experience that he had shared with King Charles IX in the aftermath of the slaughter.

A week after the massacre, a great host of crows came and settled on the pavilion of the Louvre. Their noise made people come out to see them, and the ladies sent to tell the king how frightened they were. The same night the king, two hours after he had gone to bed, leapt up, aroused all the people of his bedchamber and sent for me among others, to come and hear a great din and noise in the air, a concert of shrieking, groaning and howling voices, just like those that were heard on the nights of the massacres. The sounds were so clear that the king, believing that there was a fresh outbreak, had the guards called out to hurry into the city and stop the killing. But they came back and said that the city was at peace and that only the air was troubled; and he too remained troubled, chiefly because the noise went on for seven days, always at the same time.

❦ An emperor and a gentleman

The Emperor Napoleon III, in spite of his claims to be of humble origin, was very much a product of a bourgeois upbringing. In a world of hereditary monarchs he longed to be accepted by them as their equal.

During the visit of the French royal family to England in 1855, the main events at Windsor Castle included a ball, during which Queen Victoria danced with the Emperor Napoleon III. As she said afterwards, 'Really, to think of a granddaughter of George III dancing with the nephew of our great enemy, the Emperor Napoleon, now my most firm ally, and in the *Waterloo Gallery* is incredible.' The following day the emperor was invested with the Order of the Garter. As he received it, one onlooker commented that he had never before seen such a look of triumph on anyone's face. Napoleon was indeed delirious with joy. As he left the room, he whispered to Queen Victoria, *'Enfin je suis gentilhomme.'*

❦ The club of kings

Edward, Prince of Wales, did not come to the throne of Great Britain as King Edward VII until he was sixty years old. His prolonged period of waiting enabled him to give advice to several generations of young foreign royals.

At a regal function in London, Edward, was called on to explain to Frederick, Crown Prince of Germany, why he had been asked to yield precedence to the visiting King Kalakaua of Hawaii. Edward told his German brother-in-law, 'Either the brute is a king or he's a common or garden nigger; and, if the latter, what's he doing here?'

❦ You're a better man than I am, Caroline

Caroline Mathilda, sister of King George III, was married to King Christian VII of Denmark, who was widely held to be insane.

Caroline was packed off to Denmark without any close friends and immediately found herself the chosen target of the Dowager Queen Juliana Maria, whose son would ascend the throne if Caroline and new husband failed to provide an heir, which was all too likely as Christian was believed to be homosexual. To try to win him away from his pages and young men, Caroline took to dressing in male attire. But this merely served to make her a figure of fun. One lady of the court observed, 'If only she were well made I could understand her walking about in the costume but just think of her hips, her – quarters.' Nevertheless, Christian preferred her dressed as a man and made her ride astride, dressed as a cavalry officer. When Caroline visited England for a time, courtiers were amazed to find her wearing 'military uniform, with beaver hat, top boots, spurs and bulging buckskin breeches'. The joke among the Danes was that when they saw the king and queen together, she was the better man of the two.

❦ Clinging on to life

In March 1582, a Catholic assassin, Juan Jauréguy, had fired a pistol at William from such close range that he had set the prince's hair and beard alight. The wound in his neck seemed likely to prove fatal but through the astonishing attention of his servants, who held the wound closed with their fingers in relays for seventeen days, William's life was saved.

❦ William the Hun

At the time of the Boxer Rebellion in China, in July 1900, the Kaiser reviewed his troops at Bremerhaven and made one of the most extraordinary – indeed infamous – speeches in modern history. So passionate did the Kaiser feel on the subject of the Boxers that he allowed his emotions to get the better of him and, as a result, he tarred the German nation with the brush of barbarism of which – a century later – it still struggles to be free.

The Kaiser announced to his troops, 'You must know, my men, that you are about to meet a crafty, well-armed, cruel foe. Meet him and beat him! Give him no quarter! Take no prisoners! Kill him when he falls into your hands! Even as, a thousand years ago, the Huns under their king Attila made such a name for themselves as still resounds in legend and fable, so may the name of Germans resound through Chinese history a thousand years from now . . . ' Wilhelm's Chancellor, Prince Bernhard von Bülow, who heard the speech, described it as 'the worst speech of this period'.

❦ 10. THE WAY WE WERE

❦ The sex life of a piano

During Captain Marryat's visit to the United States in 1827, he was told by Mrs Frances Trollope, mother of the novelist, just how sensitive the Americans were about sexual matters. She told him that they rarely used the word 'leg' and even spoke of the 'limbs' of a table or a piano. Soon Captain Marryat found out the truth of this assertion for himself.

One day the captain found himself escorting a young lady to a seminary for young ladies. As Marryat wrote, he entered a room and 'conceive my astonishment at beholding a square pianoforte with four *limbs*. However, that the ladies who visited their daughters might feel in its full force the extreme delicacy of the mistress of the establishment and her care to preserve in their utmost purity the ideas of the young ladies under her charge, she had dressed all these four limbs in modest little trousers, with frills at the bottom of them!'

❦ The sound of silence

The British naturalist Charles Darwin published his On the Origin of Species *in 1859 which established the theory of evolution by natural selection.*

Charles Darwin remembered a curious dinner at his brother's house, where, amongst a few others, were Babbage and Lyell, both of whom liked to talk. Carlyle, however, silenced everyone by haranguing during the whole dinner on the advantages of silence. After dinner, Babbage, in his grimmest manner, thanked Carlyle for his very interesting lecture on silence.

❦ The fall and rise of a foote

The British actor Samuel Foote was famous in the eighteenth century for his comedy roles.

Edward Augustus, Duke of York, son of King George III, once played a practical joke on the actor Samuel Foote, who was noted as a very poor rider. The duke and his friends mounted Foote on the most vicious horse they could find, one they described as 'gentle enough to carry any lady', which promptly threw Foote off its back, breaking the actor's leg so badly that it had to be amputated. The tragic accident was redeemed when the duke persuaded his father, the king, to give the actor the patent on a small theatre in the Haymarket. Foote accepted the challenge and it made his fortune.

❦ The unspoken word

Margot Asquith, second wife of the Liberal Prime Minister Herbert Asquith, was a writer and a brilliant wit.

Margot Asquith once attended a party in Hollywood, at which she encountered Jean Harlow, the sex-goddess of the motion picture industry. When they met, Miss Harlow deliberately mispronounced Margot's name as MARGOTT, whereupon Margot replied, 'No, my dear, the "T" is silent as in Harlow.'

❦ Quick thinking

The French statesman Charles Maurice de Talleyrand-Périgord was also a brilliant socialite and wit.

Talleyrand was once sitting between Madame de Staël and the famous beauty Madame Recamier, his attention very much engaged with the latter. Madame de Staël made a bid to get into the conversation. 'Monsieur Talleyrand, if you and I and Madame Recamier were shipwrecked together and you could only save one of us, which would you save?' Talleyrand replied with his deepest bow, 'Madame, you know everything, so clearly you know how to swim.'

❦ Let the punishment fit the crime

The British prime minister Earl Russell, 1846–52, 1865–66, had a droll sense of humour.

Asked his opinion as to the appropriate punishment for bigamy, Russell replied, 'Two mothers-in-law.'

❦ Discretion

Earl Russell once recounted to a friend how at a party he had left the Duchess of Inverness and gone across to talk to the Duchess of Sutherland because the Duchess of Inverness had been sitting too close to the fire. 'I hope you told the Duchess of Inverness why you abandoned her,' said his friend. Russell thought for a moment and then said, 'No – but I did tell the Duchess of Sutherland.'

❦ Time for reflection

Erasmus Darwin, the eighteenth-century physician and botanist, was the grandfather of Charles Darwin. In spite of his great achievements he felt he was held back by a speech impediment.

A young man once asked him in, as he thought, an offensive manner, whether he did not find stammering very inconvenient. He answered, 'No, Sir, it gives me time for reflection, and saves me from asking impertinent questions.'

❦ Drunk by God!

The eighteenth-century physician, George Fordyce, was noted for his heavy drinking.

239

Fordyce was once called to see a lady patient, when he was rather the worse for drink, and quite aware that he was. First he felt her pulse, and then, finding himself unable to keep a steady count, he muttered, 'Drunk, by God!' Next morning, remembering what had happened, he was very annoyed with himself: and while he was thinking how he could explain his behaviour, a letter from the lady was put into his hand. 'She too well knew,' said the letter, 'that he had discovered the unfortunate condition in which she was when he last visited her; and she entreated him to keep the matter secret in consideration of the enclosed (a hundred pound banknote).'

❦ The bare necessity

Sir Thomas More, the author of Utopia, *was one of the greatest of Tudor statesmen. He was executed by Henry VIII for refusing to accept the Act of Supremacy.*

Memorandum that in his Utopia his Lawe is that the young people are to see each other stark naked before marriage. Sir William Roper of Eltham in Kent came one morning pretty early to my lord with a proposal to marry one of his daughters. My lord's daughters were then both together a bed in a truckle-bed in their father's chamber asleep. He carries Sir William into the chamber and takes the sheet by the corner and suddenly whippes it off. They lay on their Backs, and their smocks up as high as their armpitts. This awakened them, and immediately they turned on their Bellies. Quoth Roper, I have seen both sides, and so gave a patt on her buttock he made choice of, sayeing, Thou art mine. Here was all the trouble of the wooing.

❦ Nonsense

William Pitt the Younger was no great lover of women.

For a while Jane, Duchess of Gordon, was his favourite hostess and she was far from being a shy woman. Once when she met Pitt after a long period of separation she asked him, 'Well, Mr Pitt, do you talk as much nonsense as you used to when you lived with me?'

'I do not know, madam, whether I talk so much nonsense,' he replied. 'I certainly do not *hear* so much.'

❦ Between friends

British politician and statesman George Canning was largely responsible for British foreign policy in the period immediately after the defeat of Napoleon.

When the Bishop of Oxford was due to give his first sermon he asked George Canning to be present. Afterwards he asked his friend how he had got on.

'Well,' asked the new bishop. 'How did you like it?'

'Why,' replied Canning, 'I thought it rather – short.'

'Oh, yes, I am aware that it was short, but I was afraid of being tedious.'

'You *were* tedious.'

❦ The root of the problem

Sarah Jennings, friend and lady-in-waiting to Queen Anne, married John Churchill, who later became Duke of Marlborough. Sarah was noted for her abrasive character.

The grandson of the Duke and Duchess of Marlborough found it very difficult to make his own mind up when it came to selecting a wife. The duchess – who had been Sarah Jennings and was famous for her cantankerous personality – made the boy's life a misery by interfering in everything he did. When he eventually found a bride for himself and brought her to meet his grand-mother, she told the young couple, 'I am the root and you are only the branches and therefore you must always pay me a great deal of deference.' Jack replied in exasperation, 'That is all very well – but I think the branches would flourish a great deal better if the root was under ground.'

❦ Here, bring that back

In Victorian times, while attending royal dinners, it was the custom for guests to stop eating as soon as the queen herself stopped.

On one occasion, however, Lord Hartington quite forgot himself. Enjoying a saddle of four-year-old mutton, a speciality of the kitchens at Windsor Castle, Hartington turned his head to speak to his neighbour. When he looked back he found that his half-eaten dinner had been whisked away as the queen had finished eating. Forgetting himself he called out, 'Here, bring that back.'

❦ Deceiving the electors

Oliver Cromwell was not entirely the humourless individual that history records.

Once when Cromwell was entertaining some of his friends to dinner, a confidential servant came to him to say that 'a body of the Elect' was waiting outside for admittance. 'Tell them,' said Cromwell, looking under the table, 'that we are seeking for the Lord.' Once the servant had gone, Cromwell turned to the others and said, 'These fools think that I am seeking for the Lord while I am only seeking for the corkscrew.'

❦ A considerate judge

Justice Sir Robert Graham was regarded as the most polite judge in the country.

On one occasion it was said that he had hastily condemned a man, who had been capitally convicted, to transportation, when the clerk of the court in a whisper set him right. 'Oh,' he exclaimed. 'Criminal, I beg your pardon, come back.' And, putting on the black cap, he courteously apologized for his mistake, and consigned him instead to the gallows to be hanged by the neck until he was dead.

❦ This year's colour

By the late 1860s the influence in Paris of Germany's 'Iron' Chancellor – Prince Bismarck – was apparent in unusual ways.

The fashionable colours in Paris – primrose, blue, lavender, maize, mauve and white – were ousted between 1866 and 1868 by a very sober colour which was given the name 'Bismarck'. Never in all the annals of fashion has a colour had so long and popular a run. It was, after all, merely a kind of Havana Brown, and owed its fortune solely to its name. But in the days of Sadowa that was a name to conjure with. At first this fashionable colour appeared in a fairly warm shade, known simply as Bismarck – written Bismark, by the way; but it suddenly took a duller tone, and became known as *Bismarck malade*, until at last, assuming yet warmer tints than before, it was christened successively *Bismarck content* and *Bismarck en colère*. There were also such varieties as *Bismarck glacé* and *Bismarck scintillant*. And it was Bismarck of one or another shade everywhere; there were Bismarck silks, satins, and velvets, woollen stuffs and cotton fabrics, Bismarck boots, Bismarck gloves, Bismarck parasols and Bismarck bonnets. The last were naturally of Bismarck straw, trimmed with Bismarck lace, the only relief from the various shades of the all-prevailing colour being supplied by gold and scarlet berries. But even the Bismarck bonnet was not the 'last cry' for there came a Bismarck chignon, which compelled ladies to dye their hair the fashionable hue.

❦ A butler ousts a chamberlain

Conservative politician Austen Chamberlain was the son of Joseph Chamberlain and the brother of Neville. As Foreign Secretary in 1925, Austen negotiated the Locarno Treaty.

At an important dinner party given by Tory hostess Mrs Ronnie Greville, Tory politician Austen Chamberlain was the guest of honour. He gave a speech on the subject of 'Ireland' and was engrossed in the story of the 1886 split in the Liberal Party over Home Rule when Mrs Greville's attention was drawn to the unsteady condition of her butler, a man noted for his tendency to drink too much. Mrs Greville hurriedly wrote something on a scribbling pad and called the butler to her, handing him the message she had just written. The butler placed the note on the silver salver he was carrying and, walking with exaggerated care, took it to Austen Chamberlain and presented it to him with a deep bow. Chamberlain stopped talking for a moment, fixed his monocle in his eye and glanced at the note. It said, 'You are drunk. Leave the room.'

❧ Beneath every woman

Nancy Astor was the first woman to take her seat in the House of Commons. Her acerbic wit and boundless energy proved irritating to some of her more stolid colleagues.

Nancy Astor's arrival in the House of Commons as an MP proved to be very irritating for the anti-feminists there, of whom there were many. As a result she felt it necessary to prove herself superior to her male colleagues since, as she said, women were the superior sex. As she explained one day to a particularly chauvinist member, 'I married beneath me, you know – all women do.'

❧ A choir of angels

The great German composer Johannes Brahms was not noted for his social skills.

Brahms once found himself cornered by a group of talkative ladies. Unable to escape, he took out a cigar and began to light it. Engulfed in smoke, the ladies complained of Brahms's lack of consideration for them, saying that no gentlemen ever smoked in the presence of ladies. Brahms replied, 'Ladies, where there are angels, there must also be clouds.'

❧ A divine sense of humour

The English actress Beatrice Stella Tanner, more generally known as Mrs Patrick Campbell, was famous both for her wit and for her temper tantrums.

When asked once by a most pompous gentleman why she thought women were so devoid of a sense of humour, she replied, 'God did it on purpose, so that we may love you men instead of laughing at you.'

❦ Anything you can do

A dinner party with both Nancy Astor and Winston Churchill present was a gift from the gods for anecdotalists.

During a dinner party at which both Winston Churchill and Nancy Astor were present, sometime before the First World War, the question of female representation in Parliament was raised. Winston and Nancy were soon involved in a sharp difference of opinion. At last Nancy snapped, 'Winston, if you were my husband I'd poison your coffee.' Without a moment's thought Churchill hit back, 'Nancy, if you were my wife, I'd drink it.'

❦ A convenient affliction

François René, Vicomte de Chateaubriand, was a French author and statesman, who lived in exile in England during the period of the French Revolution but returned to France after Napoleon became emperor, occupying important diplomatic posts.

As he grew older, Chateaubriand became a little deaf, an affliction that evoked a biting comment from one of his old enemies, Talleyrand: 'He thinks he is deaf now that he no longer hears himself talked about.'

❦ Make him a bishop

The English politician Lord Chesterfield was noted for his cynical wit.

During the eighteenth century the popularity of the preacher, George Whitefield, was such that the Privy Council debated whether something should be done to stop his vast evangelical meetings. Chesterfield, however, had a better suggestion. 'Make him a bishop,' he said, 'and you will silence him at once.'

❦ Dress rehearsal

In old age, Lord Chesterfield became so frail that when he went out in his carriage the horses had to be led at a slow, walking pace. A friend, meeting him one day, commented that it was nice to see him taking the air. Chesterfield replied, 'I do not come out so much for the air, as for the benefit of rehearsing my funeral.'

❦ A prize pupil

Sir Cyril Dyson was an important British businessman and was President of the National Association of Goldsmiths.

Sir Cyril Dyson was once asked to give the prizes at the speech day of a prominent girls' school. However, after giving out a number of the awards he found it increasingly difficult to think of anything new to say to each of the prizewinners. Eventually, as a particularly attractive senior girl came up for her prize, Dyson fell back on the words, 'And what are you going to do when you leave school?' The girl fluttered her eyelashes and replied, 'Well, I *had* thought of going straight home.'

❦ A daring proposal

Princess Pauline Metternich was a leader of society in Paris during the Second Empire.

The princess was travelling on a train one day towards Compiègne. She was sharing a compartment with a gentleman, who asked politely if she would mind if he smoked. The princess, in her grandest manner, replied, 'I have no idea, Monsieur. No one has ever dared to smoke in my presence.'

❦ He stoops to conquer

Count d'Orsay was a leading French socialite who spent much time in London during the early years of Queen Victoria's reign. He lived far beyond his means and was in constant fear of being arrested for debt.

246

Count d'Orsay was once dining in London and was seated next to the flirtatious Lady Holland. The lady monopolized the count and whenever his attention strayed elsewhere she recaptured it by dropping something so that d'Orsay was forced to pick it up for her. First she dropped her napkin, then a spoon and then her fan. Eventually, d'Orsay lost patience and asked a footman to place his plates and cutlery on the floor, saying, 'I shall finish my dinner there. It will be so much more convenient for my lady Holland.'

❦ A faithful husband

The French statesman Armand-Emmanuel du Plessis, Duc de Richelieu, played an important role in the restoration of Louis XVIII in 1815.

Richelieu was married at the early age of fifteen to a deformed girl, who was only twelve. His relationship with his wife was purely platonic and she eventually took lovers. Once, when he came upon her *in flagrante delicto*, Richelieu admonished her, 'Madame, you must be more careful. Suppose it had been somebody else who found you like this.'

❦ Better dead than wet

The French writer Charles Augustin Sainte-Beuve was noted for his fastidious attention to details.

Sainte-Beuve was once involved in a duel with pistols. More at home with the pen than with the sword, Sainte-Beuve was nevertheless prepared to pursue this affair of honour to the bitter end. But at the crucial moment, just as he was preparing to fire at his rival, it began to rain. Sainte-Beuve called for a pause while he returned to his carriage to fetch an umbrella. As he said, 'I do not mind being killed but I do mind getting wet.'

❦ The ghoul

The British politician and eccentric, George Selwyn, had an obsession with death.

247

When Lord Holland was dying, Selwyn called upon him and left his card. His lordship, hearing that his old friend had just called, instructed his footman: 'If Mr Selwyn calls again, show him up. If I am alive I shall be glad to see him, and if I am dead, I am sure he will be delighted to see me.'

❦ The path to glory

The American dancer Isadora Duncan achieved worldwide fame for her new style of dancing – barefoot and in flimsy, revealing costumes – and notoriety for her flamboyant lifestyle. Her death was in keeping with her extraordinary life.

In 1925 Isadora Duncan insisted on being taken for a drive from a studio at Nice by a young Italian. As she went out of the studio she called out, 'Goodbye friends, I am going to glory.' As the car started Isadora was seen to throw the long fringed end of her shawl over her left shoulder. The car started forward at full speed and the shawl seemed to trail on the ground beside the wheel. Mary Destri screamed, 'Your shawl, Isadora, pick up your shawl.' The car stopped. The watchers thought it was to allow Isadora to pick up the end of the shawl. They walked towards it and saw that Isadora's head had fallen forward. They ran. The driver was out of the car gesticulating, howling in Italian, 'I have killed the Madonna.' The shawl had caught in the wheel of the car and her neck had been snapped, killing her instantly.

❦ Dire prospect

Irish playwright and Socialist thinker George Bernard Shaw was also noted for his sharp wit.

The famous dancer Isadora Duncan once suggested to George Bernard Shaw that they should have a child together. 'Think of it,' she said, 'with my body and your brains, what a wonder it would be.' Shaw replied, 'Yes, but what if it had my body and your brains?'

❦ Evidently confused

F E Smith, later Lord Birkenhead, was the most brilliant barrister of his day. Yet even Smith found difficulty with some witnesses.

Once when he was cross-examining a very nervous witness, F E asked him: 'Have you ever been married?'

'Yes, sir,' replied the witness, 'once.'

'Whom did you marry?'

'A – er – a woman, sir.'

'Of course, of course,' Smith said impatiently. 'Did you ever hear of anyone marrying a man?'

'Er – yes, sir,' said the frightened witness. 'My sister did.'

❦ Our queer old dean

William Archibald Spooner, who was the Warden of New College, Oxford, earned immortality as a result of his originally unintentional transposition of the initial letters of words to cause a humorous effect. However, apart from this, he was also rather an absent-minded man.

Once meeting an apparent stranger in the quadrangle at his college Spooner invited him to tea saying, 'I'm giving a little party for the new mathematics Fellow.'

'But, Warden,' said the man, 'I am the new mathematics Fellow.'

'Never mind,' replied Spooner. 'Come all the same.'

❦ Reliable servants

On his travels in North America in 1795 Isaac Weld met the Duc de la Rochefoucauld-Liancourt, who had barely escaped with his life from the Reign of Terror in his homeland. Weld was told of the aristocrat's altered circumstances. 'When I was in France,' said the Duke, 'I had sixteen servants to wait on me. Now that I have only two, I am better attended than ever I was. And here,' he added, holding up his two hands, 'are those two servants.'

❦ The biter bit

The 5th Earl of Berkeley, who died in 1810, had always declared that anyone might without disgrace be overcome by superior numbers, but that he would never surrender to a single highwayman.

As the earl was crossing Hounslow Heath one night, on his way from Berkeley Castle to London, his travelling carriage was stopped by a man on horseback, who put his head in at the window and said, 'I believe you are Lord Berkeley?'

'I am,' replied his lordship.

'I also believe you have always boasted that you would never surrender to a single highwayman?'

'That is true.'

'Well,' said the highwayman, showing his pistol, 'I am a single highwayman, and I say, "Your money or your life."'

'You cowardly dog,' said Lord Berkeley, 'do you think I cannot see your confederate skulking behind you?'

The highwayman, who was really alone, looked around in surprise, and Lord Berkeley shot him through the head.

❦ Yes, we have no 'Forbidden Fruit'

Thomas Johnson had a shop on Snow Hill in London. It was in this shop on Snow Hill that the banana was first exhibited in England. Johnson received the bunch of fruit from Dr Argent, who got it from Bermuda. Johnson hung the bunch up in his shop until it ripened. As he said: 'Some have judged it the forbidden fruit: others the grapes brought to Moses out of the Holy Land.'

❦ Lord Kitchener smiles

Lord Kitchener, Secretary for War in 1914, had few friends and was so aloof that he was thought to dislike the whole of humanity. However, his most particular hatred was reserved for what he called 'club-frequenting politicians'.

Once, when Kitchener was in a particularly bitter mood, he was asked what would make him really happy. He replied, 'First, secure a full sitting of the House of Commons, then bar and bolt all the exits and entrances except one; next place me with half a dozen men and a couple of machine guns at that one and finally set fire to the building. I think I could promise you a smile of satisfaction at the end of the entertainment.'

❦ Fresh meat

Thomas Babington, Lord Macaulay, was a Scottish writer and statesman. For four years in the 1830s he worked on the Supreme Council for India.

When Macaulay was about to leave for India in 1833, he consulted the brother of Sydney Smith – who had spent many years in the subcontinent – for advice on what to wear and how to behave. Smith told him about precautions to take against snakes and particularly mosquitoes: 'Always, sir, manage to have at your table some fleshy, blooming, young writer or cadet, just come out; that the mosquitoes may stick to him, and leave the rest of the company alone.'

❦ Must try harder

On his deathbed, John Philpot Curran, the Irish lawyer and wit, was told by his physician that he seemed to be coughing with difficulty. He replied, 'That is rather surprising, doctor, as I have been practising all night.'

❦ A ripping yarn

Madame de Staël was the daughter of the noted French statesman Jacques Necker. She was a prominent writer and political commentator and among her lovers numbered Talleyrand and Benjamin Constant. She was a noted opponent of the Emperor Napoleon.

Just two weeks after her marriage to the Swedish nobleman, Baron Eric Magnus Staël von Holstein, Madame Germaine de Staël was presented to King Louis XVI and Queen Marie Antoinette at

Versailles. She was wearing a magnificent dress, the creation of Paris's leading couturier, but Germaine was young and rather gauche and, in getting out of her coach, she had slightly weakened the seams. When she was presented to the queen she curtsied and trod on the inside of her dress so that when she straightened up she tore the bottom section away, leaving her standing in her undergarments. Seeing her shock and amazement and hearing a titter run round the assembled courtiers, King Louis commented with a smile, 'If you cannot feel at ease with us, you will never feel at ease anywhere.' The following day the Paris newspapers had the story and some of Germaine's admirers were composing quatrains on her graceful modesty at the moment of crisis, while others maliciously countered with epigrams about her clumsiness.

❦ Made to measure

In June 1811, a wager was made for one thousand guineas that a coat could not be made from freshly shorn wool between sunrise and sunset in a single day. The attempt was made on Tuesday, 25 June.

On the day at five o'clock in the morning Sir John Throckmorton, a Berkshire baronet, presented two Southdown sheep to Mr Coxeter, of Greenham Mills, near Newbury in Berkshire. The sheep were immediately shorn, the wool sorted and spun, the yarn spooled, warped, loomed and woven. The cloth was burred, milled, rowed, dyed, dried, sheared and pressed. The cloth, having thus been made in eleven hours, was put into the hands of the tailors at four o'clock in the afternoon, who completed the coat at twenty minutes past six. Mr Coxeter then presented the coat to Sir John Throckmorton, who appeared with it the same evening at the Pelican Inn, Speenhamland.

The cloth was a hunting kersey of the admired dark Wellington colour...It was supposed that upwards of five thousand people were assembled to witness this singular, unprecedented performance which was completed in the space of thirteen hours and twenty minutes. Sir John and about forty gentlemen sat down to a dinner provided by Mr Coxeter and spent the evening with the utmost satisfaction at the success of their undertaking.

❦ The naughty bits

Henry Best records an extraordinary meeting between Dr Johnson and some female admirers of his dictionary.

Mrs Brooke, authoress of *Julia Mandeville, Emily Montagu* and the musical piece *Rosina* and other works popular in their day, and of no small merit – this lady was sister to the wife of my great Uncle Joseph Digby, rector of Tinwell near Stamford...Mrs Digby told me that when she lived in London with her sister, Mrs Brooke, they were, every now and then, honoured by the visits of Dr Samuel Johnson. He called on them one day, soon after the publication of his immortal dictionary. The two ladies paid him due compliments on the occasion. Amongst other topics of praise they very much commended the omission of all *naughty* words. 'What, my dears! Then you have been looking for them?' said the moralist. The ladies, confused at being thus caught, dropped the subject of the dictionary.

❦ Hoist by your own petard

When Nancy Astor heard the rumour that David Lloyd George was living with his secretary, Frances Stevenson, she could not resist teasing the Welshman.

'L G, what is this I hear about you and Frances?' asked Nancy.

Lloyd George retorted, 'And what about you and Philip Lothian?'

Nancy was stung into replying, 'Everyone knows that my relations with Philip are completely innocent.'

Lloyd George said, with a twinkle in his eye, 'Then you should be ashamed of yourself.'

❦ Piggy in the middle

There was a lady of the West Country who gave great entertainment at her house to most of the gallant gentlemen thereabout; and amongst others was Sir Walter Ralegh.

This lady, though otherwise a stately dame, was a notable good housewife; and in the morning betimes she called to one of her maids that looked to the swine: 'Is the piggy served?' Sir Walter Ralegh's chamber was fast by the lady's, so as he heard her. A little before dinner, the lady came down in great state into the great chamber, which was full of gentlemen. And as soon as Sir Walter Ralegh set eye upon her, 'Madam,' saith he, 'is the piggy served?' The lady answered: 'You know best whether you have had your breakfast.'

❦ A custom excised

In the early years of the reign of King James I there was much rivalry between the English and the Scottish courtiers who had come south with the king. This resulted in some lively exchanges.

Shortly after the accession of James I, when Scottish gentlemen were beginning to feel at home in London, Lord Harewood gave a dinner party, to which were invited a number of courtiers and officers, both civil and military. After the bottle had circulated freely, and the spirits of the assembly had begun to rise, General S—, an English trooper of fame, and a reckless *bon vivant*, rose and said:

'Gentlemen, when I am in my cups, and the generous wine begins to warm my blood, I have an absurd custom of railing against the Scotch. Knowing my weakness, I hope no gentleman in the company will take it amiss.' He sat down, and a Highland chief, Sir Robert Blackie of Blair-Atholl, presenting a front like an old battle-worn tower, quietly rose in his place, and with the utmost simplicity and good-nature remarked:

'Gentlemen, I, when I am in my cups, and the generous wine begins to warm my blood, if I hear a man rail against the Scotch, have an absurd custom of kicking him at once out of the company. Knowing my weakness, I hope no gentleman will take it amiss.'

General S— did not on that occasion suffer himself to follow his usual custom.

❦ A woman like me

During the eighteenth century in France actresses were considered little better than prostitutes, a prejudice that quality performers like Sophie Arnould tried hard to overcome.

The French actress, Sophie Arnould, once gave a dinner party for a number of distinguished politicians. Afterwards, she received a visit from a lieutenant of police who asked her the names of the gentlemen she had been entertaining. She told him that she could not remember their names, but the lieutenant was not convinced. 'But a woman like you ought to remember things like that,' the policeman said.

'Of course, lieutenant,' said Sophie, 'but with a man like you I am not a woman like me.'

❦ Time to retire

Often called a 'monster of vice', the Prince de Conti was no worse than many other eighteenth-century noblemen in France and elsewhere, who used their inherited fortunes to indulge themselves in sensual pursuits.

The Prince de Conti, the lover of Madame de Boufflers, was greatly attached to the female sex, even when old. Perceiving that he did not succeed so well as he had formerly done, he one day said, 'It is time for me to retire. Formerly, my civilities were taken for declarations of love, but now my declarations of love are taken only for civilities.'

❦ A wise precaution

Before the development of a modern postal service the role of the trusted servant in delivering letters was open to abuse. At least Prince Talleyrand was able to see the funny side of the problem.

Talleyrand had a loyal but incorrigibly inquisitive servant. On one occasion, he asked the man to deliver a letter for him, but as he looked out of the window he noticed that the man was reading his letter. The next day, he had to send another letter to the same destination. This time he entered a postscript: 'You may send a verbal answer with the bearer; he is well acquainted with the whole business, having taken the precaution to read this letter prior to its delivery.'

❦ An identity crisis

Victorian attitudes towards sex education for children were rigid. The British novelist Samuel Butler recorded the following incident.

A little boy and his only slightly older sister were looking at a painting of Adam and Eve in the Garden of Eden.

'Which is Adam and which is Eve?' asked the boy.

'I don't know,' said his sister, 'but I could tell if they had their clothes on.'

❦ An air presumptive

The Order of the Garter was the highest award the monarch could confer on his or her subjects.

When Lady Elizabeth Seymour – the heiress to both the Seymours of Somerset and the Percys of Northumberland – married London banker Sir Hugh Smithson, Sir Hugh decided to change his name to Percy, in acknowledgement of his wife's aristocratic connections. But when he later asked King George III for the Order of the Garter he was refused. Sir Hugh was very disappointed, saying, 'I am the first Percy to be refused the Garter.' But the king replied, 'You are the first Smithson to ask for it.'

❦ An entente cordiale

The religious disputes of the seventeenth century divided many households. The dissenter, Samuel Wesley, came from a family of ministers who had been deprived of their livings by the Act of Uniformity, which had made the use of the Anglican prayer book compulsory. Samuel was therefore a supporter of William of Orange

*during the Glorious Revolution of 1688 and became one of the king's
chaplains. His wife Susanna, on the other hand, had been brought
up as a high church Anglican and still believed in the divine right of
kings, supporting King James II against the Stadtholder of Holland. As
a result, the following exchange of views took place.*

'Sukey,' said Samuel Wesley, 'why did you not say *amen* to the
prayer for the king?'

'Because I do not believe the Prince of Orange to be the king,'
she replied.

'If that be the case,' said Samuel, 'you and I must part; for if we
have two kings we must have two beds.'

And the two slept apart for a year before King William died in
an accident and was succeeded by Queen Anne, in whom neither
found offence. The result was that the couple were reunited and
Susanna later gave birth to John Wesley, the founder of Methodism.

❦ A dangerous game

*During the festivities that accompanied the Congress of Vienna in
1814 quarrels among the nobility of many nations were common
and duels subsequently a regular event.*

During an evening's entertainment at the house of the Princess of
Thurn and Taxis, the Prince Royal of Bavaria and the Crown
Prince of Württemberg quarrelled during a game of blindman's
buff. The Württemburger accused the Bavarian of moving his eye
patch so that he could capture the beautiful Countess Julie Zichy.
As a result of the accusation, the Bavarian challenged his accuser
to a duel with pistols in the Prater woods at dawn. The duel never
took place as the King of Bavaria intervened to prohibit it, but
relations between the two German states remained bad and war
was only narrowly avoided.

❦ What the butler saw

When Lord Northbrook was Viceroy of India, he invited some
Parsees to dinner at eight o'clock. As nobody had arrived by 8.20

he rang for his butler and asked if anyone had arrived yet. The butler told him that they had not. 'That's surprising,' said Northbrook, 'I thought I heard the front doorbell ring at about eight o'clock as I was coming downstairs.' 'Oh, yes, my lord,' said the butler, without turning a hair, 'some nigger minstrels called about that hour but I sent them about their business.'

❦ Where ignorance is bliss

Winston Churchill was no child prodigy. He hated his prep school and his entrance examination for Harrow provided one of the greatest arguments in favour of the public schools, though not one generally invoked in their defence by members of the Headmasters' Conference.

At twelve Winston was entered for Harrow and took the entrance examination. As he said, 'I should have liked to be asked to say what I knew. They always tried to ask me what I did not know. When I would have willingly displayed my knowledge, they thought to expose my ignorance. This sort of treatment had only one result: I did not do well on examinations.' Churchill found that the Harrow exam contained no French, no Geography, no History and just a few arithmetical questions. The bulk was simply translation from Latin and Greek. This was not to Churchill's liking. 'I found,' he said, 'I was unable to answer a single question on the Latin paper. I wrote my name at the top of the page. I wrote down the number of the question "one". After much reflection, I put a bracket round it thus "(1)". But thereafter I could not think of anything connected with it that was either relevant or true.' Harrow knew a good candidate when they saw one: he got in.

❦ Enlarging on the problem

Mrs Ronald Greville was one of the most important society hostesses in London in the 1920s. She was also extremely proud of her own jewellery collection and acknowledged no superiors.

At one of her dinners a very rich and famous American lady

discovered that she had lost the main diamond from her necklace. Soon everyone was on their hands and knees looking for it. Mrs Greville did not join them. Instead she spoke to one of her footmen. 'Perhaps this might be of some assistance,' she said, handing him a magnifying glass.

❦ A fallen angel

During the reign of King Louis XV in France, the legendary gallantry towards women displayed by General Gaillard was put to the test.

Gaillard had always insisted that there was no such thing as an ugly woman and members of the fair sex were determined to prove him wrong. One lady, whose face was spoiled by her rather short and flat nose, said to Gaillard, 'Confess, General, that you are now face to face with a really ugly woman.'

'Not at all, Madame,' replied Gaillard, with scarcely a moment's thought. 'You are like all women, an angel fallen from Heaven. Unfortunately, you had the misfortune to land on your nose.'

❦ Bear-baiting

As Boswell recounts, Dr Samuel Johnson was sometimes regarded as a target for other men's gibes. He was rarely found wanting in his response.

Admiral Walsingham, who sometimes resided at Windsor, and sometimes in Portugal Street, frequently boasted that he was the only man to bring together miscellaneous parties and make them all agreeable; and, indeed, there never before was so strange an assortment as I have occasionally met there. At one of his dinners were the Duke of Cumberland, Dr Johnson, Mr Nairn the optician and Mr Leone the singer: at another Dr Johnson etc and a young dashing officer, who determined, he whispered, to attack the old bear that we all seemed to stand in awe of. There was a good dinner, and during that important time Johnson was deaf to all impertinence. However, after the wine had passed rather freely, the young gentleman was resolved to bait him and venture out a little further. 'Now, Dr Johnson, do not look so glum, but be a little gay and lively like others: what would you give, old gentleman, to be as young and sprightly as I am?' 'Why, sir,' said he, 'I think I would almost be content to be as foolish.'

❦ Whoops!

Bishop Burnet was known for his faux pas.

The bishop was once dining with the Duchess of Marlborough, after the disgrace of her husband, and chose to compare the fate of the great duke with that of Belisarius. 'But,' said the duchess, 'how came it that such a man was so miserable and universally deserted?' The bishop replied without thinking, 'Oh, Madame, he had such a brimstone of a wife.'

❦ More brawn than brain

After the Great Fire of London an examination took place of coffins in the burned-out remains of St Paul's Cathedral. One of those inspected was of the great sixteenth-century humanist scholar John Colet. John Aubrey writes of what was found.

After the conflagration, his monument being broken, his coffin, which was lead, was full of a liquor which conserved the body. Mr Wyld and Mr Greatorex tasted it, and 'twas of a kind of insipid taste, something of an ironish taste. The body felt, to the probe of a stick which they thrust into a chinke, like brawne.

❦ The generation game

Lord Rothschild once tipped a taxi driver with what he considered a fair amount but the man was obviously disappointed and said, 'Your Lordship's son always gives me a good deal more than this.' 'I dare say he does,' replied Lord Rothschild, 'but then, you see, he has got a rich father. I haven't.'

❦ A report

The Duke of Sussex was a frequent visitor at Holkham Hall where he enjoyed some shooting with its owner, Sir Edward Coke. The problem was that, much as he enjoyed shooting, Sussex was a notoriously poor marksman.

After one day's shooting the Duke of Sussex's score card was tallied by Sir Edward Coke and was later presented to him with due ceremony. It read:

Killed of game: 0
Wounded in the legs: 1 foot-marker
Wounded in the face: 1 groom
Wounded on the head of a friend: 1 hat
Ditto on the left rump: 1 horse!

❦ Wee tim'rous beastie

When Sir Edward Coke married Jane Dutton, he hoped to provide an heir to his extensive estates at Holkham. But their only son was stillborn because of an unfortunate experience. Apparently, Jane Dutton miscarried as a result of a fright. A mouse got into her nightcap and gave her such a shock that the baby died.

❦ 11. THE ANIMALS ANSWER BACK

❦ A diplomatic incident

Prince Otto von Bismarck, known as the 'Iron Chancellor' for his famous 'Blood and Iron' speech, was a difficult man to get the better of.

While the Chancellor [Bismarck] worked, his giant dog Tiras lay on the carpet staring fixedly at his master. Tiras, known as the Reichshund, terrorized the chancellery staff, and people speaking to Bismarck were advised to make no unusual gestures which Tiras might interpret as threatening. Prince Alexander Gorchakov, the elderly Russian Foreign Minister, once raised an arm to make a point and found himself pinned to the floor, staring up at Tiras's bared teeth.

❦ Natural selection

In spite of his reputation as a frontiersman and Indian fighter, Davy Crockett also had a significant career in American politics. He died defending the Alamo in Texas against the forces of the Mexican general, Santa Anna.

At a menagerie exhibition in Washington, Crockett amused his friends by pointing out a similarity between the features of one of the monkeys on display and those of a certain member of Congress. Turning around, Crockett found the member in question standing right behind him. 'I suppose I ought to apologize,' he said, 'but I don't know whether to apologize to you or to the monkey.'

❦ Church service

In his Brief Lives *John Aubrey describes the unfortunate experiences of one proud prelate.*

This Deane was a mighty Pontificall proud man, and that one time when they went in Procession about the Cathedral church, he would not doe it the usual way in his surplice, hood, etc, on foot, but rode on a mare thus habited, with the Common prayer book in his hand, reading. A stone horse happend to break loose and smelt the mare and ran and leapt her, and held the Reverend Deane all the time so hard in his Embraces, that he could not get off till the horse had done his business.

❦ The guard dog

Napoleon suffered an early reverse at the paws of Josephine's pet pooch.

In 1795 Napoleon married Joséphine de Beauharnais. On their wedding night, engaged in vigorous intercourse, the bridegroom suddenly uttered a shriek as Joséphine's pet pug, Fortune, joined the act. Believing his mistress was being attacked the dog had jumped on the bed and then bitten Le Petit Général on his bare left calf.

❦ Give a dog a bad name

A jewel of a dog is hard to find.

Sir Isaac Newton had a favourite little dog, named Diamond: this animal ranged uncontrolled through his study; and once, during his master's absence, overturned a lighted candle which fell upon a manuscript that he had laboured many years to complete – it was reduced to ashes! The immortal Newton merely exclaimed, 'Oh, Diamond! Diamond! Thou little knowest the mischief thou hast done.'

❦ The call of the wild

Sir Edward Elgar used to telephone his Worcestershire home from London just for the pleasure of hearing his dog bark.

❦ A multiple royal birth

Vice-Admiral Grenfell kept a number of cats on his flagship, one of which he had named 'Queen Alexandra'. However, when the real queen visited the fleet with her husband King Edward VII, and took lunch on Grenfell's ship, she was told about the cat. During lunch a sailor entered the state rooms and went up to the admiral and whispered in his ear. In the next hour or so the man returned several times and repeated the performance, whispering each time in the admiral's ear. At last the queen asked Grenfell what all the whispering was about. 'Well, your majesty, if you really want to know, I must tell you. This man has just told me that Queen Alexandra has given birth to her third baby.' The true queen's expression was a picture.

❦ Requiem for a fish

Gabriele d'Annunzio was an Italian poet who was stimulated in his writing by the stillborn babies pickled in bottles that he kept on shelves in his study. The following story is typical of his outlandish behaviour.

Gabriele d'Annunzio, while staying in a hotel in Switzerland, once adopted a goldfish that he saw swimming in a tank in the foyer. Every day of his stay the poet fed the goldfish, which he had named 'Adolphus', and read it his poetry as it swam about. When he returned to Italy, he telegraphed the hotel frequently asking how his 'beloved' Adolphus was getting on. Unfortunately, the goldfish died and the hotel manager threw the body of the fish out for the cats. However, at that moment another of d'Annunzio's telegrams arrived saying: 'Feel Adolphus not well.' The manager cabled back, 'Adolphus dead. Died last night.' The distraught d'Annunzio cabled, 'Bury him in the garden. Arrange his grave.' The manager, at his wit's end, took a sardine, wrapped it in silver paper and buried it in the garden under the shade of a plant, with a little cross inscribed 'Here lies Adolphus'. The following year d'Annunzio returned to the hotel, inspected the grave, laid flowers on it and stood by it weeping.

❦ An unusual dinner guest

King Ludwig of Bavaria was enormously fond of animals, particularly his horses. On one occasion he invited his favourite grey mare, named Cosa Rara, to have dinner with him.

The dining table was laid as for a state banquet, and soup, fish, roast meats and wine were served. Cosa Rara had her own specialities and these she ate with relish. Unfortunately, her table manners left a little to be desired. Having completed her meal she proceeded to smash the priceless royal dinner service to pieces. Ludwig was not at all angry about this, explaining, 'At least she doesn't tell lies.'

❦ A flourishing amphibian

The Duke of Wellington could be very tender-hearted when dealing with young children.

One day the elderly Duke of Wellington chanced on a small boy weeping bitterly and, on asking the cause, the child began to explain that he was going away to school next day. Not waiting to hear more, the duke read him a severe lecture on his attitude, which was cowardly, unworthy of a gentleman and not at all the way to behave, etc. At last the little boy managed to explain he was not crying because he was going to school, but he was worried about his pet toad, as no one else seemed to care for it and he would not know how it was. The duke, a just man, apologized to the child for having wronged him, and being human as well as just, took down the particulars and promised to report himself about this pet. In due course, the little boy at school received a letter saying, 'Field-Marshal the Duke of Wellington presents his compliments to Master — and has the pleasure to inform him that his toad is well.'

❦ The elephant who forgot

After the conquest of Astrakhan by the Russian Tsar Ivan the Terrible, the Shah of Iran sent a peace envoy to Moscow, who brought with him the first elephant that had ever been seen in Russia.

The tsar was told by the envoy that the elephant had been taught to bow its head in the presence of the almighty Russian ruler. When people heard about the amazing creature they flooded into Red Square to see it for themselves. So large was the throng of people that the elephant became frightened. Eventually, after the elephant had been made to wait through hours of merrymaking in the square, the tsar emerged from the Kremlin and occupied a large throne in the centre of the square. The elephant was now brought forward to make its bow. In practice, all had gone well, but now the noise of so many people confused the animal and, when it was ordered to bow to Ivan, it simply stood looking at him. Showing no understanding of the animal's fear, Ivan acted hysterically, claiming that the elephant had failed to show him due reverence. 'Cut it to pieces,' Ivan yelled to his soldiers, and the elephant was promptly attacked by hundreds of men wielding axes and spears, who obeyed the tsar's order to the letter, chopping the huge creature into thousands of pieces.

❦ Pretty Pauli

*While he was in London, Prince Metternich was given an
unusual gift by an Austrian sea-captain: a parrot.*

Metternich was delighted with the parrot: 'I've been looking for
one for a long time, and I don't know how this good man was
able to guess one of my secret thoughts. They claim my bird
speaks English and Spanish. The only word I've heard him say
thus far is "Floret" – which is not a great deal in two languages.'
Metternich took the bird with him on his diplomatic journeys
and his children were particularly fond of the pet. But 'Polly', as
it was inevitably called, proved a poor linguist. As Metternich
later wrote, 'Polly is the delight of everyone in Baden, always at
one of our ground floor windows talking to everyone who
passes by, "Pauli, Pauli". He has lost his English accent and
instead of saying, "Pretty Polly" he only says "Pauli", with the
accent of an old Jew.'

❦ Bear overboard

*Queen Victoria's second son, Prince Alfred, Duke of Edinburgh,
entered the Royal Navy and rose to the rank of admiral and
Commander-in-Chief of the Mediterranean Fleet.*

Prince Alfred loved animals and allowed the midshipmen on his
flagship to keep a brown bear on board, which was called
'Bruin'. Bruin enjoyed wrestling with the sailors and his
favourite trick was, when the fleet was at anchor, to swim over
to the boats of another warship, approach stealthily and pull an
unsuspecting sailor overboard. But Bruin came to an untimely
end. He used to sleep in one of the boats on deck and one
night he woke up and got out the wrong side, falling overboard and being lost. The cry of 'Bear overboard' was raised
but the admiral in charge of Her Majesty's Mediterranean Fleet
could not risk his ships hunting for a bear and so Bruin was
drowned.

❧ Moonshine

Mrs Patrick Campbell once summoned a taxi and prepared to board with her rather disagreeable dog named Moonbeam. At first the taxi driver refused to take the dog but Mrs Campbell simply swept past him and got in, giving the instructions 'The Empire Theatre, my man, and no nonsense.' Unfortunately, on the way to the theatre, Moonbeam disgraced herself. When they arrived, the taxi driver, seeing the wet patch, gave Mrs Campbell a withering look, but she simply told him, 'Don't blame Moonbeam, I did it.'

❧ Barking mad

President Ceausescu of Romania was eccentric to the point of madness. Whereas the Emperor Caligula was supposed to have made his horse a senator, the president made his black labrador – Corbu – a colonel in the Romanian army.

Colonel Corbu was to be seen being driven through Bucharest in

a limousine, with its own motorcade. The British ambassador saw it once. 'I saw this black dog sitting all on its own in the back of a Dacia, looking rather pompous with its nose in the air, as black labradors often do.' Security was tight in case anyone tried to harm Corbu. As one of the maids later explained, 'The secret police told us never to feed the dogs. There was a special doctor who checked the food – it was the best sort of meat. Only when this doctor had tasted the food could they be fed.' Apparently the Romanian ambassador in London was under official orders to go to Sainsbury's every week to buy British dog biscuits and Winalot, which were then sent back to Bucharest in the diplomatic bag. Corbu was soon given the rank of colonel in the Romanian Army. One day he and the president visited the Brancovenesc Hospital, only to find that the hospital basement was infested with rats. The staff kept a number of cats for use against the vermin and on his visit the colonel saw one and gave chase. After a furious battle, in which both the colonel and the cat sustained some damage, the animals were pulled apart and President Ceausescu furiously drove away. The doctors were aghast. Their cat had presumed to assault a colonel in the Romanian Army and there would be repercussions. Sure enough, within days the order was sent for the hospital to be closed down. The previous year over 50,000 Romanians had received treatment there. But Colonel Corbu's nose had been bloodied and so the hospital had to go.

12. GREEK TRAGEDIES AND ROMAN FARCES

❦ A slow death

The Greek playwright Aeschylus was the most prolific of the ancient tragedians but few of his plays have survived today.

Aeschylus died and was buried at Gela in Sicily. Ancient biographies record the tradition that his death came about when an eagle, which had seized a tortoise and was looking to smash the reptile's shell, mistook the poet's bald head for a stone and dropped the tortoise upon him, killing him instantly.

❦ Ahead of his time

The Greek historian Herodotus visited the battlefield at Pelusium many years after the battle which took place there in 525 BC.

On the field where this battle was fought I saw a very strange thing which the natives pointed out to me. The bones of the slain lie scattered on the field in two lots, those of the Persians in one place by themselves, as the bodies lay at the first – those of the Egyptians in another place, apart from them: if, then, you strike the Persian skulls, even with a pebble, they are so weak, that you break a hole in them; but the Egyptian skulls are so strong, that you may strike them with a rock and you will scarcely break them in.

❦ A mother's love

Agrippina was consumed by her ambition to place her son Nero on the imperial throne. She consulted the soothsayers, who told her, 'Nero will reign, but he will kill his mother.' 'Let him kill me then,' said Agrippina.

❦ Priorities

The Greek philosopher Diogenes was the principal exponent of the Cynic school.

When Alexander the Great visited Corinth, Diogenes was living in a large earthenware tub in one of the city suburbs. Alexander went to see the philosopher and found him relaxing in the sun. Alexander politely asked if there was anything he could do for him. 'Stand out of my sun,' replied the surly Cynic.

❦ Just kidding

The great Greek lawmaker and statesman, Solon, lived in Athens, where he reformed the constitution and the administration. Of his personality we know little except that he was, perhaps, rather humourless.

271

It is said that Solon was sometime in the city of Miletus at Thales' house where he said that he could not but marvel at Thales, that he would never marry to have children. Thales gave him never a word at that present: but within few days after he suborned a stranger which said that he came but newly home from Athens, departing thence but ten days before. Solon asked him immediately, what news there? This stranger whom Thales had schooled before, answered: none other there, saving that they carried a young man to burial, whom all the city followed: for he was one of the greatest men's sons of the city, and the honestest man withal, who at the present was out of the country and had been a long time (as they said) abroad. Oh poor unfortunate father then, said Solon: and what was his name? I have heard him named, said the stranger, but have forgotten him now; saving that they all said he was a worthy, wise man. So Solon still trembling more and more for fear, at every answer of this stranger: in the end he could hold no longer, being full of trouble, but told his name himself unto the stranger, and asked him again, if he were not the son of Solon which was buried. The very same, said the stranger. Solon with that, like a madman straight began to beat his head, and to say, and do, like men impatient in affliction, and overcome with sorrow. But Thales laughing to see this pageant, stayed him and said: Lo, Solon, this is it that keepeth me from marrying, and getting of children; which is of such a violence, that thou seest it hath now overcome thee, although otherwise thou art strong and able to wrestle with any. Howbeit, for anything he hath said unto thee, be of good cheer man, for it is but a tale and nothing so.

❦ A telling testimonial

Augustus was one of the shrewdest and most successful of rulers in the ancient world.

The Emperor Augustus once dismissed a young man from his service. When the fellow asked Augustus what he would tell his father, the emperor replied, 'Tell him that you didn't find me to your liking.'

❦ The rivals

Demosthenes is often thought to have been the greatest orator of the classical period. Yet in his lifetime he had a formidable rival in the Athenian soldier Phocion. During one of their angry exchanges Demosthenes said, 'One of these days the Athenians will kill you when they are in a rage.' Phocion hit back, 'And you too, when they are in their right minds.'

❦ Only problem parents

One day a woman and a small boy came to consult Diogenes. The woman was angry and complained that her son was rude and impertinent and asked if Diogenes could suggest a way of improving his behaviour. The philosopher stepped forward and slapped the woman in the face.

❦ Principles of justice

The Roman emperor Julian – known to history as the Apostate for his attempts to restore the old pagan religions to Rome – was a man of great learning and justice. His early death on campaign in Persia robbed the empire of a great administrator.

A case of corruption was brought before the Emperor Julian. A provincial governor was accused of embezzlement, but he defended himself so vigorously that the prosecution wilted. Eventually, the judge became so irritated at the absence of any real evidence against the man that he turned to the emperor and said, 'Can anyone ever be proved guilty if it is enough just to deny the charge?' Julian replied, 'Can anyone be proved innocent if it is enough simply to accuse him?'

❦ Reading between the lines

Croesus was a ruler of legendary wealth but very little wisdom.

Croesus, King of Lydia, was torn between a policy of peace and one of war against his neighbours, the Persians. In order to decide what to do Croesus consulted the oracle at Delphi to ask if a war against the Persians would be successful. The oracle revealed to him that if he went to war he would destroy a great empire. Encouraged by this apparently good news, Croesus invaded Persia and was decisively defeated, losing his kingdom to the enemy. Croesus, believing himself to have been betrayed, sent to Delphi to ask why the oracle had misled him. But the priestess assured him that he had been well advised. He had destroyed a great empire – his.

❦ Monumental wisdom

During the period of the Roman Republic Cato, who had achieved so much for Rome, was once asked why a statue had not been erected to him. Cato replied, 'Better that question than to ask why a statue had been erected to him.'

❦ An abrupt ending

Julius Caesar was once dining with friends and the conversation turned to the subject of death. One of his friends asked what he considered the best form of death. Caesar replied, 'A sudden one.' The next day – on the Ides of March, 44 BC – he was assassinated.

❦ No substitute

During the reign of the Emperor Augustus, a veteran Roman soldier was involved in a law suit, which he was in danger of losing. He therefore appealed to Augustus, as his former commander, asking him to appear in court on his behalf. At first the emperor was unwilling to do so, offering one of his senior advisers as a substitute. But the soldier rolled up his sleeves to show the emperor his scars and said, 'When you were in peril at the battle of Actium, I did not choose a substitute but fought for you myself.' At once Augustus understood what the man was saying and appeared in court as the man had requested.

❦ The food of the gods

The Emperor Claudius's last wife, Agrippina, was determined to secure the throne for her son Nero by ousting the emperor's son Britannicus. She therefore fed the old emperor a plate of poisoned mushrooms, killing him before he was able to announce who he intended to succeed him. As a result, Nero took the throne, gave his father-in-law a splendid funeral and later made him a god. Nero later remarked that mushrooms must indeed be the food of the gods because by eating them Claudius had become divine.

❦ His master's voice

Scipio once called on his friend Quintus Ennius, only to be told by a slave that his master was not at home. As he turned to go, however, Scipio happened to see Ennius slipping into a room at the back of the house. Angry as he was, Scipio did not contradict the slave but left immediately. A few weeks later, Ennius had cause to visit Scipio. As he knocked at the door, Scipio called from within, 'Not at home.' 'You cannot expect me to believe that,' said Ennius, 'I recognized your voice.' 'You're a fine one,' said Scipio, 'I believed your slave, and yet you won't even believe me.'

❦ Nothing's plenty for me

The Greek philosopher Socrates lived a frugal life, spending no more than he needed to. With this in mind, one of his friends was surprised to see him one day studying intently some gaudy items in the market place, as if he wished to buy them. He asked Socrates why he came to the market when he never bought anything. Socrates replied, 'I am always amazed to see just how many things there are that I don't need.'

❦ The oldest joke

A talkative barber once asked King Archelaus of Macedon how he would like his hair cut. 'In silence,' replied the king.

❦ Eureka!

King Hiero of Syracuse once believed that a craftsman to whom the king had given a quantity of gold had adulterated it with silver. He therefore asked the great scientist and mathematician Archimedes if he knew of a way of testing whether his suspicions were correct. Archimedes thought long and hard about the problem but found the solution while he was in the bath. He noticed that the deeper he went into the water the more the water overflowed, and his body seemed to weigh less the more it was submerged. Jumping out of the bath he yelled, 'Eureka! Eureka! I have found the answer.' He then set off, running naked through the streets of Syracuse. As a result of his findings he was able to prove that Hiero's suspicions were right and that the craftsman had indeed cheated him.

❦ A gift of the gods

The Athenian general Themistocles alienated the allies of Athens by demanding huge quantities of gold from them. To enforce his demands he anchored a strong Athenian fleet off the coast of one small city state and told its people, 'I have two powerful deities on my side – Persuasion and Force.' The leaders of the beleaguered city replied, 'We have two equally potent gods on our side – Poverty and Despair.' Understanding their message, Themistocles withdrew his blockading ships.

❦ Beaten by fate

The Stoic philosopher Zeno once caught one of his slaves stealing from him. He gave the man a thorough beating but the slave, who had picked up some of his master's philosophical teaching, complained, 'But it was fated that I should steal.' Zeno smiled at the man's temerity. 'Just as it was fated that I should beat you,' he replied.

❦ Elder statesman

The Roman statesman Cato, at the age of eighty, announced to his friends that he intended learning Greek. Asked how he could consider such an onerous task at his age, Cato replied, 'It is the youngest age that I have left.'

🎖 13. MARTIAL ARTS

🎖 Fate lends a hand

By 1915 there were numerous critics of Lord Kitchener's conduct of the war.

On 5 June the *Hampshire*, with Kitchener on board, struck a mine within two hours of leaving Scapa Flow. Kitchener and most of the crew were drowned. So perished the only British military idol of the First World War. The next morning, Lord Northcliffe burst into his sister's drawing room with the words: 'Providence is on the side of the British Empire after all.'

🎖 A slight misjudgement

Sir Arthur Wellesley, 1st Duke of Wellington, may justly be considered Britain's greatest soldier. Undefeated throughout a long career in India, Spain and the Low Countries, he took on the best the French could throw at him and emerged victorious time after time.

In 1787, Lady Mornington did not consider the army a suitable career for young Arthur Wellesley, commenting, 'I vow to God I don't know what I shall do with my awkward son, Arthur. Arthur has put on his red coat for the first time today. Anyone can see that he has not the cut of a soldier.'

🎖 Pushing up the daisies

The Duke of Wellington was very loyal to the troops who had once served under him.

Once Wellington met a Waterloo veteran, called Sergeant Townshend, who was down on his luck and looking for employment. 'Do you know anything about gardening?' asked the duke. 'No, your grace,' said Townshend. 'Then *learn – learn* and return this day fortnight at the same hour. Take the place of gardener at Walmer Castle.' 'But I know nothing of gardening.' 'Neither do I, neither do I,' said the duke.

❦ Loyalty unto death

Many of those who fought for the king during the English Civil War did so from a sense of duty rather than from any hope of personal gain. Their loyalty to their monarch was the stuff of legend.

At the battle of Edgehill in 1642 the king's standard was carried by Sir Edmund Verney. Surrounded by Parliamentary troops he was summoned to surrender by one of their officers. Verney replied, 'My life is my own but my standard is the king's.' He died defending it and the only way his grip on the flag could be broken was to hack off his hand which still held it. When the flag was later recaptured by the Royalists, Verney's hand was still attached to it.

❦ Bed and no bawd

Lord Kitchener's austere personality and his misogyny were well known by the time that he became Secretary for War in 1914.

Lord Kitchener's first request on taking up the position of Secretary for War caused some confusion. He asked for a bed to be supplied at the War Office so that he could work throughout the night if necessary. 'Have you a bed here?' Kitchener demanded of a flustered civil servant. 'No, my lord.' 'Then get one,' said Kitchener. 'Yes, my lord. S-s-single or d-d-double?'

❦ Their visiting card

During the Irish Troubles immediately after the First World War,

"WHOM SHALL I SAY CALLED SIR?"

the British government employed ex-soldiers known as Black and Tans to combat the Irish Republican Army.

In 1921 Dunsany Castle, the home of Lord Dunsany, in County Meath, was sacked by the Black and Tans. As the soldiers left, leaving behind them a trail of destruction, Lord Dunsany's butler politely enquired of their officer, 'Who shall I say called?'

❦ Take your pick

General Robert E Lee is the only general in history to have been offered command of both opposing armies in a war.

❦ The first report

After his defeat at the battle of Prestonpans in 1745 the government commander, Sir John Cope, was one of the first to leave the battlefield. When he reached Berwick, the commander of the garrison, Sir Mark Ker, welcomed Cope with the observation that he was probably the first commander ever to bring first news of his own defeat.

❦ A father's footsteps

The British Army in the nineteenth century was rife with class distinctions and it was almost unheard of for a man from a humble background to rise to high rank. Those who tried were subject to frequent humiliation at the hands of their supposed betters. The Duke of Wellington was one of the worst military snobs, as this example shows.

During the Peninsular War, Major Todd – who was the son of a butler to one of the royal dukes – was responsible for the construction of a bridge which, unfortunately, broke down under the weight of traffic. The Duke of Wellington was at dinner when he heard the news and he was furious. When Todd tried to explain what had happened, the duke rejected all his excuses and when Todd stood speechless alongside his chair, Wellington said, 'Are you going to take up your father's trade?' The next day there was a skirmish with the French and one of Wellington's aides saw Todd standing in an exposed position. He rode up to him, saying, 'Major Todd, they can hardly miss you if you place yourself there.' 'I don't want them to,' Todd replied miserably. Only minutes later Major Todd was riddled with bullets and fell dead.

❦ Generally popular

During the Crimean War the Commander of the British Forces was the hopelessly inept but much loved General Lord Raglan.

When Lord Raglan died on 28 June 1855, his loss was felt by British and French soldiers alike. He had been in the habit of buying Christmas comforts for the soldiers of both armies and he was known to the French as '*le bon vieux Père Crees Mass*'.

♥ Laid low by a centipede

In view of the appalling suffering of the British troops during the Crimean War, and the almost total lack of medical care during the first period of the fighting, it is incredible to hear how much attention was paid to one famous invalid.

On the death of General Lord Raglan, command of the British Army went to General Simpson, who proved quite incapable of dealing with the heavy workload. Matters were made no easier for him when, on one occasion, he was awoken in the night by an urgent telegraph message from London. It was from the Secretary of State for War, Lord Panmure, and it said, 'Captain Jarvis has been bitten by a centipede. How is he now?'

♥ The grave yawns

After the Russian defeat at the battle of Narva in 1700 the Duke du Croy, fighting in the Russian service, was kept a prisoner by the Swedes at Reval.

Short of money, the Duke du Croy wrote to Peter asking for funds to pay his expenses and the tsar sent him six thousand roubles. However, in the spring of 1702 du Croy died, much mourned by Peter the Great who had valued 'the good old man, who was in truth an able and experienced military commander'. But when he died the old duke was insolvent. Peter planned to pay off his debts but before he could so du Croy's creditors in Reval invoked an ancient law that said that those who died in debt could not be buried. As a result, the body was placed in a church vault in Reval, where in the dry atmosphere it did not decay but mummified. Eventually, it was removed from the church and placed under glass. For more than two centuries visitors to Reval were able to see the body of the duke, still in the wig and uniform of a seventeenth-century general. Just before the First World War, the Russian government decided it was unseemly for the duke to be exposed to visitors as a tourist attraction and the body was finally buried.

❦ A prickly situation

During Louis XI's struggle against the League of the Public Weal, the king found himself besieged in Paris by the forces of Duke John of Burgundy.

One day a great cannonading was heard, convincing both sides that they were about to be attacked. To see if the king's troops had left the city, Duke John sent out scouts and the weather being cloudy and duskish those who got nearest the city discovered a party of horse upon the patrol and beyond them (as they fancied) they perceived a great number of lances standing upright, which they imagined to be the king's battalions drawn up in the field and all the people of Paris with them.

And, being come up to us, Duke John said: 'Well, gentlemen, we are now where we desired to be; the king and all his army (as our scouts inform us) are drawn out of Paris, and marching to engage us; so let us each behave with courage and goodwill, and as they march out we will march in.'

By this time our scouts, perceiving the enemy were weak, began to assume a little more courage, ventured something nearer the town, but still found the battalions in the same place and posture in which they had left them which put them into a quandary. However, they stole up to them as near as they could, but could make nothing of them; till at length the day cleared and they discovered them to be tall thistles.

❦ The inexperience of youth

During the Seven Years' War, George Washington fought with the British Army in America and Canada against the French and their Indian allies. There is some evidence to suggest that George Washington may actually have fired the first shot in the war, on the Ohio River in 1754.

At the start of the Seven Years' War, a London magazine quoted young George Washington as saying, after a skirmish with the French and Indians, 'I heard the bullets whistle and believe me there is something charming in the sound.' King George II sharply observed, 'He would not say so, had he been used to hear many.'

❦ The relief of Lady Smith

This anecdote is probably the most famous to emerge from the annals of the whole Peninsular War. In April 1812 the British finally took Badajoz after a prolonged siege, and then subjected the city to an appalling sack. For three days the place was the scene of murder, looting and rape and yet out of the horror walked two ladies, completely unscathed, who surrendered themselves to the first British officers they saw. The younger of the two, Juanita, eventually became the wife of Harry Smith of the Rifle Brigade, followed him on his campaigns for the next forty years, and finally had a town in South Africa named after her. It was a happy outcome to a siege that had blackened the name of British soldiery. This account is told by Smith's fellow officer, John Kincaid.

I was conversing with a friend the day after at the door of his tent, when we observed two ladies coming from the city, who made directly towards us; they seemed both young, and when they came near the elder of the two threw back her mantilla to address us, showing a remarkably handsome figure, with fine features; but her sallow, sunburnt and careworn, though still youthful, countenance showed that in her 'the time for tender thoughts and soft endearments had fled away and gone'.

She at once addressed us in that confident, heroic manner so characteristic of a high bred Spanish maiden, told us who they were – the last of an ancient and honourable house – and referred to an officer high in rank in our army, who had been quartered there in the days of her prosperity, for the truth of her tale.

Her husband, she said, was a Spanish officer in a distant part of the kingdom; he might or he might not still be living. But yesterday she and this her young sister were able to live in affluence and in a handsome house; today they knew not where to lay their heads, where to get a change of raiment or a morsel of bread. Her house, she said, was a wreck; and, to show the indignities to which they had been subjected, she pointed to where the blood was still trickling down their necks caused by the wrenching of their ear-rings through the flesh by the hands of worse than savages, who would not take the trouble to unclasp them!

For herself, she said, she cared not; but for the agitated and almost unconscious maiden by her side, whom she had but lately received over from the hands of her conventual instructresses, she was in despair, and knew not what to do; and that, in the rapine and ruin which was at that moment desolating the city, she saw no security for her but the seemingly indelicate one she had adopted – of coming to the camp and throwing themselves on the protection of any British officer who would afford it; and so great, she said, was her faith in our national character, that she knew the appeal would not be made in vain, nor the confidence abused. Nor was it made in vain! Nor could it be abused, for she stood by the side of angel! A being more transcendingly lovely I had never before seen – one more amiable I have never yet known.

Fourteen summers had not yet passed over her youthful countenance which was of a delicate freshness – more English than Spanish; her face, though not perhaps rigidly beautiful was nevertheless so remarkably handsome and so irresistibly attractive surmounting a figure cast in nature's fairest mould, that to look at her was to love her; and I did love her, but I never told my love, and in the meantime another and a more impudent fellow stepped in and won her! But yet I was happy for in him she found such a one as her loveliness and her misfortunes claimed – a man of honour and a husband in every way worthy of her.

That a being so young, so lovely, and so interesting, just emancipated from the gloom of a convent, unknowing of the world and to the world unknown, should thus have been wrecked on a sea of troubles, and thrown on the mercy of strangers under circumstances so dreadful, so uncontrollable, and not have sunk to rise no more, must be the wonder of everyone. Yet from the moment she was thrown on her own resources her star was in the ascendant.

Guided by a just sense of rectitude, an innate purity of mind, a singleness of purpose which defied malice, and a soul that soared above circumstances, she became alike the adored of the camp and of the drawing room and eventually the admired associate of princes. Yet she lives in the affection of her gallant husband in an elevated situation in life, a pattern to her sex and everybody's *beau idéale* of what a wife should be.

❦ Buttons

The Duke of Wellington once related an extraordinary story of the battle of Waterloo.

In the middle of the fighting Wellington had seen a man in plain clothes, riding about on a cob in the thickest fire. During a temporary lull, the duke beckoned him and he rode over. He asked him who he was, and what business he had there. The man replied that he was an Englishman, accidentally at Brussels, that he had never seen a fight and wanted to see one. The duke told him he was in instant danger of his life; he said, 'Not more than your Grace,' and they parted. But every now and then he saw the cob man riding about in the smoke and at last, having nobody to send to a regiment, he again beckoned to this little fellow and told him to go up to that regiment and order them to charge, giving him some mark of authority the colonel would recognize. Away he galloped and in a few minutes the duke saw his order obeyed. The Duke asked him for his card, and found in the evening, when the card fell out of his sash, that he lived at Birmingham and was a button manufacturer! When at Birmingham, the duke enquired of the firm, and found he was their traveller and then in Ireland. When he returned, at the duke's request, he called on him in London. The duke was happy to see him and said he had a vacancy in the Mint of £800 a year, where accounts were wanted. The little cob man said it would be exactly the thing and the duke installed him.

❦ Fair shares for all

The British seaman was a stout fighter but a democrat.

When the British under Lord Nelson were bearing down to attack the combined fleets off Trafalgar, the first lieutenant of the *Revenge*, on going to see that all hands were at their quarters, observed one of the men devoutly kneeling at the side of his gun; so very unusual an attitude exciting his surprise and curiosity, he went and asked the man if he was afraid? 'Afraid!' answered the honest tar, with a countenance expressive of the utmost disdain, 'No; I was only praying that the enemy's shot may be distributed in the same proportion as the prize money, the greatest part among the officers.'

❦ The honour of the regiment

New officers were frequently subjected to practical jokes on joining their regiments.

Colonel Guise, going over on campaign to Flanders, observed a young raw officer, who was in the same vessel with him, and with his usual humanity told him that he would take care of him and conduct him to Antwerp, where they were both going; which he accordingly did, and then took leave of him. The young fellow was soon told by such arch rogues, whom he happened to fall in with, that he must signalize himself by fighting some man of known courage, or else he would soon be despised in the regiment. The young man said he knew no one but Colonel Guise, and he had received great obligations from him. It was all one for that, they said in these cases; the colonel was the fittest man in the world as everyone knew his bravery. Soon afterwards, up comes the young officer to Colonel Guise, as he was walking up and down the coffee room, and began in a hesitating manner to tell him how much obliged he had been to him, and how sensible he was of his obligations. 'Sir,' replied Colonel Guise, 'I have done my duty by you, and no more.' 'But colonel,' added the young officer faltering, 'I am told that I must fight some gentleman of known courage, and who has killed several persons and that nobody —' 'Oh, sir,' interrupted the colonel, 'your friends do me too much honour; but there is a gentleman (pointing to a fierce-looking black fellow that was sitting at one of the tables) who has killed half the regiment.' So up goes the officer to him and tells he is well-informed of his bravery, and for that reason he must fight him.' 'Who, I, sir?' said the gentleman. 'Why, I am the apothecary.'

❦ A fully equipped army

Complete with napkins.

As every schoolboy knows, King George II was the last British monarch to lead an army into battle, which he did at Dettingen in 1743. But if anyone thinks he endured the hardships of his soldiers, like a Henry V or an Edward III he is very much mistaken. King George was well insulated against the rigours of a campaign. His baggage required the use of 662 horses, 13 Berlin carriages, 35 waggons and 54 carts. Among his essential equipment was 900 dozen napkins!

❦ Blindingly obvious

In wartime the first casualty is common sense.

An American newspaperman in England during the Second World War, John Gunther, fell foul of the censors when he asked to see the text of the leaflets that the British were dropping over Germany. His request was refused. When he asked why, he was told, 'We are not allowed to disclose information which might be of value to the enemy.' An astonished Gunther pointed out that over two million of the leaflets had just been dropped on the enemy. The civil servant blinked. 'Yes, there may be something wrong there.'

❦ Fashioning a farewell

When Lord Kitchener was lost in the cruiser *Hampshire* in 1915, Lady Violet Bonham-Carter asked Margot Asquith, the Prime Minister's wife, if she planned to wear a certain hat, trimmed with ostrich feathers, at the memorial service for the Secretary for War. 'How can you ask me that?' Margot replied. 'Dear Kitchener saw me in that hat twice.'

❦ A swift reverse

Sir Redvers Buller had been an effective junior officer, but when he became a general he proved to be totally incapable.

On one of the occasions that Sir Redvers Buller was forced to retreat during the Second Boer War, he told his superiors in London that he had accomplished the task without losing a man, a flag or a cannon. On hearing of the story Whistler acidly added, 'or a minute'.

❦ The voice of reason

Britain claimed to be fighting in 1914 to defend civilization against the Germans.

A distinguished classical scholar was stopped in a London street by a woman who tried to give him a white feather as he was not in uniform. 'I am surprised that you are not fighting to defend civilization,' she said. 'Madam,' replied the scholar, 'I am the civilization they are fighting to defend.'

❦ A one-track mind

General Ulysses S Grant once admitted that he had no appreciation of music and tried his best to avoid concerts. When asked for his favourite music, he replied, 'I know only two tunes; one of them is "Yankee Doodle" and the other one isn't.'

❦ The deserter

In 1812, during the dreadful retreat from Moscow, Napoleon abandoned his army in Poland and hurried back to France.

Reaching the River Neman, Napoleon asked the ferryman there whether many French deserters had passed that way. 'No,' replied the man, 'you are the first.'

❦ Telling a story

During the Second World War Picasso stayed in Paris and was frequently visited by the German secret police.

One particular German officer, while searching Picasso's apartment, seemed intrigued by a photograph of the painting entitled *Guernica*. 'Did you do that?' the officer asked Picasso. 'No,' he replied. 'You did.'

❦ The sound of battle

The Duke of Wellington was no lover of music. During the Congress of Vienna in 1814 he was obliged to sit through a performance of Beethoven's *Battle of Vittoria*, or *Wellington's Victory*. Afterwards, a Russian diplomat asked him if the music had been anything like the real battle. 'By God, no, sir,' said the duke. 'If it had been that bad I would have run away myself.'

❦ Army grub

American soldiers in the Civil War remembered their food with horror.

During the Union siege of Petersburg in 1864 troops were issued with wormy hardtack or ship's biscuit. It was almost universally unpopular with the men, who were sickened by finding live worms when they broke open the biscuit. Most of them simply threw away the biscuits in the trenches where they were doing duty, although they had been ordered to keep the trenches clean, for sanitary purposes. One day a senior officer was passing a group of men and noticed biscuits lying everywhere in the trench. He shouted at the soldiers, 'Throw the hardtack out of the trenches. Don't you know better than to just drop it anywhere?' At which one of the soldiers reasonably replied, 'We've thrown it out two or three times, sir, but it just goes on crawlin' back.'

❦ Soldiers in swarms

During the Peninsular War Wellington's soldiers were adept at living off the country.

Once Wellington caught a soldier staggering along with a stolen beehive.

'Hallo, sir, where did you get that beehive?' asked the duke.

The soldier clearly did not recognize his commander nor understand his question, so he replied, 'The beehives, sir, are over that hill. But you'd better hurry before they've all been taken.'

❦ Preserving a legend

After the battle of Trafalgar Nelson's body was placed in a cask of brandy before being taken back to England for burial. Sir William Beatty described what happened to it on the journey.

In the evening after this melancholy task was accomplished, the gale came up with violence, and continued that night and the succeeding day without any abatement. During this boisterous weather Lord Nelson's body remained under the charge of a sentinel on the middle deck. The cask was placed on its end, having a closed aperture at its top and another below; the object of which was, that as a frequent renewal of the spirit was thought necessary, the old could thus be drawn off below and a fresh quantity introduced above, without moving the cask or occasioning the least agitation of the body.

On the 24th there was a disengagement of air from the body to such a degree that the sentinel became alarmed on seeing the head of the cask raised. The spirit was drawn off at once and the cask filled again, before the arrival of the *Victory* at Gibraltar on October 28th, where spirit of wine was procured; and the cask, showing a deficit produced by the body's absorbing a considerable quantity of the brandy, was then filled up with it.

❦ At home

Admiral Tryon was the most famous British sailor of his time.

On the day of the disastrous loss of HMS *Victoria* in 1893 when she was rammed by HMS *Camperdown* in the Mediterranean, Admiral Sir George Tryon, who was drowned in the incident, was seen on the stairs of his wife's house in Eaton Square, London, by a number of guests at one of her 'at homes'.

❦ Chinese take-away

At the battle of the Yalu River in 1894 between the Chinese and Japanese navies, the Chinese flagship of Admiral Ting was unable to fire all of its guns because the crew had sold the ship's gunpowder and replaced it with cocoa. They had also pawned one of their heavy guns and used the other to store pickles, rice and chopsticks.

❦ In a spin

The Russian navy once built a circular battleship named the *Admiral Popov*. Unfortunately, it could not steer straight and most of its crew were too seasick to operate it as it spun round in circles.

❦ Winds of war

During September 1940 the Royal Navy transported General de Gaulle and his Free French troops to Dakar in West Africa. The operation, known as Operation Menace, was of utmost secrecy.

Unfortunately, when de Gaulle and his staff left Euston Station in London for their journey to embark from Liverpool, a porter pushing a trolley full of cases tipped one on to the ground, causing it to burst open. The wind blew into the air hundreds of red, white and blue leaflets headed, *Aux habitants de Dakar*, soon spreading them all over London.

❦ Naafi Française

During Operation Menace in 1940 the French transport ships refused to sail from Liverpool until their kitchens had been supplied with *pâté de foie gras* and champagne for the French troops aboard.

❦ Red badge of courage

During the battle of Fredericksburg a Zouave from Philadelphia, fleeing from the battlefield to the pontoon bridge, was arrested by a guard and asked to show his pass or his wounds. Throwing down his gun and raising his hands to his hips, the Zouave responded, 'Let me pass. I am demoralized.'

❦ Long service

General Rosecrans was once dining with his staff at a hotel. Unfortunately, he tasted the Tennessee butter. He immediately rose and saluted the plate in front of him, saying, 'Gentlemen, that butter outranks me.'

❦ Red herrings

During the Russo-Japanese War of 1904–5 the Russian Baltic fleet sailed halfway around the world only to be defeated by the Japanese at the battle of Tsushima.

As the Russian fleet passed through the North Sea at night they mistook the Hull trawler fleet for Japanese torpedo boats and attacked them, sinking several and scoring many hits on their own ships.

❦ All at sea

The battle of Tsushima in 1905 was a national disaster for Russia and cost her the lives of many of her most prominent sailors. Memorials took place, some by mistake.

When the defeated Russian admiral Rozhdestvensky returned home he was sent an invitation to a memorial service held in honour of his own death.

❦ Pompo

In the 1880s Admiral Sir Algernon Charles Fiesché Heneage was known in the Royal Navy by the nickname 'Pompo' as result of his eccentricities.

Heneage took to sea aboard his flagship twenty dozen shirts which he refused to allow any of his sailors to wash and sent home when dirty on every available ship bound for England. Once, during heavy weather, a ship's carpenter was clapped in irons for entering the admiral's cabin to shut his portholes and prevent Pompo's apartments being flooded.

❦ Magnificent men in their flying machines

Some First World War planes were notoriously unstable.

Captain L A Strange was flying his Martinsyde on 10 May 1915, and was in action against a German Aviatik two-seater. He had just fired off a drum of ammunition from the Lewis gun and therefore had to stand up in his seat, reach up to the wing and try to unjam the drum before reloading. But the screws were crossed and the drum would not loosen. While he was struggling

with the gun, he was holding the joystick between his knees. Suddenly the plane was lifted by the wind and was sent into a spin. Strange lost hold of his stick and was thrown out of the plane, hanging on to the Lewis gun by his fingertips at 5,000 feet. Then the plane turned over on its back with Strange hanging underneath. Incredibly he held on to the ammunition drum and was able to struggle back into his flying seat, and turn the plane upright. The Germans had flown off at the point that his plane turned over and he was flung out, counting him as lost. But Strange survived although he was too exhausted to continue the battle with the Hun and happy enough to fly back to base in one piece. Strange survived the war and actually flew during the Second World War.